DOGMATIC
WISDOM

Also by Russell Jacoby

*Social Amnesia: A Critique of Conformist Psychology
from Adler to Laing*

Dialectic of Defeat: Contours of Western Marxism

*The Repression of Psychoanalysis:
Otto Fenichel and the Political Freudians*

The Last Intellectuals: American Culture in the Age of Academe

RUSSELL JACOBY

DOGMATIC

WISDOM

HOW THE CULTURE WARS
DIVERT EDUCATION
AND DISTRACT AMERICA

ANCHOR BOOKS
DOUBLEDAY
New York   London   Toronto   Sydney   Auckland

An Anchor Book
PUBLISHED BY DOUBLEDAY
a division of Bantam Doubleday Dell Publishing Group, Inc.
1540 Broadway, New York, New York 10036

ANCHOR BOOKS, DOUBLEDAY, and the portrayal of an anchor
are trademarks of Doubleday, a division of
Bantam Doubleday Dell Publishing Group, Inc.

Dogmatic Wisdom: How the Culture Wars Divert Education and Distract America
was originally published in hardcover by Doubleday in 1994.
The Anchor Books edition is published by arrangement with Doubleday.

The Library of Congress has cataloged the Doubleday hardcover edition as follows:
Jacoby, Russell.
Dogmatic wisdom: how the culture wars divert education and distract America /
by Russell Jacoby.
p. cm.
Includes bibliographical references.
1. Education, Higher—United States—Philosophy. 2. Education,
Humanistic—United States. 3. Education, Higher—Social aspects—
United States. 4. Education, Higher—Political aspects—
United States. 5. United States—Intellectual life—20th century.
I. Title.
LA227.4.J33   1994   378.73—dc20   93-36382
CIP

For my parents, Betty and Daniel

ACKNOWLEDGMENTS

I have long objected to the new style of encyclopedic acknowledgments—vast catalogs of friends, associates, reviewers, deans, chancellors, institutions, foundations, conferences, and grants. Do these listings bespeak of generosity or calculation? I am grateful to the teachers, administrators, and students who met and talked with me. I also want to thank James LaSpina at UCLA and Charles Conrad, my editor at Doubleday. I am especially indebted to William Hackman, Perry Anderson, Brian Morton, and above all Naomi Glauberman for the scrupulous and unstinting attention they gave to my manuscript. Although I sometimes ignored their excellent advice, I could not ask for better readers.

CONTENTS

PREFACE

WHILE I WAS VISITING an old industrial city in upstate New York, a friend took me to see his high school, a massive structure a block square and three stories high. The son of Italian immigrant tailors, he had entered high school thirty-five years earlier and made his way through college and graduate school, eventually earning a doctorate. Today he is a publisher and writer. In a small way he illustrates the truth in the American myth of success.

As we approached the school, I could see a large sign near the front entrance. I assumed it announced school activities or achievements, perhaps "Congratulations to the Senior Class!" I was wrong. The sign read: "*For Sale*: For information on purchasing this building and site, contact the Board of Education." The school was nailed shut.

Shuttered, beleaguered, abandoned schools: it wasn't always so. For centuries the United States conducted a love affair with education. Early American educators championed universal education as the stuff of democracy and individualism. "Education must be universal," stated Horace Mann in the 1830s, because we are all citizens and voters. "The whole land must be watered with the streams of knowledge. It is not enough to have, here and there, a beautiful fountain playing in palace-gardens . . ."[1]

Today, amid recriminations, the love affair is over. No one talks of fountains and streams of knowledge; the talk now is of metal detectors, privatization, hopeless schools, falling test scores, and the breakdown of public education. The news from schools is every day a little worse than the day before; and few can doubt that the corrosion of education mirrors a larger corrosion. Books like Jonathan Kozol's *Savage Inequalities* that address American education address American society. Arthur M. Schlesinger, Jr.'s reflections on a fragmenting curriculum are titled *The Disuniting of America*. If the title is overdramatic, the assumption is sound: education and society reflect each other.

This is obvious; and I offer no apologies for moving between society and education. Issues of multiculturalism surface in schooling, museums, and employment; disputes over "bias-free" language trouble the government, the media, and universities. Questions about student performance arise in Congress and national newspapers. The speed and size of the beast, in fact, keeps observers scrambling.

In the rush vital things get lost or forgotten. Too many critics are scoring points; too few are considering the whole situation. Contributions remain blinkered and insular—not wrong, but narrow, confounding surface and substance. Conservatives protest that education has lost its mind. Radicals respond that it is better than ever. The debate stays within the boundaries of curricula, books, and speech. Both sides suffer from nearsightedness.

The essentials recede from sight. Public discussion seems governed by a "law" of displacement: secondary issues displace primary issues. We fight over form and forget content. The "law" also means that the present deflects the past. Overwhelmed by urgent crises, we push aside history and lose the ability to sort out what is new or old, fundamental or tangential. We mistake bypasses for shortcuts, speeding toward our destination on an endless detour.

I do not pretend to command a direct line to reality or to the past. I do oppose litigating over property lines when the house is on fire. In the following chapters I call attention to the fire and explain why the "culture wars" are diversionary or misleading. Conservatives, liberals, and radicals argue over which books should be taught in schools; meanwhile few books are read, and a liberal education shatters under the weight of commercialism. Faculty and students dispute which words violate the rights of which groups; meanwhile society turns increasingly violent. Psychologists preach the virtues of a healthy self-esteem; meanwhile the world of the self

—education and jobs—collapses. Citizens wrangle over multiculturalism, arguing how, when, and if diverse cultures should be studied; meanwhile the irresistible power of advertising and television
converts multiculturalism into a monoculture of clothes, music, and
cars.

Without a wide-angled and historical view we risk making stands
on secondary problems, avoiding the main ones. It matters when
we focus energies on a violent vocabulary and forget a violent
world; or when we discuss a few books taught at a few schools and
ignore the state of liberal learning at most schools; or when we fight
for blacks and Latinos in textbooks and are silent about their fate
in society. "It sometimes seems," remarks Henry Louis Gates, Jr.,
"that blacks are doing better in the college curriculum than they are
in the streets."[2]

Until recently primary and secondary schools provoked the most
attention from writers and observers—for an obvious reason; few
Americans went to college. In the course of the twentieth century,
and especially since World War II, this has shifted. From less than
one in ten Americans attending college, the numbers progressed to
three, four, and five out of ten. And not only do students proceed
directly from high school to college; millions of Americans return to
campuses for courses they want or must obtain to advance their
careers.

If only by virtue of this influx, the college experience alters. Images of dotty college presidents, absentminded professors, and
prankish students have vanished, supplanted by a harder and less
amusing reality. The first freshman orientations in the 1920s included lectures on "Taking Notes and Examinations," "Use of Library," "College Duties and Responsibilities," and devoted evenings to "Athletic Rally and Songs" and "Dance and Games." Now
arriving students receive talks on sexual harassment and date rape,
films on drug abuse, and raps on race.[3]

A revamped higher education has elicited many reports of students not learning; teachers not teaching; college presidents not pre-
siding. Observers detail nasty campus feuds stoked by race, sex,
and ideology. Incidents of racism and violence seem to multiply;
faculty and students squabble bitterly about curriculum, free
speech, ethnic studies, admissions and hiring practices.

This situation has inspired many books and endless articles blasting colleges and universities. *The Closing of the American Mind,*

Profscam, Tenured Radicals, Illiberal Education, and other tracts
raise an alarm. American higher education is in a crisis due to invaders with a political agenda. Who are the new barbarians? Academic leftists and radicals. At best ideologues, at worst relativists,
hypocrites, and new totalitarians, these academics gut higher education. They wreck a traditional liberal curriculum with leftist propaganda; they denigrate Western civilization and worship everything non-Western. They toss out standards and truth, prizing
books only for political messages. Impatient with free speech, they
impose a political "line" about the oppression of women and minorities.

Editorialists decry what they see as a reign of leftist dictators in
the universities. While silent about the federal government, alumni,
corporations, or Wall Street itself, *The Wall Street Journal* identified
political radicals as the campus "powers that be."[4] In the same
spirit, Hilton Kramer, editor and art critic, charged that radicals
control a "large academic empire."[5] Commentators trace the
source of evil to the sixties; the present professors and administrators, children of that decade, moved up through the institutions;
they traded little red books for appointment books, Volkswagens
for Volvos, and street protests for hotel conferences, but they have
not fundamentally changed. They subvert American education with
leftist claptrap.

A reader of these books and commentaries would conclude that
leftists have seized control of major American universities, undermining traditional scholarship and Western culture. The stakes are
significant. Higher education, a vast heterogeneous affair, encompasses 3,000 colleges, 800,000 instructors, almost 14 million students, and some $95 billion in expenditures a year. Conservatives
accuse radicals and sympathizers of dominating this turf or a significant portion of it, choking a liberal education with stale leftism.

The broadsides exuded the triumphant conservatism of the Reagan-Bush era. At the same time—and this was puzzling—the critics
presented themselves as a beleaguered minority attacking a well-
entrenched majority. Yet for a quarter century, at least since
Nixon's presidency, conservatives dominated the political scene.
"Conservatism has gained control over national elections and, to a
significant degree, over the national agenda," concluded the Edsalls
in *Chain Reaction*, their best-seller that surveyed new political realities.[6] In political discourse, liberalism became an epithet, "the

L-word," which denoted wimp and which sidelined careers. The other "L-word" (leftist) spelled nothing and meant nothing.

The conservative majority appeared built on rock, a permanent foundation of political loyalties and realities. Is it necessary to recall this today? *Chain Reaction*, published in 1991, sought to explain what everyone took as a given, the lasting decline of liberalism. After the war in the Persian Gulf and well into 1992, virtually all observers assumed that the Reagan-Bush reign would continue, a string of conservative Presidents and policies reaching far into the future.

A new liberalism in presidential politics puts an end to a conservative era, giving another cast to its educational criticism—or does it? The lingo coming out of Washington about public education, health care, and abortion has altered. Perhaps deeds and actions will alter as well: it is too soon to say. Even hard-nosed liberals can believe that presidential appointments, like those to the Supreme Court, might profoundly affect national life.

In his uncompromising *Savage Inequalities*, Jonathan Kozol attributes the sanctioning of stark educational injustices to a single Supreme Court decision with a five-man majority that included all four Nixon appointees. In *Milliken* v. *Bradley* the Supreme Court overruled a district court's desegregation order that had directed Detroit to integrate by including the largely white suburbs outside city limits. "If only one of the concurring justices had accepted the opinions of the four dissenting judges . . . an entire generation of black children in such cities as East Orange, Paterson, Detroit and East St. Louis might have had an opportunity for very different adult lives."[7]

Kozol may overstate the matter. Neither national elections nor Supreme Court judges reverse long-term trends, which are here the issue; nor do they change the past. Decades of educational woes do not vanish because of a new President or shifts in electoral sentiment; past grievances over educational and cultural disarray are as current as tomorrow's weather.

The debate over culture and education has largely been driven by conservatives, and it is impossible to think about schooling without assessing their criticisms. They lay a bill of goods at the office doors of leftists. These itemize charges about a liberal education, free speech, curriculum, and the politics of knowledge. What have leftist professors said to refute the accusations? Very little.

This too is puzzling. Many critical reviews and essays have appeared, but for years nothing more. No leftist stepped forward with a book as sweeping and compelling as those by the conservatives. Academics sprinkle "critique" all over their writings, but where is the "critique" of the education conservatives? The smartest and sassiest contribution to appear so far, *The Culture of Complaint*, is by an art critic and journalist, Robert Hughes.

The editor of an academic collection which seeks to fill the breach admits, "The academy simply hasn't responded forcefully to the multiple attacks against it."[8] The recent appearance of several books may indicate a belated but effective marshaling of energies. Perhaps. A notable bid by a leading academic opponent of the conservatives, Gerald Graff's *Beyond the Culture Wars*, which I discuss in Chapter 6, does not inspire confidence on this score.

Left academics may have been too busy with their own projects to enter the fray of public debate. Radicals and postmodernists have been making giant theoretical steps; they attack "hegemonic discourse," "deconstruct" the gender system, "bracket" Western civilization. Categories like liberal and conservative, and even Marxist, have been discarded as hopelessly retrograde. Firing away at the assumptions of society, the new academics establish hierarchical institutes where they attack hierarchy. They found academic centers where they "decenter." They celebrate authors who deride authorship. From chaired positions at elite universities they assail domination. By their own account they are more profoundly revolutionary and sophisticated than previous radicals. One problem: few know it.

Embarrassment may contribute to the silence of radicals. Conservatives have seized the offensive by assailing higher education. To join the quarrel means defending the university. By rallying to a major institution of American life the radicals become willy-nilly the conservatives. This might give a hacking cough to Marxist or post-Marxist professors. No one can forget that many of these professors began as radicals attacking the university. Protesting against universities as imperialist tools is more fitting on a leftist résumé.

A quarter century later, hip academics might find defending the university difficult to square with their past, their selves—or their illusions. Some swallow hard and admit it. "It used to be," writes a young English professor, "that any self-respecting leftist criticized the university as a place that perpetuates privilege. Today things have turned around, and I find myself in an awkward position, summoning up as many resources as I can to defend the university against the blunt-edged polemic now wielded against it."[9]

The fate of education alarms parents, teachers, and observers throughout the country, not only conservatives and academic radicals. My children attend public schools in Los Angeles. With the government virtually bankrupt and the social fabric unraveling, we parents half joke about a future with no schools. Will there be education next month? Next year? Is public education finished, already abandoned by all who can afford private schooling? Amid all the hoopla of "Rebuild LA," the campaign launched after the Los Angeles riots, the school system visibly falls apart. Few public figures seem to notice or care. Officials proposed shortening the school year to save money; and mandatory salary cuts elicited strike votes from teachers. How does one rebuild a city while dismantling its schools?

Higher education presents different problems, yet the differences are easily exaggerated. Conflicts over curriculum, economic costs, correct language, and multiculturalism permeate all education. While I focus on colleges and universities, I am loyal to the issues; and these ignore distinction between levels of education.

I do not pretend to offer dazzling new insights. I only try to use both eyes, keeping in view both the cultural smog and the polluting industries. The amount, and sometimes the quality, of writings on education intimidates even the most self-assured. Somewhere everything is said and argued. "Education is a subject which has been exhausted by the ablest writers, both among the ancients and moderns," wrote Noah Webster two centuries ago. "I am not vain enough to suppose I can suggest any new ideas upon so trite a theme as education in general." Of course, Webster continued, "but perhaps the manner of conducting the youth in America may be capable of some improvement."[10]

I first joined the debate on education in 1963 as a freshman at the University of Chicago, when I unhappily encountered remnants of its Great Books curriculum. I have returned occasionally to educational matters, but only the permanent crisis warrants adding to the mountain of print.[11] Yesterday a student was gunned down in class; today underfinanced state colleges turn away disappointed students; and public schools abandon art and music classes. Tomorrow, what? Gated schools for the elite, and barracks for the rest? Meanwhile in one of the world's richest societies high school students increasingly work part-time in service industries, relinquishing studies for cars and designer clothes. To reflect on liberal education today is to consider not only its demise but the reason for its demise, an illiberal society.

DOGMATIC
WISDOM

1

OFFICE MANAGEMENT 101

AMERICANS DREAM OF COLLEGE. For one social stratum finishing high school is the supreme goal. For the rest, however, the object of kindergarten through twelfth grade is simple: college. My daughter, who attends public school, began taking the PSAT examinations, the preliminary to the SATs required by many colleges, in the sixth grade. The school counselors recommended that students get "comfortable" with the format and the experience.

The counselors are not alone; teachers, parents, and students themselves assess high school courses and activities with an eye to college. They ask, "What are colleges looking for?" "Is a high grade average with easy courses better than a lower average with hard ones?" "Is working on the school yearbook preferable to playing on a team?" Parents want, and high schools routinely provide, information not simply on how many students proceeded to college but how many went to which college. How many were accepted by Harvard or UC Berkeley or the University of Michigan?

No one contests the college fixation. If anything, the current runs the other way. Universities are more explicit in what they want; and secondary schools are more anxious to please. Everyone admits, even celebrates, the fact that the object of high school is college; and the object of college is, well, good jobs.

The obsession is new. Not so long ago, standard wisdom pronounced higher education a squandering of time and money. "Men have sent their sons to colleges," stated Andrew Carnegie ninety years ago, "to waste their energies . . . They have been 'educated' as if they were destined for life upon some other planet . . . In my own experience I can say that I have known few young men intended for business who were not injured by a collegiate education. Had they gone into active work during the years spent at college they would have been better educated men."[1]

This widespread sentiment kept the college-going population small. Before World War I, virtually any interested student could attend any college. A parent, principal, or headmaster wrote a letter about the pupil to the school; the student arrived, took an examination, paid fees, and enrolled. Even the elite colleges turned away few applicants. In 1920 Yale accepted all eligible students. Up through the 1930s only a handful of schools established formal selection procedures. Colleges needed students more than students needed colleges. "In no other civilized country," commented a 1911 Carnegie Foundation report, "do institutions of higher learning compete for students."[2]

"I'd never admit it publicly," confessed Sinclair Lewis's Babbitt to his son Ted, "fellow like myself, State U. graduate, it's only decent and patriotic for him to blow his horn and boost the Alma Mater—but smatter of fact, there's a whole lot a valuable time lost even at the U., studying poetry and French and subjects that never brought in anybody a cent." The words are revealing. In 1922 Lewis's Babbitt, a caricature of a midwestern businessman, would not state his doubts publicly. Today private doubts would not bother him. He would be singing the virtues of a college education, and probably urging his boy to enroll in a private course to elevate his SAT scores.

Why the shift? Why the obsession with college admissions? Several reasons might be offered. Babbitt has heard the news; studying French and poetry brings in the bucks—at least finishing college does. Like much economic information, the numbers speak from both corners of the mouth. Everyone knows that college graduates wander about looking for employment. A baccalaureate hardly ensures a job. At the same time the earning gap between high school and college graduates steadily widens. In the mid-1970s white male college graduates earned only 18 percent more than white male high school graduates. By 1989 the difference had jumped to 45 percent. For women and blacks the gap is even more dramatic. For instance, in 1989 the "earning advantage" for white and black college women over white and black high school graduates reached an extraordinary 75 and 92 percent.[3] For Babbitts or poets a college degree spells money and good careers.

These realities propel students to college. They know that without a college degree they relegate themselves to second-rate jobs and salaries. The myth of the self-made man who spurns schooling to hurry up the employment ladder is not even a myth anymore; it has vaporized. No one counsels skipping college to jump straight into the whirlwind of life. Today a Carnegie would exhort the young to obtain a master's in business administration (MBA). While a college degree hardly ensures a good career, the reverse imprints itself upon young and old: a high school education constitutes a one-way ticket to nowhere.

A practical impulse is hardly new among students; nor is it bad. Students attend college to obtain good jobs. Who can argue with that? Over a century ago, Henry Adams, a scion of Presidents who was teaching at Harvard, wondered what his students "could do with education when they got it." He "put the question to one of them, and was surprised at the answer. 'The degree of Harvard College is worth money to me in Chicago.' "[4]

Continuities mask changes, however. Students have always been broadly practical; today they may be utilitarian. Adams posed his question to a student enrolled in a medieval history course. Nowadays history does not exactly rope in students. In the last fifteen years traditional majors like philosophy, history, and English have declined, while business and management majors have doubled. Students believe that more practical studies lead to well-paying jobs. The shape of higher education reflects these beliefs, which are widely shared by parents and others.

Commercial and pragmatic pressures on education are hardly new. Richard Hofstadter's 1962 *Anti-Intellectualism in American Life* deplored the rise in high school of "life adjustment" courses that crested in the 1940s and 1950s. Reformers, who distrusted academic subjects as useless, successfully boosted utilitarian training as the replacement for the classical curriculum. A 1911 report, extolling practical education, charged that "by means of exclusively bookish curricula false ideals of culture are developed."[5]

For much of this century, secondary education reformers sought to minimize "bookish" culture and maximize useful studies. The reports came thick and fast. Perhaps the most influential recommendations on secondary education, the U.S. Bureau of Education "Cardinal Principles Report" of 1918, called for downgrading traditional subjects and promoting practical studies. The challenges of modern life, stated the authors, require that schools stress "health, worthy home-membership, vocation, citizenship, the worthy use of leisure and ethical character."

History and mathematics almost disappeared as an objective. What was an education in "worthy home-membership"? For girls it meant "the household arts should have a prominent place." Boys should be taught appreciation of "the value of the well-appointed house and of the labor and skill required to maintain such a home . . . For instance, they should understand the essentials of food values, of sanitation, and of household budgets."[6]

The report reflected the thought of David Snedden, a state education commissioner and professor, who prized "social efficiency" in education; he neatly sectioned education into two parts, each with a specific goal. Vocational education made the individual an "efficient producer," liberal education an "efficient consumer." In this scheme, little place could be found for studies valued for themselves. Snedden discounted academic subjects, judging the study of history a great disappointment with "no real purpose." Up through the 1950s reformers like Snedden championed a "life adjustment" curriculum, regretting only its slow progress though the educational system.[7]

The old curriculum had peaked in 1910, when academic course enrollments easily exceeded nonacademic. Afterward modern languages, algebra, and sciences dropped precipitously. "During the following forty-year span [after 1910]," wrote Hofstadter, "the academic subjects offered in the high-school curricula fell from three fourths to about one fifth." Other subjects like home economics, bookkeeping, and typing took up the slack.[8]

"Life adjustment" and practical courses never lacked forceful critics. The popular tide did not run against it, however, until 1957. On October 4, as rumors swirled that the Dodgers might abandon

Brooklyn for Los Angeles, Americans learned that the Russians had launched the first satellite. Not only did the satellite circle the globe every ninety minutes, beeping taunts at the Americans; one month after Sputnik, the Russians sent a second and much larger satellite into orbit. For Americans, this spelled humiliation. The culprit was close at hand: education.

"In a national torrent of self-abuse," writes the historian Loren Baritz, "Americans suddenly awoke to the crisis of the schools because Sputnik evidently proved that Russians were smarter and more serious." *Life* magazine ran a series on the "Crisis in Education," and scores of commentators joined in. *Life* contrasted the lives of two students, a serious and somber tenth-grader, Alexei of Moscow, and a good-natured and easygoing eleventh-grader, Stephen of Chicago. Six days a week Alexei carried heavy-duty courses like Russian literature, sixth-year English, fifth-year physics, and fourth-year chemistry. After long homework assignments, Alexei relaxed by going to concerts or playing chess with his best friend. Stephen lived in a different world, his courses more elementary and practical, his life more comfortable. "Stephen . . . starts out almost every school day by meeting his steady, Penny . . . and heading for Austin High. Ten minutes later he gets to the Typing II class, slips behind a large electric typewriter and another pleasant school day begins."[9]

Journalists discovered that American report cards graded "getting along with others" and sometimes "cheerfulness" next to "spelling." Russian youth studied calculus and English, while American students learned how to smile. Spurred by the cries of doom, Congress resolved to mend American education by federal action. The year after Sputnik, Congress passed the National Defense Education Act, funding science, mathematics, and languages. "A severe blow—some would say a disastrous blow—has been struck at America's self-confidence and at her prestige," stated the chairman at the Senate hearings, referring to the Soviet satellites. "We must give vastly greater support, emphasis, and dedication to basic scientific research, to quality in education, to instruction in the physical sciences, to training in foreign languages . . ."[10]

In the long view, however, Sputnik hardly slowed a spreading mercantile ethos in education. Stephen's college successors are not taking chemistry or Japanese or even English, but Managerial Economics and Introduction to Office Administration. The crisis of higher education is that there is no crisis, only business as usual. The curriculum fractures under the weight of professional and practical studies. Education looks less like liberal studies than a grab bag of offerings; it seems to have lost its coherence, perhaps its mind.

Colleges add more courses like Commercial English and Principles of Management. From an old curriculum little is dropped, but in the name of choice, new fields and subjects are added. College catalogs come to resemble fat telephone books. Any inner unity or even logical progression of courses evaporates, leaving behind a residue of "general education" or "distribution" requirements, the ghost of the liberal arts.

The specific requirements of each school result from departmental power and bickering; administrative diplomacy; and demands of students, parents, alumni, and outsiders. They change regularly, and like tax regulations, they seem designed to baffle. No one can quite figure out what is necessary to graduate; usually the required courses are listed under several categories in classic Chinese menu style, and students must choose one from column A, two from column B, and so on—except there are more columns and subcolumns.

Menu-style education is not new; it encourages tinkering—add a course here, subtract there—and allows the student the freedom to wander about. Abraham Flexner's 1930 survey of American universities slammed the multiplication of illiberal courses. Flexner, who had gained national attention with a devastating criticism of American medical schools, noted that "a student of Columbia University may study serious subjects in a serious fashion." This student may also, Flexner complained, "complete the requirements for a bachelor's degree by including in his course of study 'principles of advertising,' 'the writing of advertised copy,' . . . 'business English,' 'elementary stenography,' . . . 'wrestling, judo and self-defence.'" Flexner charged that "a sound sense of values has not been preserved within American universities . . . They have thoughtlessly and excessively catered to fleeting, transient, and immediate demands."[11]

Flexner joined other early-twentieth-century critics like Irving Babbitt—not to be confused with Sinclair Lewis's fictional George Babbitt—in decrying the corruption of liberal education by utilitarianism and cheap vocationalism. Citing a college catalog, Babbitt, a literature professor, remarked that students could obtain a BA with courses like "The killing, trussing, and marketing of fowl." "The change that has been taking place in our education is . . . not simply a modernizing and adjusting to new conditions," stated Babbitt, but the "substitution" of a "new spirit." The "old education" aimed at "wisdom," the new at power and cash.[12]

Babbitt, who inspired a "new humanism" protesting relativism and utilitarianism, wanted universities to foster cultural standards, not serve as utility shops for farmers and mechanics. He bemoaned that the traditional liberal BA meant nothing and anything. He condemned "the sapping of the sense of moral responsibility" and "the stupid drift toward standardization." "The very idea of liberal education is in danger of perishing in America in the midst of a great bewilderment . . . We seem to be witnessing today the consequences of a weakening of standards."[13]

Since Flexner and Babbitt the situation has hardly improved. Oddball courses have become main courses; main courses have become majors; majors have become departments. On this score conservatives raise an alarm; they assail the splintering of the humanities. With passion Allan Bloom in *The Closing of the American Mind* indicted universities for failing to provide even a minimal liberal education; the vast number of courses mystify students. "And there is no official guidance, no university-wide agreement, about what he [a student] *should* study." For Bloom "it is become all too evident that liberal education . . . has no content, that a certain kind of fraud is being perpetrated."[14]

Conservative critics pound away at this charge, complaining of cafeteria-style education where students select only what is appealing. If "Western Civilization" doesn't entice, a student might sample "Social Anthropology of the Caribbean" or "Leisure in Contemporary Society." A conservative handbook, *The Common-Sense Guide to American Colleges,* lambasts the course structure of most schools; for instance, the guide attacks the University of North Carolina at Chapel Hill, which abandoned a "core curriculum" and now allows students to select from "a wide array of courses . . . Predictably, many students choose the easiest classes and learn little. The legacy of this 'salad bar' approach . . . is thousands of graduates who have no understanding of Western culture." The authors note that "it is not uncommon for a political science major to graduate without having read John Locke, Adam Smith, or Thomas Jefferson, and most students don't seem to mind."[15]

The charges hit home. The only problem is that they do not go far enough. For all their verve, the new conservative critics like Bloom in *The Closing of the American Mind* and Dinesh D'Souza in *Illiberal Education*[16] lack the bite of Flexner or Irving Babbitt. The earlier conservatives targeted a grubby commercialism for undermining education; they protested a utilitarianism rooted in an industrial age. Flexner believed that American universities had become "merely administrative aggregations, so varied, so manifold, so complex that administration itself is reduced to budgeting, student accounting, advertising, etc. . . . Their centres are the treasurer's office, in which income flows, out of which expenditure issues."[17]

In the course of seventy years the situation has worsened, and the successors to Flexner and Babbitt rise to the occasion by boldly attacking—what? English professors. Rock 'n' roll. Feminist studies. Relativism. "There are attempts to fill the vacuum," Bloom wrote, with "fancy packaging," and "Black Studies and Women's or Gender Studies, along with Learn Another Culture." This is the conservative refrain: illiberal academics destroy a liberal education.

Yet these conservative critics barely breathe of the real force corroding liberal education: an illiberal society. They sputter about tenured radicals and stay mute about an instrumental society. An unbridled desire for practical knowledge and good money recasts higher education, as it has for decades, even centuries. Among students, a drive for fat jobs may be commendable or deplorable: that is not the point. Flexner and Babbitt sputtered also; but they realized that an exclusively commercial and instrumental vision degraded education; and they called for the universities to resist, not pander to this spirit. Students did not and do not take courses on "trussing poultry" because of a Marxist or feminist professor; they want to go into the poultry business.

Most students care nothing for Gender or Peace Studies; most do not care much for history or philosophy or religion. That is why enrollments in the humanities have dropped sharply. Students prefer Business Psychology or Management Economics. These courses constitute a real "illiberal education," but D'Souza's *Illiberal Education* never even mentions them. By 1984, notes one higher education commentator, "we passed the point at which 50 percent of our nation's undergraduates had chosen to major in vocational or occupational fields."[18]

An annual survey of incoming freshmen, drawing on 250,000 students, confirms a striking increase in business majors over the last twenty-five years. "The field which has experienced the largest and most consistent surge in student popularity . . . has been business." Conversely, "the biggest overall losses have involved education and the traditional liberal arts and science fields . . . These declines have averaged 50 percent" over the same period.[19]

The bachelor's degrees awarded over almost twenty years verify this shift. A breakdown by discipline shows a sharp increase in the business and management degrees to the point that they far outstrip other majors. Of the million-odd bachelor's degrees awarded in 1991, some 250,000 were conferred in business, compared with 7,300 in philosophy and religion and 12,000 in foreign languages.[20] These numbers speak volumes about liberal education today, but no-nonsense conservative critics are oblivious. Instead, D'Souza cries foul when an English professor assigns Hollywood movies and popular novels.

The most careful examination of what students study is *Tourists in Our Own Land,* sponsored by the U.S. Department of Education. Clifford Adelman, its author, drew upon a continuing "longitudinal" examination of 22,000 high school students representing nearly three million high school seniors. The study tabulated the courses taken by the students as they made their way through college. Unlike less reliable surveys that examine college catalogs or query administrators as to educational requirements, Adelman used the actual transcripts of students, which listed the specific courses taken. With these records he compiled accurate registers of courses students enrolled in.

What he found confirms the wide drift away from "bookish" humanities to practical and professional studies. Adelman and his staff discovered that the total credits of the humanities and social sciences amounted to less than a third of the credits that students took. "The sheer amount of time," he observes, that this generation "spent studying accounting, marketing, physical education, nursing, and basic electrical circuits, for example, absolutely dwarfs the amount of time it spent in the formal streams of explicitly cultural information."

Indeed, the news is even worse. When the cultural courses are examined, with few exceptions they are the most basic and introductory courses, such as Introduction to Sociology and General Biology, which are required in order to study something else. Very few students take advanced courses in these areas. "If roughly one of five bachelor's degree holders studied accounting, only one out of 20 studied European history since 1789 . . . Based on the records of their course-work alone, college graduates of this cohort are far more likely to use the term 'leveraged buy-out' . . . than 'Waterloo.' "[21]

The most poisonous conservatives would be hard put to indict feminists or deconstructionists for encouraging students to study Real Estate Economics or Business Communication. Why don't conservatives bring up the sharp jump in business majors and the general triumph of commercial education? Perhaps the conservatives themselves are implicated—or at least conservative foundations and ideology that crow about the virtues of the market. The Free Enterprise Institute, the American Heritage Foundation, and the Olin Foundation all fund the conservative education critics; and the foundations bless the free enterprise system.

Students get the same message everywhere: go for the money. After a while it is difficult to resist. A major in American literature does not spell a job, perhaps not even a credit card. From the University of California at Berkeley comes an illuminating tale. Citibank, America's largest banking company, set up a table on the UC Berkeley campus for the purpose of signing up graduating seniors for a MasterCard or Visa Card. A sign stated: "No Previous Credit History Required."

One student, a former math major and already a reputable Visa Card holder, applied for a MasterCard and was turned down. Why? He had changed majors from mathematics to rhetoric, a less remunerative field of study. The Los Angeles *Times* discovered that the bank followed its standard procedure. "The bank has routinely rejected students who listed majors in the humanities, such as English, history or art." The bank calculated that these students are less likely to repay debts because they will not land the high-paying jobs that go to business or engineering graduates. "It is obvious discrimination," said one art history major, who was turned down for a card just before graduation. She reported that "a friend who majors in business got one [a credit card] as a freshman."[22]

The bank revised its policies, but not the reality. I ask my best

students, "What is your major? What are your plans?" Fifteen
years ago, they frequently hesitated, and answered that they were
not certain; or that they wanted to study history or philosophy, but
were unclear as to what end. Now they respond promptly with a
field, an employer, sometimes a salary range. "Prelaw. I hope to
study international law and work for a New York firm." "Commercial art. I want to go into product design and marketing." "Business. I plan to work in the bond division of a San Francisco bank."

A professor new to a small liberal arts college met with communications students he was advising, expecting them to offer airy
generalities about their future. "One of my students declared, 'I
want to be an *anchorwoman!*' I was stunned."[23] Yet exact career
goals are common, surprising only to new professors. If a bright
student states that he or she wants to get a master's in business
administration, we nod, "Yes, of course." If a bright student wants
to study art history or philosophy, we are startled, as if encounter-
ing an individual who is out of touch, which is frequently the case.

To be sure, a single cause or a single politics cannot be blamed
for the long-term trends of American education, but this is the
point: the steady dismantling of the curriculum is an old story. It
predates leftist professors and feminist theorists. It has more to do
with the professionalization of labor, consumerism, utilitarianism,
and market forces. Earlier conservatives, less enamored with capitalism, knew this. More recent conservatives are not only more
timid but more ambivalent; they worship the market and bemoan
the education it engenders. They blast BMW radicals, not a BMW
society.

Bad conscience and feeble efforts plague the conservative effort
to revitalize liberal education. Conservatives may suspect that the
very cultural tradition they prize harbored no love for industrial
civilization and its values. For this reason, instead of outlining a
liberal education, they vaguely refer to a "core curriculum" or
"classics" of Western civilization or to Matthew Arnold's criterion
of "the best that has been thought and said." This should settle the
question of what a liberal education is. It doesn't. D'Souza is typical; his book is even called *Illiberal Education,* but what is a liberal
education? He refers to Arnold and the classics, but little more.

An honest appraisal of Arnold and nineteenth-century conservatives must recognize their profound distaste for industrial society. If
they loved culture, they disdained the illiberal economic system

with its "free-trade, unrestricted competition, and the making of large industrial fortunes." For all his spirituality and elitism, or because of it, Arnold judged a money-obsessed civilization a threat to "culture." "The commonest of commonplaces," wrote Arnold, "tells us how men are always apt to regard wealth as a precious end in itself; and certainly they have never been so apt thus to regard it as they are in England at the present time. Never did people believe anything more firmly, than nine Englishmen out of ten at the present day believe that our greatness and welfare are proved by our being so very rich."[24]

Culture for Arnold breathed of another world, not simply "sweetness and light" but a universe antagonistic to grubby materialism. "Culture" protested against those "who most give their lives and thoughts to becoming rich." It "begets a dissatisfaction which is of the highest possible value in stemming the common tide of men's thoughts in a wealthy and industrial community." Arnold's language bears repeating: "Culture begets a dissatisfaction . . ." It nurtures a protest against a commercial ethos.

This tradition that runs from Burke to Arnold, wrote Raymond Williams, set "culture" against "the powerful Utilitarian tendency which conceived education as the training of men to carry out particular tasks in a particular kind of civilization."[25] Liberal culture was something to be studied for its own sake, not a means toward another goal. A liberal education does not make an individual more wealthy or more slender. "Knowledge Its Own End," reads a chapter title from John Henry Newman's classic *The Idea of a University* (1852).

Some nineteenth-century liberals like John Stuart Mill also distrusted a utilitarian education. Mill defended an education at odds with adjustment and practicality. He was "glad" to join a conservative critic of English universities who savaged Oxford and Cambridge for seeking to "turn out clever lawyers and serviceable Treasury clerks," instead of "great men, whom the age will scorn." The university prepared "youths for a successful career in society," but this critic wanted universities to move in the reverse direction, enabling them to "resist the influences of society." Mill concurred, though he believed the critic understated a dire situation.

Mill regarded Oxford and Cambridge with "utter abhorrence." "We do not conceive that their vices would be cured by bringing their studies into a closer connexion with what is the fashion to term 'the business of the world.' " Rather, Mill prescribed the opposite: add studies "more alien than any which yet exist to the 'business of the world.' " The whole problem of education, he wrote, is that educators believe its object is to inculcate conventionality, "not to qualify the pupil for judging what is true or what is right." They want to produce students in agreement with "the opinions of the small minds."

This tenet is so widely held and has been so successful that Cambridge and Oxford not only graduate generations of mediocrities but fill its faculties with them. "Has Cambridge produced, since Newton, one great mathematical genius?" asked Mill. "How many books which have thrown light upon the history, antiquities, philosophy, art or literature of the ancients, have the two Universities sent forth since the Reformation?"[26]

The attack on an illiberal and commercial education did not close with Arnold and Mill. At the turn of the century, W. E. B. Du Bois in *The Souls of Black Folk* added his passionate and lucid voice. No matter the pressing need, he objected to an industrial or practical education for a black population. "The picture of a lone black boy poring over a French grammar amid the weeds and dirt of a neglected home" might seem the "acme" of absurdity to some. Not to Du Bois.

He resisted the utilitarianism idealized by Booker T. Washington. Black people—all people—needed the knowledge and culture that a liberal education, especially higher education, sustained. "The function of the university is not simply to teach bread-winning, or to furnish teachers for the public schools or to be a centre of polite society." Rather, universities sustained ideas of Truth and Freedom. "And the final product of our training must be neither a psychologist nor a brickmason, but a man. And to make men, we must have ideas, broad, pure and inspiring ends of living—no sordid money-getting, not apples of gold."[27]

In an address to a black Boston group in 1891, Du Bois forcefully presented the case for a liberal education. He recognized and sympathized with his audience's skepticism. "Grandfather says, 'Get a Practical Education, learn a trade, learn stenography, go into a store, but don't fool away time in college." Du Bois understood, but dissented:

The general argument for so-called practical education really lies upon the postulate that the object of life is bread and butter and ultimately money. Well, it isn't; they are but the means to life . . . Learn a trade, by all means, and learn it well, but Get a Liberal Education . . . Never make the mistake of thinking that the object of being a man is to be a carpenter—the object of being a carpenter is to be a man . . . Don't forget that you do not live to get rich, but that you get rich to live; and that in order to live the sort of life which the spirit of all the ages tells you it pays to live, you must know what Aristotle thought, what Phidias carved, what Da Vinci painted, what Bacon knew, what Leibnitz created, what Kant criticized, how Jesus Christ loved—this is education, this is life.[28]

There is no going back to Arnold (or to Mill and Du Bois), but the effort to resuscitate a liberal education must not stop at vague references to the Englishman and the "classics." The nineteenth-century conservatives, and some liberals and radicals, repudiated the instrumental education of a commercial civilization. Today's conservatives, on the other hand, damn marginal leftist academics, not an expanding commercialization, as the threat. They bless the market economy and curse the educational system it engenders. This is a problem of stringency or courage, flinching in the face of unwelcome truths.

Leftist critics are no better; with less excuse, they are often worse. Conservatives eloquently lament a decaying university and its fragmenting curriculum, but rarely mention the economic cannon that has blown up the canon. Leftist, Marxist, and post-Marxist professors miss the report amidst the theoretical explosions and partying. The new academics advance not only beyond Marxism but beyond materialism, except for their own. In celebrating academic writings and progress, a gut feeling for the larger realities wanes.

Gerald Graff's recent *Beyond the Culture Wars* is a case in point. Graff, a left-leaning English professor who teaches at the University of Chicago, happily discusses "culture wars" at elite schools like Stanford, Duke, or Chicago but hardly alludes to the rest of American higher education, where culture, in Adelman's words, "takes a back seat." "The curriculum of students at elite colleges," notes Adelman, which composed only 3% of the bachelor's degrees in his sample, "is so different from that followed by the other 97% that it is irrelevant to discussions."[29] Few academic leftists attain this lucidity.

Anyone who challenges the narrow practicality that dominates education will be suspected of elitist or aristocratic pretensions. The risk should be run. For if a liberal education is to regain its vitality, it must recapture its nonutilitarian dimension. Thinking, reading, and art require a cultural space, a zone free from the angst of moneymaking and practicality. Without a certain repose or leisure, a liberal education shrivels.

Today, to mention leisure evokes images of retirement communities or television viewing. Leisure has lost meaning, succumbing to the general fetish of leisure in a consumer society. In America leisure usually means buying or doing or watching something. The 1911 commission that validated an educational shift from academic to useful subjects listed the "worthy use of leisure" as one goal. "This objective calls for the ability to utilize the common means of enjoyment, such as music, art, literature, drama and social intercourse, together with the fostering in each individual of one or more special avocational interests."[30] The terms are revealing: leisure, the very antithesis of utility, must be "useful."

Sebastian de Grazia, in his *Of Time, Work and Leisure,* sought to disentangle leisure from "free time," an empty category. "Free time refers to a special way of calculating a special kind of time. Leisure refers to a state of being." Originally leisure signaled something like quiet reflection. As the point of work and life, leisure or contemplation sustained Western culture.[31] "Leisure" provided the space for education and schooling. As the theologian Josef Pieper wrote:

> And even the history of the word attests the fact: for leisure in Greek is *skole,* and in Latin *scola,* the English "school." The word used to designate the place where we educate and teach is derived from a word which means "leisure." "School" does not, properly speaking, mean school, but leisure.[32]

The link was not accidental. An essential character of the liberal arts emerged from its contrast to practical arts. Schools devote themselves to knowledge in itself, not useful trades, which were judged inferior; knowledge depends on leisure, a certain freedom from constraint. Pieper cited Aquinas's commentary on Aristotle: "Only those arts are called liberal or free which are concerned with knowledge; those which are concerned with utilitarian ends that are attained through activity, however, are called servile." They are servile because they reflect servitude and work, not leisure and liberty.

Leisure, on the other hand, implies autonomous activity; it enters the liberal arts or the *artes liberales* both from "school," a site of leisure, and from the term *liberalis,* which refers to "free men" or men with leisure. As one historian of liberal education put it, the allusion to "free men" "implied both the status of social and political freedom, as opposed to slavery, and the possession of wealth, affording free time for leisure. Thus, *liberalis* characterized the *liber,* the free citizen."[33]

The language is sticky, compressing the entire development of freedom and slavery, but fundamental; the liberal arts, sustained by leisure, do not consist of courses—to cite some typical examples— like Tax Accounting I or Principles of Public Relations. If these are necessary, they do not belong to the liberal arts, which are devoted to nonutilitarian knowledge, things valued for themselves. "Some of us are enslaved to glory, others to money," stated Cicero. "But there are also a few people who devote themselves wholly to the study of the universe . . . These call themselves students of wisdom, in other words, philosophers."[34] To criticize this as elitist or hierarchical would miss the point. It obviously is, but only because it is better to be free to study and reflect than to be dominated by work and money.

The contrast between knowledge "in itself" and utilitarian knowledge can be overstated; a sharp distinction between "liberal" and "useful" is more recent than ancient.[35] For instance, Newman offered a harsh critique of utilitarianism in his *Idea of a University*. He attacked the idea that education should be confined to a "narrow end, and should issue in some definite work, which can be weighed and measured." He criticized those who argued that "every thing, as well as every person, had its price" and those who asked "what is the real worth in the market of the article called 'a Liberal Education' "; and he protested saddling in advance a liberal education with a "business, or profession, or trade, or work . . . as its real and complete end."[36]

Yet he did not think that a liberal education was useless. The utilitarians "frighten" us with this charge; but Newman believed that a liberal education was "truly and fully" a useful education. It was useful in a larger sense for every office or activity. "I say that a cultivated intellect, because it is good in itself, brings with it a power and a grace to every work and occupation which it undertakes, and enables us to be more useful."[37]

On the other side of the aisle, John Stuart Mill, a classic liberal, virtually agreed. "Universities are not intended to teach the knowledge required to fit men for some special mode of gaining their livelihood . . . Men are men before they are lawyers, or physicians, or merchants, or manufacturers; and if you make them capable and sensible men, they will make themselves capable and sensible lawyers or physicians."[38]

The history of education cannot be condensed into a battle between liberal and utilitarian education or classical and practical schooling. The categories are too broad, and their meaning does not remain constant; and neither the defenders nor the critics of a classical education can claim to be on the side of the angels. Justifiable reforms were often enacted in the name of rendering education more useful. When he faced the crying needs of Ireland, Newman himself veered from his purist ideas in shaping the Catholic University of Ireland.[39]

On the other hand, with erratic countermovements practicality has dominated education in the twentieth century, and especially higher education in the last twenty-five years. An instrumental ethos is nourished not simply by market forces but also by parallel pressures of specialization and professionalization. The invasion of the liberal arts by vocational and preprofessional studies constitutes the real illiberal education. Nor does it seem accidental that the invaders carry the label "business majors." Business derives from a "busyness" that undermines "leisure" or *skole,* the space to think, read, and contemplate. Students are too busy to think.

They may be also too busy to study. International surveys highlighting the poor achievements of American students have been widely publicized; even when roughly similar school populations are contrasted, the Americans wind up on the bottom. Probably no single factor explains this, but some observations about American students are extremely suggestive: many more American students work for wages on a weekly basis than their counterparts in Europe or Asia. This is certainly true in high school and is most likely true in college; as tuition inexorably increases, students scramble for part-time jobs. With outside work obligations, something suffers, usually the unstructured time to read and study.

Several studies confirm that American high school students, unlike students elsewhere, hold jobs in significant numbers. A North Carolina study of high school juniors found that half worked, with two-thirds holding jobs twenty hours or more a week. The number and amount of high school students working troubles Scott D. Thomson, director of a national school principals' association; he notes that in "other nations school is considered too important for students to work." And it used to be, he says, that kids worked just on weekends; now they work throughout the week.[40]

As American society grows richer, and cannot employ all who want to work, more and more students dish out ice cream and ring up sales. Why? Not to chip in for home or food expenses, but to obtain $100 sneakers and designer jeans, as well as pay for their own car and car insurance. The North Carolina study found that only 5 percent of the students held jobs to support families. Thomson estimates that family expenses or college savings make up only 15 percent of student outlays; the rest is for themselves. A survey of high school students in Austin, Texas, concluded that 80 percent held some sort of job after school; moreover, the more affluent students were more likely to work. "It is indifference to their education," comments one education observer, "that seems to motivate many students to join the job market."[41]

These observations tally with those of Juliet B. Schor in her *Overworked American*. Since the mid-sixties the number of teens holding jobs has increased ten percentage points. "Not only are more of the nation's young people working, but they are working longer hours." She also concludes that "much of this work is motivated by consumerism: teenagers buy clothes, music, even cars." Throughout society, hours of work multiply, and leisure diminishes.[42]

Newsweek recently featured the topic of students working. Drawing on market surveys, it estimated that teenagers are twice as likely to work now as they were in 1950. A 1989 study in New Hampshire found that 77 percent of seniors worked, and more than half worked over twenty hours. Again, only a small percent said they worked to help the family or to save for college; for the vast majority, work meant sweaters, cars, lavish dates. After interviewing several score of working students, the *Newsweek* reporters concluded that they "take jobs by choice, not necessity."

The impact of work on studies is not arcane: sinking grades and easy courses. Yet some students hold jobs and do well; others without jobs do poorly. An attitude toward knowledge, as much as the absence of leisure, undercuts learning. Still, only so many hours exist in a week. After fifteen hours serving hamburgers, the average twenty-odd hours a week watching television, a few more shopping, plus eating and sleeping: nothing is left. Leisure has evaporated and with it the time to study and read. A full week suffocates schooling. To add three hours a day of work is to subtract three hours students do not have; it comes directly out of the time and energy for schooling. No wonder American students sleep through class and skip homework.

The Educational Testing Service determined that students working long hours are less likely to take biology and chemistry, and are more likely to score poorly in math, science, history, literature, and reading. A study of teenagers in Wisconsin and California finds declining grades with increasing work. As one psychology professor commented, "Everybody worries why Japanese and German and Swedish students are doing better than us. One reason is they're not spending their afternoons wrapping tacos."[43]

"Leisure," wrote de Grazia, "is a state of being free from everyday necessity," a state "rarely approached in the industrial world."[44] Leisure is obviously not an answer to the ills of education, yet it may illuminate those ills. A liberal education requires a cultural breathing space, a small refuge. Reading, writing, and thinking are delicate activities, easily numbed by the din of money, shopping, and jobs. This is not a judgment on individuals, who live as they must, but a judgment on a society that constricts the education it provides.

If the plain figures on good money and jobs for college graduates explain a tidal wave of students seeking admission, they do not explain the frenzy. Higher education is vast enough to absorb all students. Many schools have unfilled slots; most colleges recruit and drum up trade. Why the obsession? Everyone can find a seat.

Of course, not everyone can obtain a place in the school they deem essential. The general obsession turns into a special obsession of some students over a few colleges; and the fixation is fed by an economic reality. College costs rise at the same time government support declines and family income stagnates. This has led to some expected and unexpected results: more student loans; more students working; reduced course offerings; and increasing years required to graduate. It also leads to something else.

Gargantuan tuition at elite private schools frightens the families of bright students who are neither very rich nor very poor. Stanford's annual tuition approaches $20,000. Throw in living expenses —dormitories or apartments, food, books, and travel—and the yearly bill for schooling at Stanford inches toward $30,000. Four years at Stanford will set back a student well over $100,000. Many comfortable families assume they will not be eligible for scholarships—and their children are unable to attend without them.

They turn not simply to public schools but to the best in their states, like the University of Michigan at Ann Arbor or the University of Texas at Austin or the University of Massachusetts at Amherst or the University of California at Berkeley. These are no longer cheap; tuitions run from $3,000 to $5,000 a year, plus $10,000 for lodging, food, and books. Yet for many families this is possible because it is essential; they are desperate to gain entry to what they consider the best campuses of the public university system. Even with excellent incomes they cannot handle the costs of select private schools. This population demands a seat in the select public universities.

As they push their way in, the economic profile of the top public schools shifts. The "middle" middle class, once the backbone of these universities, is being priced and forced out. Middle-income students, concludes one report, "have faced stagnant family income, dramatic increases in the cost of college attendance, and a diminishing access to financial aid." As a result, they register "dramatic declines" in enrollment. Conversely, upper-income students are attending select public universities at rates "well above" the growth of their income groups; and even when middle-income students seek places at the Ann Arbors and Berkeleys, their lower test scores and grades means they "get squeezed out."[45]

Administrators use their financial resources to increase the least represented, lowest-income and minority ethnic groups. Why help the middle class? In the pressure to demonstrate school diversity, a middle class counts for naught. No one hauls out the profile of the campus population and proudly indicates the numbers of middle-income students; everyone wants to know the attendance of the lowest-income groups, usually African-American and Latino. Despite stalling and reversals, that presence has increased. However, more dramatically but less visibly, the wealthier have taken over the select public schools. Even as they become more diverse, the elite public universities are becoming economically more homogeneous.

For instance, over 60 percent of the incoming freshmen at UCLA in 1991 had family incomes above $60,000; and 40 percent of these had family incomes over $100,000.[46] This seems generally true throughout the state and nation. In California the attendance of low-income students at four-year public universities has increased; but the big increases come from children of families earning over $75,000. For comparison, the average family salary of students attending the African-American and Latino two-year Compton College is $23,000; 60 percent of the predominantly Latino East Los Angeles College, a community college, have family incomes of less than $24,000.

This process may be the "gentrification" of higher education, but it is also a restratification, both within top schools and across higher education. The striking range of tuition—from $20,000 at the elite private schools to several hundred dollars at community colleges—spells economic stratification. Public two-year community colleges demonstrate the greatest growth in recent years; in an era of static or declining family incomes, they are most accessible. Within the elite private and select public schools an opposite development takes place; an enlarging group of affluent students obtain spots. Enough places exist across the country for all freshmen, but not enough at prestigious schools within economic reach. Among the upper middle classes this fires the frenzy of college admissions.

Berkeley may exemplify the pressures. From its origins through much of the sixties, Berkeley admitted virtually any student meeting the basic requirements, mainly graduating in the top eighth of a high school class. By the 1980s this completely turned about; only about 16 percent of those applying (and meeting the general requirements) were being admitted. In the fall of 1989 some 21,300 high school seniors applied to Berkeley for 3,500 freshmen openings. Moreover, of those applying almost 6,000 boasted straight-A high school averages.[47]

D'Souza in *Illiberal Education* recounts a poignant tale of an Asian-American, first in his class, a straight-A student, who was turned down by Berkeley. That seemed astounding, and D'Souza attributes the rejection to the ills of affirmative action, which unfairly punishes the best-prepared to make way for lower achievers from other ethnic groups. Yet D'Souza misses something: there are not enough places for the all straight-A students. With 3,500 spots and 5,800 straight-A students applying, even if it were the single criterion for admission over 2,000 would still receive rejection letters. That produces hordes of unhappy students and families.

What to do? It seems futile to point out some obvious truths; reputation in higher education is circular. The best schools are best because they attract the best faculty and students, runs the argument. To ask if the teaching and classes are the best, however, cracks the tautological logic. Will students receive the best education at the best schools? This is far from certain. Many students who transfer from community colleges to the elite public universities complain of the huge classes, the use of graduate students as teachers, and the indifference of professors. Few observers contest this; and many appeal to a cynical truth. The reason to attend a select university is not to receive a superior education, but to receive a superior diploma.

The obsession with a few schools forgets the rest. Defenders and critics view higher education through the lens of the Stanfords, Harvards, and Berkeleys. When they refer to American campuses they summon up images of grassy quadrangles, stately buildings, and vast libraries. College catalogs sent to prospective students confirm these images. In these publications thoughtful students stride across vast lawns, study beneath soaring towers, or converse in well-appointed classrooms. Nor is this simply false advertising. A skeptical visitor will be surprised to find that many colleges look like colleges. In the fall parents drive up to discharge their children to schools that very much resemble images of what colleges should look like. Either colleges copy stereotypes or stereotypes copy reality—or both.

D'Souza's book on higher education opens with these familiar scenes from America's opulent and green campuses, which he calls "tributes to the largesse of democratic capitalism." Gigantic auditoriums, gymnasiums, and libraries "sprawl across the landscape" indicating a "tremendous investment of resources." Some schools boast "impressive domes and arches" which exude "old money and traditions." Students wander across the campus, nodding to friends, evidently "conscious of being part of a community." If these pictures are accurate, they are hardly the whole story.

I'm standing in a parking lot looking up at West Los Angeles College, a predominantly African-American school. Scattered across the surrounding hills are oil rigs. Next to the main building stand temporary structures and a series of trailers serving as offices and classrooms. Although it's the first week of a semester, the place seems deserted. It could almost be a futurist movie set: the oil wells, the sun, blowing wind and trash, and no people. I figure some activity might be found at the library. Nothing much. A small sign on the door lists hours. The library closes at noon on Friday and all day Sunday; the hours for Saturday are crossed out, and the words "To be announced" are written in.

I locate the bookstore, a beehive of activity on many campuses. This one could fit into two minivans, and contains only the barest necessities. The student cafeteria and union prove equally dismal. I talk with a dean. "Where are the students?" Most attend in the evening. The dean complains about the unfinished buildings and temporary structures that have become permanent. He recalls that a new student asked him point-blank, "Is this really a college?" Assured it was, he demanded, "How come it doesn't look like one?"

It's neither new nor specifically American, but most people prefer to hear (or read) about the rich rather than the poor, the successful rather than the unsuccessful. Only drama or disaster draws the media to the poor, as if to emphasize their difference from others. With mixed success social historians have sought for decades to redirect attention from the few to the many.

Higher education reflects this skewed attention. We pay attention to the few, presumably the best, and ignore the rest. What happens at Harvard or Princeton or Stanford or UC Berkeley is national news. If a lawsuit is filed at Harvard or a professor charges harassment at MIT or a UC Berkeley group protests a course: these events merit national attention.

Even a memo at an elite school elicits news reports. An ironic memo on "abolishing" evil circulated by the new president of Yale caused numerous journalists to take note. In his first day as president, A. Bartlett Giamatti issued the following memo:

> In order to repair what Milton called the ruin of our grandparents, I wish to announce that henceforth, as a matter of University policy, evil is abolished and paradise restored. I trust all of us will do whatever possible to achieve this policy objective.

This communication prompted an open letter to *The New York Review of Books* and news reports and editorials in the New York

Times, the Washington *Post, The Wall Street Journal, The New Yorker,* as well as discussion in a nationally syndicated column by George Will. *The Wall Street Journal* grumbled, "What we need is not more talk about evil, but some decent courses in risk arbitrage." The wide response amazed Giamatti.[48]

But Pima College in Arizona or Triton College in Illinois—both schools with over 20,000 students enrolled—will never draw a single national reporter with a memo or a lawsuit. They will go unnoticed unless a mass murderer guns down thirty students or a natural-gas explosion levels the campus. If a tomato is thrown at Harvard, the nation will read about it: "Irate Student Heaves Tomato at Harvard Prof." If student protesters shut down Tulsa Junior College in Tulsa, Oklahoma, a large place with some 18,000 enrolled, only Tulsa residents will know.

Virtually all the media reflect this bias. A national magazine asked me for an article on today's universities with a focus on the new type of college president. Yet it turned out that the magazine's editors wanted something on only a few schools: Harvard, Yale, Princeton, or Stanford and perhaps a couple of others. They claimed their readers couldn't care less about what was happening at the University of Wisconsin at Madison, much less at New Mexico State at Las Cruces.

Another reason for focusing on the top few assumes that what happens there reflects or anticipates what happens elsewhere. This partial truth does not justify ignoring the larger world of higher education that faces different realities. A study of American society confined to a Donald Trump or David Rockefeller, assuming each reflected common realities, would get blasted by reviewers. Yet the conservatives savage higher education by way of a few elite schools, supposing they reflect the general condition. The books engender much discussion, but few contest the flawed proposition.

Allan Bloom here is typical, honest, if condescending, in his attitude. He wrote that *The Closing of the American Mind* will concentrate on the "thousands of students of comparatively high intelligence" who people the "best universities." Why only these? Because these students "have the greatest moral and intellectual effect on the nation." They are "materially and spiritually free to do pretty much what they want" during their college years. In other words, the costs of schooling do not burden them. He admitted that other types of students exist. "They have their own needs and may

very well have very different characters from those I describe here."
This is a genteel way of stating that other students require economic
support and, in Bloom's terms, may lack intelligence.

Few students populate "the twenty or thirty best universities,"
which are Bloom's concern. Many of the "best" schools—for instance, Amherst or Williams College—enroll just several thousand.
What can this select crowd from twenty-five schools tell us about
the 14 million enrolled in American higher education? Moreover, in
practice, the conservative critics remain fixated on far fewer than
twenty-five. D'Souza takes up six schools: Berkeley, Stanford,
Howard, Michigan, Duke, and Harvard.

Vocal leftist academics might not see the elitism of the conservatives because they share it; they teach at the same schools and evidence little concern for the community colleges and commuter state
universities. In a celebrated comment, a leftist English professor at
Princeton stated, "I teach in the Ivy League in order to have direct
access to the minds of the children of the ruling classes."[49] This
could be a statement by Allan Bloom's radical brother: only the
elite students matter, an odd sentiment for a Marxist, though perhaps apt for a post-Marxist.

Even at the elite schools, those not born to wealth may be invisi-
ble. Benjamin deMott, who teaches at Amherst College, a select
private school, recalled a tragic incident. "A black freshman named
Gerald Penny went down the hill to the gym with his classmates,
during 'orientation,' to take a compulsory swimming test. Rows of
larking students—mainly children of affluence—dove one after another into the pool, filling the lanes. Penny dove with the others,
and, not knowing how to swim, drowned."[50]

Countless editorials, essays, discussions, and conferences have
dealt with the curriculum revisions at Stanford University. Many
have found them ominous for American education. The critics
charge that a coherent Western Civilization course has been diluted
into a trendy multicultural offering, which is required of all undergraduates. This may be bad, this may be good, but what is its
impact on American higher education? The total (undergraduate)
enrollment at Stanford is about 6,500. As Clifford Adelman comments, drawing on a representative sample of 20,000 transcripts,
only several percent attended elite schools like Stanford. "When
one looks at the archive left by an entire generation, it should be
rather obvious that Stanford is not where America goes to college."

He adds, "Whether Stanford freshmen read Cicero or Frantz Fanon is a matter worthy of a raree show."[51]

Community colleges often have enrollments three and four times larger. For instance, Northern Virginia Community College enrolls over 30,000. Shouldn't its course requirements engage the concerns of educational commentators? When was the last time a national news story appeared about curriculum revisions at Northern Virginia Community College?

This can be made more exact. Down the road from Stanford is Mission College, a community college, with twice the number of undergraduates as its more famous neighbor. Since 1986 "cultural pluralism" has guided curriculum revisions at Mission. Its general catalog advertises the college's commitment to "cultural pluralism," perhaps because over 50 percent of its 11,000 students are Asian or Latino. Its basic humanities courses now compares "traditions of different ethnic groups with the study of classical and European cultures."[52]

One might imagine that these changes would trigger an immediate response. One might suppose that reporters would descend on Santa Clara, California; commentators would comment; editorial writers would editorialize; conservatives would bemoan. "Western Civilization Demoted at Mission College," a headline might scream. What has been the national response? Nil. No one cares.

Numbers bore and can mislead, but a valid criticism of higher education requires a sense of its size and shape. Any survey of higher education, for instance, that does not mention community colleges may crash into several new mountain ranges. In 1920, they enrolled under 2 percent of all college freshmen; today over one-half of college freshmen are found in community colleges.[53]

California education, because of its size and structure, illustrates the numerical configuration of American colleges. At its top rest the campuses of the University of California; these are well known because of scholarship, politics, or sports. They include UC Berkeley, UCLA, UC San Diego, and six other campuses; they restrict their students to the best high school graduates. While several are vast campuses, with large medical and graduate schools, they enroll relatively few of the state's undergraduates, under 120,000.

The next tier of the system is the four-year state college system. These colleges command a much smaller public profile, but are the backbone of California undergraduate higher education, twenty four-year schools with limited or no graduate schools. They call themselves "the largest system of senior higher education in the nation." With lower admission requirements than the University of California campuses, their total undergraduate enrollment is almost three times larger, about 340,000.[54] Finally, the community colleges, open to all high school graduates, dwarf the other two systems with about 1.2 million students.

Why do students across the nation attend community colleges and four-year commuter state universities in such numbers? The answer is simple: costs and access. They are usually close, easy to get into, and, most of all, cheap. Total cost at the top state universities runs about $15,000; and at top private schools, $25,000 to $30,000. Community colleges and lower-echelon state universities belong to another world. Numbers like $20,000 a year look like funny money. Where would students get these sums? Fees for tuition at two-year colleges are correspondingly low. Until recently California community colleges charged $5.00 a credit. Because of strapped budgets, this was raised by one dollar. Tuition for a full load of courses sets a student back a maximum of $120 for a year, somewhat less than Stanford's $20,000.

California community colleges are exceptional in their low costs —or were, since steep hikes in costs are in the offing—but most community colleges charge well under $1,000 for a year. For instance, tuition at Pima Community College in Tucson runs about $600. Four-year state schools charge more, but dramatically less than the elite schools. A year's tuition at University of Texas Pan American, with an enrollment twice that of Stanford, costs about $1,000. Moreover, non-elite colleges draw upon students in the surrounding area, who commute to school. By staying at home, students save a bundle, as living costs are the major expense of attending a public university.

The gentrification of higher education—the increasing dominance by the wealthy of the select universities—is troubling. Everyone applauds the ethnic and racial diversity of American campuses, visible in faces and skin hues. Economic diversity or its absence does not catch the eye in the same way. Yet within the augmented ethnic diversity exists its opposite, an augmented affluent homogeneity; even as students are more different, they are more alike.

As elsewhere in American society, food indexes class differences. Once upon a time, student unions served more or less the same fare in colorless cafeterias; uniformed workers ladled out soup or plucked a hot dog off a grill; students chose a ready-made sandwich off a counter and got coffee from stainless-steel vats. These outfits still exist, but mainly at community and commuter colleges, campuses where students do not live, stick around little, and have less money for eating out.

The major universities have undergone "boutiquization"; drab cafeterias are long gone, replaced by custom-made sandwich shops —six kinds of bread, three condiments, with or without cheese, tomatoes, and lettuce; coffee bars with ten brews, cappuccinos and espressos; falafel vendors, mini-delis, salad eateries, pizzerias, and more. Campus food has unquestionably improved, but like the food offerings in malls, the variety also represents a homogenizing consumerism. The diversity is no illusion, but depends on an affluent uniformity that reduces cultural differences to shopping whims and preferences. No one could interpret a wall of food vendors—Thai, Mexican, Ethiopian, Italian—as anything more than food choices for a hungry Western consumer.

A monochromatic affluence, or desire for it, renders false the claims of vast cultural differences among students, and indeed among the American population. Inasmuch as this encroaches upon complex issues of cultural identity, the proposition is not something that can be dispatched in paragraph or a book.[55] It is striking, however, that amidst the barage about diversity on and off campus, few bother—or dare—to argue the reverse: that American society, perhaps the world, is not becoming more diverse, but more uniform. This does not simply mean that in Tokyo, Chicago, Rio, and Prague people buy the same goods and dress the same, which they do; it means that cultural differences are weakening, not intensifying.

Cultural homogeneity coexists within economic stratification, and doesn't lessen it. With its equalitarian garb America has long deceived visitors, and some inhabitants. Both rich and poor wear Levi's, but live in different neighborhoods and attend different colleges. With important exceptions, the curricula of the schools they attend are similar; they testify to a blaring mercantilism that leaves a liberal education pinched and gasping.

2

THE FREE SPEECH
MOVEMENT,
PART TWO

"IT WAS A TENSE SITUATION, but what was more vivid at the time was a peculiar fact: this was my first speech in stockinged feet. Or from the top of a police car."[1] Inside the car were two police officers and an ex-student arrested for violating campus regulations. As the news spread of the arrest, thousands of students converged, trapping the vehicle. The blocked car served as a podium, and onto its roof clambered a series of students and professors. The standoff lasted some thirty hours and engendered the Free Speech Movement (FSM). The place? University of California, Berkeley. The date? October 1, 1964.

Those were the bad-good old days. Speakers took off their shoes to avoid marring the automobile; and students collected $334.30 to pay "for damage to the police car."[2] All was not benign, however. The Free Speech Movement, a key chapter in the sixties, unleashed a series of acrimonious confrontations that led to several sit-ins and eight hundred arrests on the Berkeley campus. "One of the world's largest and most famous centers of learning was brought to the edge of collapse," wrote two Berkeley professors.[3] Berkeley was under siege.

Although the FSM moved beyond a single issue, university restrictions on free speech gave rise to it. The University of California had long regulated campus speech, film showings, invited speakers, and political recruiting. On a small tract of land at the entrance to the university, however, student politicking and speechifying flourished; this was considered public and free space. "In the official mythology of that now distant era," writes the philosopher John Searle, "the land did not belong to the University but to the city of Berkeley and so a citizen could there exercise at least certain of his rights."[4]

In September 1964, the administration served notice that the tract belonged to the university, and campus restrictions on political speech would apply. The following month the university arrested in this area an ex-student for distributing political literature. For many Berkeley denizens the university's actions violated their rights; the arrest triggered the confrontation between the administration and what became the Free Speech Movement.

"The issue is free speech," stated an FSM leaflet. "Civil liberties and political freedoms which are constitutionally protected off campus must be equally protected on campus . . . The administration . . . may not regulate the content of speech." The FSM accused the university of succumbing to "right-wing political pressure" in restricting free speech. Conversely, critics of the FSM like Sidney Hook, the American philosopher and longtime critic of Marxism, considered "preposterous" the idea "that the *content* of speech should be beyond any restriction by the University." As an educational institution the university has not only the right but the obligation, Hook believed, to regulate speech and behavior by a standard "higher" than obtains outside the campus.[5]

Out of the FSM emerged an eloquent spokesman, Mario Savio, who gave a speech that would be quoted endlessly: "There's a time when the operation of the machine becomes so odious, makes you so sick at heart, that you can't take part . . ." Savio identified the southern civil rights movement as the root of the Berkeley protest. "Last summer I went to Mississippi to join the struggle there for civil rights." On his return he found the same violations of rights in Berkeley. "In our free speech fight at the University of California

. . . we have encountered" the "same organized status quo" that we found in Mississippi.[6]

For a moment, America watched with fascination. The Berkeley events included scenes that would become increasingly familiar: students jammed into a campus building; a huge mobilization of police; Joan Baez singing "Blowin' in the Wind" and "We Shall Overcome"; and, finally, hundreds of students hauled off and arrested. With its vitality and esprit the Free Speech Movement spread the message of the sixties far and wide. Two sympathizers stated in 1966, "On campuses all over the nation faculties and administrations have combined to prevent themselves from becoming Berkeleys. The FSM succeeded in bringing the key feelings, ideas, and moods of the Movement to the attention of the entire national student body."[7]

Fast-forward to the present. Free speech is again a campus cry. In almost thirty years little has changed—except this: the players have exchanged roles. Now conservatives accuse the university and academic leftists of censoring speech. "Visiting a campus these days," writes the conservative columnist Michael Novak in a piece entitled "Thought Police," is "a little like visiting Eastern Europe before the fall of communism." Everywhere "politically correct" (PC) leftist dogma threatens freedom. "To stray from PC, one fears, will bring down public humiliation, even ostracism, maybe a disciplinary hearing."[8]

The radicals, loosely the graduates of the Free Speech Movement, advance positions that once were conservative; they want speech regulated by codes that proscribe certain language. They see free speech as at best a delusion, at worst a threat to the welfare of minorities and women. "Nowadays," writes Stanley Fish, a leftist English professor, "the First Amendment is the first refuge of scoundrels." We need campus speech codes because of the "lacerating harms that speech of certain kinds can inflict." "Ever wonder," asks the feminist law professor Catherine A. MacKinnon, "why men are so passionate about the First Amendment?" For MacKinnon free speech "means free sexual access to women." A campus gay activist complains that anytime their group tries to block a speaker "the right wing" screams about "freedom of opinion" and "threatens to bring in the ACLU."[9]

What happened? Why do academic leftists deride and conservatives prize free speech? Why do campus liberals want speech re-

stricted and conservatives champion the First Amendment? Why
does the conservative Supreme Court offer a defense of free speech,
while leftist law professors grumble? In 1992 the Supreme Court
struck down a law that banned certain hate symbols and words.
"The First Amendment," wrote Justice Scalia for the majority,
"does not permit . . . to impose special prohibitions on those
speakers who express views on disfavored subjects." Advocates of
campus speech codes were not happy. A Stanford law professor
objected that the court has no notion of the "real injury" speech
can cause.[10]

This most obvious (and cynical) explanation for the switched
positions is the switched situations. Protesting students became established professors and administrators. For outsiders, free speech
is bread and butter; for insiders, indigestion. To the new academics,
unregulated free speech spells trouble. They want to codify and
limit speech. Conversely, curbs on free speech seldom agitated conservatives in the past; historically they sought to limit subversive
and obscene speech. Now, on campuses, they doggedly uphold unrestricted language. As leftists migrated from outside to inside, have
conservatives traveled in the reverse direction?

The obvious explanation, however, may not dig far enough. In a
society obsessed with media and images, the boundaries of "free
speech" may alter. Left and right rethink the contested arena of
language because the world is now constructed out of language; or,
at least, some leftists and liberals reassess free speech in an age of
speech. Are violent words acts of violence in a society that trades in
words? Yet before considering these matters, the decks should be
cleared. What transgressions have the new guardians of free speech
found? How serious is the situation?

The conservative journal *The American Spectator* announced that
"our universities are in crisis." Radical dogmatists restrict free
speech. "More than 130 universities have issued codes barring free
discussion of dozens of topics." One school established "university
thought patrols" to monitor faculty and students. "The real question," declare the editors, is: "Will anybody be able to rescue the
universities from PC's anti-intellectual radicals of the 1960s?" Will
things just get worse?

"At *The American Spectator* we have decided that something will
be done." But nineties conservatives are not sixties radicals. Instead

of launching an anarchistic Free Speech Movement, the conservatives set up something befitting the times: they establish a "toll-free human rights hotline" to field calls on campus free speech violations. With heavy irony, the editors encourage students to report "the imminent arrest of a Shakespearean scholar or the brutal interrogation of a student caught whistling the National Anthem on campus."[11] Conservatives are manning the lines; they are defending liberties.

The cases frequently aired to illustrate a dire situation are instructive. In his *Illiberal Education,* D'Souza begins with two incidents from Harvard. Black students criticized Stephan Thernstrom, a well-respected and liberal professor, for "racial insensitivity." Apparently in his American history class Thernstrom read aloud from a plantation owner's journal, which angered some students. He first learned of his misdeed from the campus newspaper; a university-wide controversy erupted about what could be said in college courses, and implicitly whether students could censor course material. Thernstrom felt abandoned by the university, which failed to forthrightly defend him.

In a second incident a student head of the Harvard Women's Law Association accused visiting law professor Ian Macneil of sexism. In a quasi-open letter she accused Macneil of two misdeeds: his law textbook contained a line of poetry from Byron's "Don Juan" that she considered offensive to women; and in class he made "flippant" remarks about possibly sexist language, such as "That would be a straw man—or do we use that word anymore?" "Sauce for the goose, sauce for the gander—I don't know, is that sexist?" As with the Thernstrom incident, the campus newspaper ran headlines like "Law Prof Denies Sexism Charge," which legitimized the accusation; Macneil also felt that the university failed to defend his rights and integrity.

This only begins the list; but for D'Souza as well as Thernstrom and Macneil the implications are ominous. Student vigilantes roam the campuses, looking for transgressions of a new code. The administration, as well as most professors, either actively promote the new despots or look the other way. In the name of sensitivity to race and sex, academic freedom withers.

The critics may be right; it does not take much to thwart academic freedom—or any freedom. Few are heroes; and no matter how outrageous or unjust the charge, no one wants to risk the label "racist." The stories that D'Souza and others recount support these observations. The accusations hang in the air; the students and allies are righteously angry; the accused seemed damned without any recourse. They, and others, draw the lesson to steer clear of controversial subjects, to keep silent.

Yet before announcing a new leftist McCarthyism, some important distinctions must be made. McCarthyism was orchestrated from above by government officials and agencies with fairly wide popular support. It had at its beck and call the full powers of government: investigators, subpoenas, state police, jail, and the electric chair. It used them all. In 1949 the House Committee on Un-American Activities requested information on the social studies textbooks assigned in some universities.[12] The impact of this request by a federal committee with the right to issue subpoenas and jail witnesses is somewhat different than an "open letter" from a student group.

Leaving aside jailings, McCarthyism caused numerous firings as well as a system of blacklisting, keeping those discharged out of work. Estimates are very imprecise, but everything from schools and labor unions to Hollywood were investigated; those fired, forced to resign, or blacklisted ran into thousands in the entertainment business alone. Government loyalty investigations led to over ten thousand firings. "Between 1947 and 1953 over twenty thousand other people were subjected to formal filing of charges in the federal loyalty program alone." In the field of education, David Caute in *The Great Fear* estimates that "at least six hundred, and probably more, teachers and professors" lost their jobs.[13]

The loss of livelihood eviscerates freedom; and only the obtuse could miss the news that during the late forties and early fifties teachers were losing their jobs. To be simply summoned by a federal, state, or city committee investigating subversive activities constituted a crime in many school systems; and acts as minor as signing a petition in favor of world peace brought teachers to investigators' attention. "New York City's Board of Education dealt swiftly with its recalcitrant professors," writes the historian Diane Ravitch, "by invoking a section of the city charter that permitted automatic dismissal of those who refused to testify in official inquiries."[14] Teachers needed no additional prompting to avoid certain topics and people.

The current alarm of conservatives about free speech would be more convincing if they demonstrated an even historical hand. Allan Bloom objected to the widening range of "things unthinkable and unspeakable" in today's universities, but he also commended McCarthyism as a wonderful tonic for higher education. Bloom denounced as "mythology" the belief that McCarthyism injured the university. "Actually the McCarthy period was the last time the university had any sense of community." McCarthyism "had no effect whatsoever on curriculum or appointments. The range of thought and speech that took place within [the major universities] was unaffected." Bloom brazenly stated, "Professors were not fired, and they taught what they pleased in their classrooms."[15]

This is an extraordinary statement from a new steward of campus freedom. Where had Bloom been? Several contemporary studies of McCarthyism found faculty stayed away from controversial issues inside and outside the classroom. A careful survey of several thousand professors in 1955 concluded that the majority felt "the intellectual and political freedom of the teaching community had been noticeably curtailed, or at least disturbingly threatened."[16]

This same study, *The Academic Mind*, tallied 990 incidents in which teachers were accused of leftist politics or Communist Party membership, and found that over 20 percent led to a firing or forced resignation. Lionel Lewis's *Cold War on Campus* studied 126 cases at fifty-eight universities and colleges. During the height of McCarthyism, over two hundred cases claiming violations of academic freedom piled up in the offices of the American Association of University Professors. Few institutions of higher education went uncited.[17]

Bloom must at least have been familiar with a well-known case in his own field. In 1952, M. I. Finley, a classicist, was called before the Senate Subcommittee on Internal Subversion. He answered some questions, and declared that he was not a Communist. However, to the question whether he had ever been a member of the Communist Party, Finley invoked the Fifth Amendment. For this, Rutgers University fired him; unable to find work, he moved to England, where he pursued an illustrious career at Cambridge University.[18] "Professors were not fired"?

The current situation differs. The censors are not government agents or police with subpoenas. They are students with some faculty and administrative allies who yell, literally or in the press. The impact is hardly the same. It may be extremely unpleasant, and occasionally leads to a limited administrative action, but it is difficult to find cases of a firing or forced resignation of a regular faculty member.[19]

For instance, Thernstrom was hardly threatened with unemployment; rather he concluded that teaching about race today "isn't worth it" and he will no longer offer the course that provoked the controversy. Macneil, bitter about his experience as a visiting faculty at Harvard, chose, according to D'Souza, "not to seek an extension of his teaching appointment but to move on to Northwestern University School of Law."

Compare these burdens to the fate of professors grilled during the McCarthy period. At the University of Washington six faculty were investigated as Communists; eventually three were put on probation and three fired outright. A historian of the cold war notes, "None of the three dismissed faculty ever got jobs in higher education again. [Professor] Butterworth wrote to two thousand members of the Modern Language Association, but though there was a demand for Old English specialists in the 1950s, he never got an offer. Without severance pay from the University, he subsisted on odd jobs and eventually went on public assistance . . ."[20]

The recent cases belong in another category. Those targeted do not become unemployed; sometimes they move from one department or school to another. Julius Lester, an African-American professor and writer, earned the wrath of his colleagues in Afro-American Studies at the University of Massachusetts. Lester, who converted to Judaism, attacked as anti-Semitic some remarks of James Baldwin. His colleagues attacked him in return, and the atmosphere heated up. Relations deteriorated to the point that his colleagues suggested to the administration that Lester might be "more comfortable in a different location in the University." Lester agreed, and transferred from Afro-American Studies to Judaic and Near Eastern Studies.[21] End of tale.

Newsweek's cover story on the leftist dogmatists ("Is this the new enlightenment on campus or the new McCarthyism?") reported various unpleasant incidents, but again none led to unemployment or blacklisting. The *Newsweek* account opened with presumably the most significant or representative case. A homemade poster on the dormitory door of a University of Connecticut student provoked an objection by gays. The poster, a sophomoric effort at humor by a sophomore, listed "preppies," "bimbos," "men without chest hair," and "homos" as "people who are shot on sight." Campus gays charged a violation of the university behavior code, which prohibited slurs and insults based on race, sex, ethnicity, and sexual orientation. The student was found guilty and ordered to clear out of university housing (not the school); she sued in federal courts and was allowed to move back.[22]

Newsweek also reported the tale of a UC Berkeley professor, Vincent Sarich, a physical anthropologist, who researches the relationship between race and innate abilities and concludes that some races have a genetic advantage. Seventy-five students marched into his anthropology class and drowned out his lecture. As with Thernstrom, the university waffled in coming to his defense; it pledged to look into student complaints. Conclusion? "Sarich was left in doubt whether he would be allowed to teach the introductory anthropology course." *Newsweek* did not mention that the university condemned the interruption of his class and disciplined students who participated.[23]

Other cases more or less follow this pattern. The *National Catholic Reporter* told of a student who expressed "an unpopular view" and was "drowned out by a fellow student with a chant of 'wrong, wrong, wrong.' "[24] The complete episode consisted of one student yelling at another. *National Review* offers a more serious story. A male University of Washington student who enrolled in Introduction to Women's Studies "endured" various outrages. "But when it was asserted that lesbians actually make the best parents, he asked, after class, his feminist professor for some proof. 'Why are you challenging me?' she asked indignantly. At the next session, Mr. Schaub found himself barred by campus police from entering the classroom."[25]

Of course, many cases follow no pattern; some seem like jokes; others are indecipherable webs of charges and countercharges. From St. John's University in Minnesota emerges a story of "ostracism" of the "politically incorrect." A student felt "oppressed" because the administration banned her posters backing college Republicans. Why the ban? Because the Republican elephants " 'were dancing suggestively and one elephant had nipples.' "[26]

From Texas comes news of a "political correctness" victim which seems more like a case of acrimonious disagreements. Professor Gribben, a member of the conservative National Association of Scholars, taught at the University of Texas at Austin; he resigned, fleeing to a position at a smaller school. The reason? According to Gribben, political persecution. Gribben opposed several curriculum revisions; his English Department colleagues turned intolerant and hostile. As one of his supporters put it, "There have been no shouting matches in the halls, but there has been animosity. There are faculty members who won't speak to other faculty members."[27]

Even the most sympathetic presentation of Gribben's plight does not go much beyond listing slights and grimaces. Gribben cast the single dissenting vote against a new graduate program in Third World and minority literature; he believed that master's degree students needed a better grounding in European and American literature before tackling this new field.

After the vote he "noticed that attitudes toward him were changing." The "hits were subtle but palpable," writes the conservative journalist Peter Collier, who describes an incident: "Gribben was talking to a student near the department's mailroom door and a colleague came by and brusquely asked him to move out of the way, even though Gribben wasn't blocking his access, and then said, 'I said, *please* move!' when he didn't shuffle fast enough." That's the whole of the event, which a Gribben backer interprets this way: "It was that special sort of cruelty of which only literature professors are capable."[28] Maybe, but when it comes to cruelty telephone operators or postal workers seem just as skilled.

Gribben suffered other attacks, but nothing beyond angry comments and stares. After losing an unpleasant round in the controversy to revamp the freshman English course, a Gribben ally commented, "Now I understand fascism a little better."[29] This refers to a departmental meeting! In the controversy over the revised English course, Gribben became more outspoken, appearing on local radio and television talk shows. To alumni contributors of the university, he wrote that a "highly politicized faction of radical literary theorists" dominated the English Department, which should be put in administrative "receivership." These interventions did not endear Gribben to many colleagues; the blood became so bad that Gribben found a position elsewhere. The problem is this: Even if Gribben was completely in the right, cold shoulders, mortifying looks, and nasty comments do not constitute an infringement of academic freedom, much less fascism.

More recent tallies of campus political persecution have not come up with much. *The American Spectator,* which set up the hotline and an organization, Amnesty in Academia, to monitor the situation, took stock after a year, stating that "hundreds of informants" have called in to report "human rights abuses."[30] Yet the magazine is sketchy about details; the serious cases of campus repression it cites are familiar, false, or not serious. The first three episodes it offers are: the writer Edward Hoagland "not reappointed" at Bennington College "because of un-PC sentiments"; Lawrence Millman "fired" at Goddard College because of criticism of a woman's class work; Alan Gribben "forced to resign" in Texas because of opposition to ethnic and Third World studies for graduate students.

"Forced to resign" is a bit embellished as the caption for the Gribben story. After finding another position, he resigned from Texas because departmental relations turned unpleasant. The firing of Lawrence Millman at Goddard is a tough one: the college reports that no one with that name belonged to its regular faculty since 1938. To be sure, it is possible that Millman was a part-time, adjunct, or extension instructor whom the college barely knew existed.

In order to save money, all schools have multiplied their part-time staffs, which exist in a gray world, deliberately ignored by the administration; these instructors lack long-term contracts (and regular salaries and health benefits). Inasmuch as they are hired only temporarily, they do not have to be fired; rather they are let go unless they are reappointed. They flow in and out of American higher education like the tides. Occasionally a part-time instructor claims he or she was "fired" for political, racist, or sexist reasons. Inasmuch as no reasons have to be presented for not rehiring a short-term employee, these situations prove almost impossible to resolve.

The Hoagland incident may be a veritable case of harassment. In an article for *Esquire* magazine, Hoagland wrote in passing that anal intercourse was rare among animals and for physical reasons damaging among humans. These two statements upset the Lesbian/Gay/Bisexual Alliance, which dubbed him homophobic; with faculty help or leadership the group managed to get his department to reverse a vote reappointing him. "I never imagined such frankness could get me into so much trouble," mused Hoagland. One colleague congratulated Hoagland "on being the first person ever fired from Bennington for opposing sodomy."

Unfortunately for *The American Spectator,* the story does not unfold according to script. The incident unleashed a small storm of memos, position papers, and letters. While all that ends well is not necessarily well, the college, pressured by Hoagland, a faculty review committee, and PEN, reversed itself and rehired the writer. Hoagland agrees that "free speech did indeed win out at Bennington," though he remains concerned. "Nationwide and at Bennington, I don't think the lesson's been learned."[31]

This only ices the cake for Amnesty in Academia, which is also bringing "the firings of fourteen other university professors under consideration." This sounds impressive, but the organization tantalizes us with information about only two of these cases: Tim Osterholm, who was " 'forced' to resign" from Western Washington University, and James Sellers at Rice. If these are the most dramatic or illuminating of the fourteen firings, Amnesty in Academia needs its own defense committee.

For starters, Tim Osterholm was not a professor; he was a student who worked in the Veterans Outreach Center, administered by the Associated Students of the University. According to the associate director of the student union at Western Washington, Osterholm, himself a veteran and an undergraduate, manned the Veterans Outreach Center, one of many student organizations with a paid staff person. He resigned his position in his second year mainly because he objected to pressure by other groups to enlist the Center in AIDS and feminist educational activities.

A regular full-time faculty member figures in the second case. Yet this professor, James Sellers, was not fired or threatened with firing. As in many bitter controversies, a new faculty appointment fueled the flames. The Department of Religious Studies needed to fill a position, an endowed chair of Western religious thought. According to Sellers, a professor of ethics in the department, the job description advertising the position shifted the focus from Western religion to a more politically correct multicultural orientation. This slight but significant modification minimized Western religion. Sellers and his supporters believed that "to take a chair of Western religious thought and turn it into chair of comparative religious thought" depreciated Western religion.

Sellers protested the job description in several ways, including a letter to *The Wall Street Journal.* "The wish to be 'Politically Correct' has taken a novel turn in the department of religious studies at Rice University," he wrote. "Incredibly, it now appears to be

viewed as undesirable to teach theology in a religious-studies department."[32] For his outspokenness Sellers suffered "various forms
of harassment." The departmental chair promptly released Sellers
from his position as a PhD thesis director. Since overseeing doctoral
students is sometimes considered an honor, the action might have
been an administrative slap. However, Sellers was hardly fired; both
the president of the university and the dean affirmed his right to
protest the job description. He looks forward to a reconciliation or
at least an understanding.[33]

From these dramatic and fictitious tales of fired university professors Amnesty in Academia turns to stories of student intimidations,
"suspensions and expulsions." Again the organization cries foul,
but hardly follows through. It offers no information on student
suspensions and expulsions, presumably because it has none; rather
it presents a list of miscellaneous reports and odd sightings. A female applicant for a scholarship was rebuked by letter for the "inappropriate use of the term 'chairman.' " Another student applying
for a scholarship was asked some "weird" questions about sex. A
student at Harvard suffered "threats and indignities" for displaying
a Confederate flag. Elsewhere a student "innocently entered a seminar where she was encouraged to air her independent views, only to
be targeted by PC Thought Patrollers for the rest of the seminar."
So much for the most horrifying tales of political persecution by
leftists among the more than 14 million students in American
higher education.[34]

Another matter should be raised: the general accuracy of the reports. An eagerness to find leftist censorship gives rise to distortions
and serious exaggerations. For instance, *The Wall Street Journal*
recounted an egregious violation of free speech with the headline
"Return of the Storm Troopers." In editorializing about a lecture
sponsored by a conservative group at a SUNY campus, it evoked
the "reign of Hitler's brownshirts." According to the *Journal,* two
hundred radical students, "some carrying canes and sticks," roared
into a quiet lecture violently threatening the speaker. "The threat of
violence is clear and soon fulfilled. The mob disrupts the talk, jeers
the speaker. An elderly, distinguished professor in the audience
barely escapes a beating . . ." A similar account appeared in the
New York *Post,* headlined "Outrage at SUNY-Binghamton" and
"The Brownshirts and the Cowards."

Yet careful examinations of the event in *Newsday* and *Mother*

Jones, based on audiotapes and videotapes of the incident as well as interviews, found that account mainly fanciful.[35] True, hostile students had crowded into a lecture hall; a single student, later disciplined by the university, caused an unpleasant disturbance for four minutes. That was all. The lecture proceeded; no one was hurt; the sticks were apparently one walking stick and some fraternity pledge canes. A local TV station, which showed up looking for some action, reported that an expected confrontation did not take place.

Scrutiny of the Thernstrom incident also reveals significant distortions. "Almost every element of the story D'Souza tells [about the Thernstrom incident] is erroneous," states Jon Wiener, a *Nation* columnist. D'Souza and others have trumpeted it as a clear case of a liberal administration caving in before totalitarian minorities. But the administration hardly stated or even hinted that Thernstrom should not teach the course; even Thernstrom agrees with this. According to Thernstrom, the administration told the students, " 'We don't take complaints against the faculty; have you talked to him? If not, do so.' That was the end."[36]

A male student at the University of Washington was barred from a Women's Studies course; but standard references to leftist intolerance hardly do justice to the reality.[37] An instructor blocked a student from attending the class because of his threatening demeanor and obnoxious questions. His alleged misdeed hardly required the campus police. For instance, hand raised for a question, he sought recognition by repeating "ma'am, ma'am." The instructor responded, "Don't call me 'ma'am'; that's sexist." He replied, "Excuse me, sir." His humor won few friends.

However, the university—after hesitating—reinstated the student, directing that he receive full credit for the course. At the same time, the university did not simply bury the incident, but established a committee of professors to investigate, not the student, but the Women's Studies course. What it found was more damning about higher education than about leftist dogma.

Typically in big universities regular professors teach large introductory courses. Students meet weekly in small classes with a graduate student to discuss the material; and these graduate students mark papers and examinations. This is already a poor state of affairs inasmuch as too much responsibility falls upon overburdened and undertrained graduate students. As its own committee discovcied, the University of Washington went further than this in Women's Studies.

In the introductory Women's Studies course, a graduate student gave the lectures, while undergraduates conducted the weekly discussion sections and graded the students. For this work these undergraduates were "paid" by receiving academic credits. A freshman who had taken the course the previous semester taught the section of the barred student. That is, a freshman, the same age as or younger than those enrolled, had primary responsibility to lead discussions and grade. This was a situation designed for disaster.[38]

To call this a case of leftist intolerance misses the essence. If it was so, it went nowhere. The university flexed its muscle against the petty tyrants by reinstating the student and moving to restructure the introductory Women's Studies course. The incident illuminates, not the strange behavior of some feminist academics, but the degraded condition of teaching. That an introductory course could be taught by a graduate student with a staff of undergraduates suggests that some schools have abandoned teaching.

Not only are single incidents misinterpreted or fabricated; the entire "crisis" resists accurate surveying, even confirmation. A national campus "crisis" of political dogmatism may have been as much fantasy as reality. Very few events are necessary to create what journalists consider a national trend; an incident here or a happening there gets picked up and circulated throughout the press, appearing as a national problem. "Crises" of political persecution, racism, and speech codes may plague American campuses. Yet often these "crises" are based on self-referential reports, accounts that gain credibility only by citing other accounts that refer to a closed circle of reports. It is possible to count traffic accidents, drive-by shootings, AIDS deaths, but it is far more difficult to tally up incidents of political harassment or racial hostility on campuses. These depend far more on who is doing the reporting and what happens with the report. A few events are transmuted into cultural reality.

For instance, a sentence about "date rape" in a campus publication traveled through the media gaining more and more credibility; it seemed to demonstrate a deranged feminist ideology. In 1985, students at Swarthmore wrote and produced a video on "acquaintance rape." This was sent out to other schools with a two-page student-written discussion guide. In one sentence the students suggested that "acquaintance rape" should be situated in a "spectrum of behavior" running from overt violence to "inappropriate innuendo."

Five years later a columnist for *U.S. News & World Report* stumbled upon this guide. He sought verification from Swarthmore that its official policy deemed inappropriate innuendos a form of rape. He did not obtain confirmation, but he wrote it up anyway as an example of campus "feminist ideology" gone nuts. From there the story took on a life of its own; it was picked up by a small libertarian magazine; then it moved to the Washington *Times* and into the mainstream press. The incident found its way into a column syndicated by Knight-Ridder, *Playboy, New York* magazine, the Detroit *News and Free Press,* and finally *Time.* Reporters and editors all judged extremely revealing a single sentence written by an undergraduate five years earlier.[39]

The same problems bedevil more serious issues, like violations of free speech, racial hostilities, and even speech codes. How are these measured or counted? What constitutes a trend? Speech codes might seem cut-and-dried—they either exist or not—but vast uncertainties surround even their numbers. The Washington *Post* estimated that 200 campuses enacted speech codes; the New York *Times,* 100. Other accounts repeat these figures, referring to the Washington *Post* or the New York *Times* or, even more authoritatively, to the Carnegie Foundation for the Advancement of Teaching. Nat Hentoff claims that over 60 percent of 355 colleges the Carnegie Foundation surveyed have speech codes.[40] Another count draws upon the Carnegie to affirm that speech codes are spreading to over 70 percent of institutions of higher education.

If several hundred schools have passed these codes, commentators, faculty, and students assume the situation must be serious; campuses face an epidemic of hate speech and speech codes. But is it so? When news stories offer details of speech codes, only five or six schools—usually Michigan, Wisconsin, Texas, Connecticut, Brown, and Stanford—are mentioned. Presumably the reporters can find no other speech codes to analyze. Why? The American Council of Education, which sponsored the survey with the Carnegie Foundation, believes the number of schools with speech codes is wildly inflated.

The survey conducted by the Council and the Carnegie never inquired about speech codes. It polled colleges about the existence of a "written policy" on racial harassment and intimidation. A written policy might include speech codes, but is a much wider category, encompassing, for instance, racial and sexual harassment in the workplace. Federal law prohibits workplace harassment, and many schools with federal contracts enact anti-harassment policies. Sixty percent of surveyed institutions had policies prohibiting "acts" of racial hostility or intimidation, but this implies neither speech codes nor an epidemic of racism. "The survey results," states David Markowitz of the Council, "are being distorted and presented as evidence that suppression of free speech is rampant on college campuses."[41] The number of schools with speech codes may be far lower than the numbers usually cited, perhaps closer to a dozen.

Calculating the incidents of political censorship runs into the same problems: who is counting what? At what point do a few facts become mythological? One survey interviewed over 200 full-time faculty about their current concerns. Over 90 percent were familiar with the debates about political dogma and censorship; and two-thirds even believed it was a real issue on their campuses. Yet none had been directly affected. "The perception was that it was others elsewhere on campus or in other universities or colleges who had" direct experience.[42]

Of course, both right and left trumpet their own causes. On the basis of a handful of facts, conservatives avow that the left tyrannizes the campus; this becomes a national crisis, and a past President himself referred to it. On the basis of a handful of facts, the left avows that racist violence sweeps through campuses. To be sure, the truth does not simply rest in the middle: these are not symmetrical distortions. Campus racism has a gravity far beyond campus censors.

Nevertheless, not every incident of political censorship is fictitious or misreported. An atmosphere of charges and countercharges permeates some campuses, suggesting that campus freedoms are not flourishing. Yet distinctions between "unfreedoms" are critical. Disgruntled students or an "open letter" in a campus newspaper command vastly different power than a subpoena served by the FBI. The former may bring about meetings, memos, and headaches; the latter, disrupted lives and unemployment. These are not minor differences. Any serious observer of social and political life must be able to distinguish despotic students with press statements and state investigators with search warrants.

Confusing tanks and pea shooters, however, seems endemic to conservatives. Bloom compared students and youth of the sixties to Nazis of the thirties. "The American university in the sixties was experiencing the same dismantling . . . as had the German university in the thirties . . . Whether it be Nuremberg or Woodstock, the principle is the same."[43] It may be fair game to compare movements that appear very different, such as Nazis of the thirties and American students of the sixties, but only if some fundamental distinctions are acknowledged. For starters, the sixties students were a minority protesting the state; the Nazis were the state. Sixties radicals commanded mimeo machines, posters, music, drugs, automobiles, and a handful of guns and bombs. These do not match the resources of the Third Reich.

"Woodstock" gathered several hundred thousand young people on a muddy farm listening to music and, often, getting high. "Nuremberg" gathered several hundred thousand people in a highly orchestrated and disciplined party congress to celebrate the victory of the Nazis and their allegiance to the Führer, Adolf Hitler. During the party congress, the decrees known as the Nuremberg laws were passed; these deprived Jews of citizenship and expelled them from social life; this has been called a "definite step on the road to Auschwitz."[44] Woodstock was anarchistic and benign; Nuremberg, authoritarian and menacing. Is a movement to end a war (in Vietnam) or protest racism the same as a movement to spread war and racism?

Bloom hardly made these distinctions. For this reason, the burning down of the Reichstag (the German parliament) in 1933 and the takeover of a Cornell University building in 1968 by gun-toting black students struck him as parallel affairs. Reality eluded him. One event triggered the eclipse of democracy in Central Europe, leading to a global war and millions dead; the other precipitated a faculty vote in Ithaca, New York, leading to Professor Bloom's move to Toronto University (and then to the University of Chicago).[45] Bloom considered these comparable events in twentieth-century history.

Too often conservatives blur critical differences between the state police and university committees or between censorship and opinion. They seem to suggest that an irritating or idiotic opinion is a form of censorship. "When a group of dining-hall workers at Harvard held a 'Back to the Fifties' party, Minority Affairs Dean Hilda Hernandez-Gravelle denounced them for racism on the grounds that their nostalgia for the 1950s probably included segregationist sentiments." Or: "In December 1989 Linda Wilson, the new president of Radcliffe . . . was denounced by feminists" who charged she did not call herself a feminist.[46]

These are just passing lines in D'Souza's book, but they indicate a worrisome confusion. Many of the cases cited as evidence of the new leftist censorship are of this ilk; someone is denounced as a racist or sexist. Yet surely for an individual or a group to damn someone or something—no matter how ridiculous the charge— does not constitute censorship. After all, the way is open for a reply; dining-hall workers might attack the dean as a petty tyrant, a little Stalin, or a busybody; the university president might denounce the feminists as phonies. Public discourse entails not simply polite exchanges around a table; it also means bellowing. Freedom of speech includes the freedom to be a fool. To object to public idiocy as a threat to freedom implies a censorship code. Who will decide what is idiotic?

Though the current malpractices do not compare to McCarthyism or government repression, they still might be significant. A mugging is still a mugging, even if it is not murder; and on the leafy campus byways a cultural stickup is fairly easy to pull off. In this operation the left is implicated; a long affinity for humorless dogma serves it well. Moreover, the left cannot have it both ways. It sometimes argues for speech codes, reasoning that language can injure individuals. However, this argument can be reversed. If a certain vocabulary constitutes aggression, the language of a campus left itself might cause harm.

Ian Macneil, the law professor attacked as sexist by the Harvard Women's Law Association, believes the whole affair "reeks of McCarthyism" with "One Simple Truth," "faceless informers," mudslinging, and unfair procedures. He may have a case. With no warning or airing of complaints, he received a letter that informed him of alleged improprieties; the letter alluded to previous discussions about which he knew nothing. The letter began: "Repeated instances of sexism in both your contracts textbook and your classroom discussions have been brought to the attention of the Women's Law Association. Furthermore, the Women's Law Association understands that student discussions since October with you and with members of the administration have failed to effect improvement."

This is the language of the commissars of the future—or past. "You are under arrest, certainly," stated the police to Kafka's Joseph K, "but not as a thief is under arrest." Yet this misleads, as if the issue were arrests and indictments; it is not. If there is any reality to the PC scare, it exists as a phenomenon of group psychology—an atmosphere informed by cheers and jeers. Students and faculty respond not simply to laws and regulations but to derision. The threat is less criminal penalties than social opprobrium.

It is worth recalling that the classic modern statement on freedom, John Stuart Mill's *On Liberty* (1859), addressed, not the legal restrictions, but the group restrictions on freedom. Mill hardly thought it necessary to defend the "liberty of press" against a tyrannical government, both because this had been lucidly done by previous authors and because in England, except during some momentary panic or crisis, the government did not censor the press. The real danger to liberty came from elsewhere, the community or the majority pressures.

Mill took the idea of the tyranny of the majority from Tocqueville.[47] This oppression differed from the traditional despotism of kings and hangmen inasmuch as it reached further and deeper. The community monitored comments and opinions, not just behavior. Democratic society, wrote Mill, can practice "a social tyranny more formidable than many kinds of political oppression." Though not backed by "the extreme penalties," it "leaves fewer means of escape." The issue is this:

> Protection, therefore, against the tyranny of the magistrate is not enough; there needs protection against the tyranny of the prevailing opinion and feeling, against the tendency of society to impose, by other means than civil penalties, its own ideas and practices as rules of conduct on those who dissent from them.

For Mill, the situation was serious, and getting worse. This "encroachment," supported by "some of the best and by some of the worst feelings incident to human nature," is growing "more and more formidable." The "tendencies of the times" cause the public to "prescribe general rules of conduct and endeavor to make everyone conform to the approved standard."[48]

To jump from Mill's *On Liberty* to campus liberty may seem unwarranted. Yet if there is a threat to freedom on American campuses, it resides, not in laws and penalties, but in group opinion; this intimidates, especially fainthearted students. Mill was on target: students do not fear the authorities or the dean, who seem distant and irrelevant, but the ridicule of other students. Anyone who teaches knows that getting students to participate is the challenge.

"The real danger we run today," writes Benjamin R. Barber, "is not the closing of the American mind but the closing of the American mouth. Open mouths, noisy classrooms, impolite questions, impertinent noisiness: these are hallmarks of youthful curiosity and democracy as well."[49] Students most frequently cite embarrassment to explain their deep reluctance to ask a question or offer a comment; they think other students know more and their question or comment will sound "dumb." In the terrain of racial and ethnic and sexual relations this is intensified. Every word or step is charged. Conclusion? Stay mum.

A national threat to the First Amendment is difficult to discern; free speech seems secure, especially in comparison to fundamentalist Islamic regimes or past Stalinist governments. A book (*Satanic Verses*) that precipitates an official call for the death of its author (Salman Rushdie), riots, bombings, and several assassinations is inconceivable in North America or Western Europe. "For anyone accustomed to freedom of speech," Daniel Pipes has written, "Rushdie's novel seems child's play." Pipes notes the irony: where freedom of speech is fragile, speech is explosive. "In the Muslim world . . . where repression is common, books have a power rarely felt in the West." Rushdie himself observed that in "a predominantly illiterate culture the respect for the written word is enormous."[50]

Visitors to Stalinist Eastern Europe sometimes envied the lack of free speech, since it implied that speech mattered. Writings were extensively monitored and censored; they also radiated energy. Devoted readers carefully studied materials that writers managed to circulate. Words and ideas meant something. The proof? Imprisoned authors. Banned books. "The Western intellectual," wrote Timothy Garton Ash in 1985, "who visits his colleagues in Poland feels admiration, excitement and, yes, envy. Here is a place where people care, passionately, about ideas . . . And often he returns to view with weary disdain our workaday world of Western culture, with its hypermarket profusion of ideas, for none of which anyone risks anything . . ."[51]

From this perspective, with or without speech codes, free speech is hardly threatened in the United States. The free market allows almost everything; it also devalues everything. Serious writings must compete with pornography and slick television shows—and inevitably lose out. Subversive or provocative or obnoxious speech is not curbed, but ignored. In the Western democracies almost anything can be said or written; the problem is reaching an audience.

The boundaries of free speech remain contested, however; issues arise about free speech and television, shopping malls, libel, copyrights, obscenity, government funding, and teaching.[52] Of these free speech within schools has proved the most explosive. In 1925 Tennessee authorities arrested a young science teacher, prompting one of America's most celebrated trials. John Scopes had used a textbook, George William Hunter's *A Civic Biology*, to teach evolution, which the state deemed contrary to divine truth. The act Scopes violated stated that "it shall be unlawful for any teacher in any of the Universities, Normals and all other public schools of the State which are supported in whole or in part by the public school funds of the State, to teach any theory that denies the story of Divine Creation of man as taught in the Bible."[53]

People get excited about teaching in schools. No one would have objected if Scopes had lectured on evolution in the Dayton town park; he would have been ignored or heckled, not arrested. The lecture became illegal inside a school. Here society passes along its knowledge and traditions to a captive audience. Public funds and taxes are spent; parents try to stay abreast of what is happening in schools. They ask their children, "What did you learn today?" or "What did you read today?" In schools and colleges words still matter.

On this, left and right can agree. The agreement marks a momentary convergence of divergent logic. Yes, in schools words matter. But for conservatives, this sanctions scrutinizing and, if necessary, censoring textbooks and teachings. For liberals, at least in primary and secondary schools, this justifies defending books and teachings as the inherent rights of individuals. Nat Hentoff's history of the First Amendment, *The First Freedom,* opens with recent violations of free speech, all of which took place in schools. For Hentoff the issues are simple; the First Amendment guarantee of free speech includes the rights of students and teachers to say, read, and write what they please.[54]

Conservatives have never accepted this argument. Their recent appeal to the First Amendment brushes against their own history and loyalties. The relationship of conservatives to free speech defies a simple formulation. Yet from the Council of Trent in the sixteenth century, which established an index of prohibited books, to Hollywood censors in the twentieth, they have often challenged freely circulating ideas in the name of religion, state, or family.

Before championing free speech on campus, D'Souza edited several conservative periodicals that regularly pilloried human rights and celebrated opponents of free speech; he also wrote a sympathetic study of the Reverend Sun Myung Moon's Unification Church as well as an adoring biography of Jerry Falwell, the conservative evangelist, who is hardly known for defending free speech. Falwell's private jet is "fully equipped" and he "frequently phones from 50,000 up," D'Souza enthused; he did not mention that Falwell frequently calls about religious correctness. Christian education, Falwell has stated, "is not a moral and intellectual quest . . . It is simply the process of learning, or teaching, the right answers . . . The students don't have any vote on what's right or wrong . . . We tell them . . ."[55]

Falwell tells them at his own school, an oasis of free inquiry modestly called Liberty University. He apprised the incoming freshmen that the church would control the college and that the students would find no diversity or differences among the faculty. "Any time [the faculty] start teaching something we don't like, we cut the money off. It's amazing how that changes philosophy."[56] So much for liberty at Liberty.

These are not just idle remarks—or just confined to faculty. Liberty University, which received $15 million in federal student aid in 1991, expelled three students for attending an off-campus Pentecostal church. Falwell claimed that this Pentecostal church's teachings were "incompatible" with Liberty's. Moreover, to attend off-campus services "a student must obtain written permission" from the administration.

The students consider their dismissal an infringement of rights. One student recounted that the administration "kept saying repeat-

edly that they weren't trying to challenge me for what I believe in
. . . yet all of their questions were about what I believe, like 'Do
you believe in the Trinity?' . . . Then they handed me a form and
asked me to renounce my beliefs." "I don't think it is fair," protested another student, "that they take away my scholarship and
kick me out for my different beliefs. All I want to do is finish my
education." Religious heresy demands action, however. "I wish
they would've let me finish out the semester," lamented the third
expelled student.[57] Where were the conservatives when this oc-
curred? Were they ringing up their toll-free number?

Probably not, for an old distrust of free speech compromises the
new conservative commitment to campus freedoms. Falwell himself
sued Larry C. Flynt, publisher of *Hustler,* for a parody which
mocked the evangelist as a drunk having sex with his mother in an
outhouse. To Falwell his mother marks the limits of freedom of
speech. There is "a line where the media may not go, and that line
was crossed by Mr. Flynt when he attacked my mother." "Academic freedom" also rubs Falwell the wrong way; he considers it a
cover for "radicals and revolutionaries" to plunder American universities.[58]

This places Falwell well within a conservative tradition denounc-
ing academic freedom. William F. Buckley's first book, *God and
Man at Yale,* is subtitled *The Superstitions of "Academic Freedom."*
For Buckley, Yale's mission is to inculcate certain values, not pander to professors. He contrasted "value orthodoxy" to the "hoax of
academic freedom," which allows professors to teach anything they
want. University scholars "have constructed an appealing and com-
pact philosophical package, labeled it 'truth,' and tossed it for en-
shrinement to that undiscriminating fellow, the liberal." This is
Buckley on the origin of academic freedom. "It is time," Buckley
advised, "that honest and discerning scholars cease to manipulate
the term academic freedom."[59]

Conservatives have not only traditionally distrusted "academic
freedom"; they have long suspected that under its cover radicals
undermine education. To read today's conservatives, however, is to
believe this is a new phenomenon; they charge that aging sixties
leftists corrupt American higher education. "It is important to appreciate," writes the conservative journalist Roger Kimball in *Tenured Radicals,* "the extent to which the radical vision of the sixties
has not so much been abandoned as internalized by many who

came of age then and who now teach at and administer our institutions of higher education." This cabal expounds fancy theories attacking the "hegemony" of Western culture; it possesses "a blueprint for a radical social transformation that would revolutionize every aspect of social and political life."[60]

It is also important to appreciate the extent to which this nightmare regularly troubles the sleep of decent citizens. Fear of the university succumbing to radicals arose in the thirties and fifties. In 1935 Charles R. Walgreen, a drugstore magnate, accused the University of Chicago of spreading subversive ideas. Walgreen, who pioneered the American pharmacy with a food counter, announced he was withdrawing his niece from the university because of her exposure to un-American ideas.

These were not simply the rantings of an oddball. With local newspapers feeding the flames, the state government decided to investigate whether subversive teachings would render the University of Chicago ineligible for tax exemptions as an educational institution. In a hotel the principals assembled, including Walgreen, his niece, and Chicago's president, Robert Maynard Hutchins, along with various faculty members. The stakes were high, because to lose tax exemption would effectively close a school like Chicago. Referring to Walgreen's drugstore lunch specials, a University of Chicago official sighed, "To think that the higher learning in America is at the mercy of the man who thought up tuna-fish marble cake."[61]

Walgreen testified that in talking with his niece he discovered she parroted leftist dogma. "She told me," he said, "that in a lecture marriage was described as an institution that was not universal, that there were varying standards of morals." He examined some of her books and found that her English textbook was really a Soviet primer. A supporter of Walgreen deplored that "under the guise of so-called freedom of thought" "insidious propaganda against the home and our government" was being spread. His niece reported that some professors advocated "free love"; others repeatedly stated that "the family is disintegrating." Her "confidence in the perfection of our government" had been undermined.[62]

Conservatives hardly succeeded in crippling the University of Chicago. The state committee found no basis for the charges, but instructed the university to conform to the law on sedition. For months, however, front-page news stories trumpeted discoveries of

subversive student groups, Communist professors, left-wing textbooks, and radical off-campus associations. The incident high-
lighted the general fear of higher education as subversive and anti-
American.[63]

After World War II conservatives frequently accused schools and
colleges of sheltering liberals, socialists, and Communists out to
corrupt, sink, or transform America. In 1949 the Conference of
American Small Business Organizations launched a journal (*The
Educational Reviewer*) expressly to unmask radicals in the
schools.[64] Its opening issue explained why businessmen and parents
were upset: "The questions [by their children] at the family dinner
table, the quotations from certain teachers, began to sound
strange." One businessman was "shocked when his daughter came
home from college" full of political and economic nonsense. He
examined her textbooks and found that "the history books were
slanted toward the revolutionary 'new order.' The textbook on government pleaded for 'change' and for giving more power to the
government." And he really "hit the ceiling" when he discovered
that the economic textbook damned the "system of which he is a
part."[65]

For four years, this review examined textbooks and denounced
subversion in the schools. For instance, a review of a political science anthology began this way: "This book is poison. It is poison
unless you believe that students should emerge from their introductory college course in political science with the general impression
that man is an irrational animal, that morals are relative, religion
outmoded . . ."[66]

Of course, the students of the sixties could not be held responsible for educational decline in the fifties. What was the cause? Conservatives had a short answer: the thirties. The worldwide depression and the rise of fascism drove a generation leftward in the
thirties. In subsequent years these individuals became teachers and
professors, bringing about the same type of damage that agitates
today's conservatives.

The issues were parallel, and even the titles of the conservatives'
books were parallel. Felix Wittmer's 1956 *Conquest of the American Mind* suggests Bloom's 1987 *Closing of the American Mind*.
Along with others like E. Merrill Root's *Collectivism on the Campus,* Wittmer's book denounced liberals, collectivists, and Communists for taking over American colleges. The leftists gutted stan-

dards, politicized knowledge, and spread subversive ideas. For instance, Wittmer complained that liberal teachers want to abolish grades and tests in order to advance their real aim: to spread mediocrity and replace capitalism with socialism.[67]

E. Merrill Root's argument also anticipated that of later conservatives. Under the cover of academic freedom, radical professors spread leftist propaganda. Like today's conservatives, he was struck by a paradox: radicalism was ebbing worldwide, but apparently intensifying on American campuses. He endorsed the opinion of an English observer of American colleges: "In the thirties . . . a substantial element among the university population . . . adopted Marxism." Today—the early fifties—Communism is discredited; and at least in England radical professors have lost influence. "This appears to be the happy development of events in Britain, but is far from true, alas, in the United States . . . *where academic Marxism —or crypto-Marxism—is stronger than ever.*"[68]

For these authors subversive professors gave academic freedom a new meaning; it now spelled academic license. College presidents, alumni, parents, and faculty should be on the alert, ferreting out disloyal instructors. E. Merrill Root quoted approvingly from a job description of a small New Jersey college looking to hire a professor. One qualification read: "Definite, positive loyalty to American political ideals and traditions. Reds, pinks, near-pinks and 'fellow travellers' will not fit into the policy of Bloomfield . . ." Root rejected arguments that such an advertisement violated academic freedom.[69]

These efforts to rid schools of subversive instructors and ideas do not stand out as exceptional; for many conservatives and religious fundamentalists censoring is a familiar pastime. Moreover, they do not object simply to readings they judge seditious, un-Christian, and anti-family; they often object to textbooks that allow students to draw their own conclusions. A group advocating conservative textbook revisions put it this way: "Too many discussions and textbooks leave students to make up their minds about things. Now that's just not fair to our children." It's worse than unfair: when a student learns in a math book that "there are no absolutes, suddenly every value he's been taught is destroyed. And the next thing you know, the student turns to crime and drugs."[70]

The American Library Association lists books banned or removed from library shelves; the inventory runs almost fifty pages and includes over a thousand titles. In virtually all cases, conservative groups or individuals object to immoral books in school libraries. For instance, an elementary school library removed *The Stupids Step Out,* by Harry Allard and James Marshall, because "it described families in a derogatory manner and might encourage children to disobey their parents." Promoting disobedience is not taken lightly. Shel Silverstein's *A Light in the Attic* was challenged because it "encourages children to break dishes so they won't have to dry them."[71]

One reason for conservative censorship is almost honorable; conservatives revere ideas—and, conversely, fear them; ideas can be dangerous. This is a brand of distorted idealism; conservatives prefer to target ideas and values over social facts and forces; they favor talking of idleness rather than unemployment, pornographic books rather than a sexually violent society. Words and images provoke them more than deeds and behavior.

Edmund Burke, in that classic of conservatism, *Reflections on the Revolution in France,* charged that the ideas of philosophers and literary men gave rise to the French Revolution. The tilt here is typical; corrosive realities recede before corrosive ideas. *Ideas Have Consequences* runs the title of a modern American conservative book.[72] If ideas have consequences, some ideas have destructive consequences. How does one prevent or minimize the destruction? Here conservative idealism turns malignant. Too many ideas or the wrong ideas, they believe, undermine the moral order.

In 1992 a controversy erupted over the song of a black rap singer, Ice-T. Many thought that his song "Cop Killer" promoted the killing of police and should be withdrawn; others believed that no matter how offensive the lyrics, they fell squarely under First Amendment protection. The song provoked the National Rifle Association (NRA) to demand its recall. Their stance illuminates the paradox of a certain conservatism, allergic to words, oblivious to reality. The NRA damned lyrics as brutal, not bullets. The parallel is almost perfect: the NRA attacked as too violent the "Cop Killer" song and defended as legitimate so-called "cop killer" ammunition, bullets capable of penetrating armor that police commonly wear.

The NRA issued statements and took out newspaper advertisements offering "full legal and financial resources" to police or their kin "shot or killed by someone shown to be influenced by this incitement and provocation." The NRA affirmed "this isn't about freedom of speech." And in a nice touch, the rifle group drew upon academics for support: "Researchers indicate a causal link between violent behavior and violence in the media. These songs are an outrage." This organization opposes banning assault weapons.[73]

Evidence from history may support or undermine an argument, but does not constitute proof. An old affinity of conservatives and censorship does not invalidate their criticism of campus leftists. Conservatives may be hypocritical or inconsistent, yet still on the mark; perhaps leftist students and academics do choke discussion. If conservatives break with their own history in appealing to the First Amendment, liberals and radicals who favor speech codes and censorship part from theirs.

"November 2nd. Free Speech Day. All lovers of free speech are asked to be in readiness to be in Spokane on that date." The Berkeley "free speech movement" comprised only one chapter from a thick volume about leftists defending First Amendment rights. This call for action dates from 1909, and formed part of the IWW (Industrial Workers of the World) or Wobbly "free speech campaign" that spread to twenty western cities before World War I. The Wobblies sought the right to give speeches on city sidewalks, where they would denounce the evils of capitalism and recruit members. Local authorities did not appreciate these political orations and responded with jailings. The Wobblies in turn called for supporters to gather in certain towns and cities, give sidewalk speeches, and fill the local jails.[74]

Today this legacy is weak. When a staunch proponent of free speech, Nat Hentoff, visited colleges he thought he would find what he usually finds: conservatives banning books and speakers, liberals and radicals upholding the First Amendment. He was wrong. He discovered "liberals fiercely advocating censorship of 'offensive' speech and conservatives merrily taking the moral high ground as champions of free expression."[75] Why have campus leftists abandoned their traditional commitment to free speech?

In front of the UCLA Law School students loll about in lush grass under sunny skies. It looks like a postcard or an advertisement, but as I talk with a law student I met at a forum on the "racist speech controversy," stereotypes melt away. His parents are Bolivian and Nicaraguan. He went to high school in Nicaragua and Costa Rica, and then attended the University of Michigan at Ann Arbor. He considers himself a leftist, but he eloquently criticizes leftist pieties. At Ann Arbor, he regularly ran up against political dogma, especially among younger professors and teaching assistants. In one of his classes the instructor stated at the first meeting that "any sexist, racist, homophobic comment, and you're out of here." This rendered the atmosphere tense; students were nervous as to what constituted a racist or sexist comment. They clammed up; discussion languished.

Several weeks earlier at the meeting on the "racist speech controversy," we heard a bevy of law professors pour scorn on the "mantra" of free speech. To an appreciative audience the professors denounced free speech as never really "free." State or economic "power" determines its limits. Speech is always restricted, these professors maintained. The issue is not about pure free speech, which does not exist, but how speech should be regulated. Speech codes penalizing racist or sexist speech were necessary, they believed, inasmuch as racial and sexual harassment was increasing—and speech can constitute harassment.

This forum represented more than an isolated phenomenon; many professional groups have debated speech codes, and some campuses have passed them. The leading association of professors (AAUP) proposed a campus speech code to its membership. "The principle that colleges and universities must be open to all ideas does not imply that they must tolerate every speech act." Speech designed to "degrade or humiliate" or make students feel "unwelcome" should be penalized; and this speech includes not simply direct personal attacks but "written communications" like leaflets and posters. The association eventually rejected the proposals, affirming freedom of speech even for "ideas we hate."[76] Still, if some professors have proposed curbing speech, and some campuses have done so, perhaps something worrisome is happening, but what and why?

3

SAY THE RIGHT THING

"A LITTLE PALE-FACED MAN came into the office" with a slip of paper, recalled an old Vermont printer. The message read: "My lad, when you use these words, please oblige me by spelling them as here: *theater, center,* etc."[1] This was Noah Webster indefatigably promoting an American spelling and pronunciation. In the Republic's early years, Webster, whose name became synonymous with dictionaries, sought to reform spelling; he also devoted himself to establishing, in tandem with the American Revolution, an American English separate from the English of England.

Webster's mission to reform American English put him in good and increasingly crowded company. In the 1790s as in the 1990s, reformers posited a belief that few dispute: the importance of language; to contest this belief confirms it. Language distinguishes humans from fish, butterflies, and dogs. Moreover, during the course of civilization language seems to expand. In the beginning there was the word; at the end there are words. Once labor consisted of weaving, plowing the land, or pounding a nail; it still does, but for fewer and fewer. More people work with words through telephones, paper, computer monitors, conferences, and discussions. There are more teachers than coal miners, more secretaries than farmers. During and after work, we are inundated by words, chatter, memos, images, commercials, news, sound bites, recordings, messages, printouts, mail.

These shifts reshape our view of reality. The changes have been called many things: an information revolution, media explosion, a wired society, postindustrial or postmodern world. Philosophers emphasize the "linguistic turn"; literature professors underscore "discourse" and "text"; sociologists study "role definitions" and group images; psychologists survey "labeling" and self-conceptions; social theorists ponder "the monopoly of the code"; and even economists reflect on the "rhetoric" of economics. All infer that the new reality is largely linguistic.

A heightened attention to speech and its impact redoubles efforts to reform, revise, and clean up language. This project falls into two categories: prescribing and proscribing. A new literature advises what is the correct or "bias-free" way to write and talk. At the same time, campuses debate "speech codes" and anti-pornography measures which prohibit language that might offend minorities and women. Numerous questions cluster around these projects. What are the principles of a bias-free speech? Does better speech lead to better social relations? Does a monitoring of speech suppress speech? Might an improved idiom mask an unimproved reality? When is "free speech" more than speech? Do the reformers and speech coders transform a truism—the significance of language—into a myth?

A campaign for linguistic reform paralleled—or tried to parallel—the American Revolution. Some eighteenth-century scholars pondered the ultimate direction of American English. Would or should it become a separate language? John Witherspoon, one of the earliest commentators on American English, coined the term "Americanisms" to refer to phrases "different from the use of the same terms or phrases . . . in Great-Britain." He thought the languages might eventually diverge. "Being entirely separated from Britain," he wrote in 1781, "we shall find some centre or standard of our own, and not be subject to the inhabitants of that island, either in receiving new ways of speaking or rejecting the old."[2]

This was too passive for Webster, who sought to shape and codify a standard "American" tongue that differed from English. He never doubted the gravity of his life project. "An attention to literature must be the principal bulwark against the encroachments of civil and ecclesiastical tyrants." If he wrote a valuable book on some "abstruse philosophical subject," he believed, few would read it. A book on language, however, casts light everywhere. Webster wanted to create a strong and egalitarian national union by reforming language. The goal was simple: "America must be as independent in *literature* as she is in *politics.*"[3] The means were also simple: language reform and correction.

Even before his Dictionary, Webster achieved astounding success with his *American Spelling Book* (1783). After the Bible and *McGuffey Readers,* his speller attained the greatest sales for an American volume. It went through almost 400 printings during Webster's lifetime, and sold well over 50 million copies in the nineteenth century. More than a speller, it was reading textbook, primer, and moral catechism. Webster infused the speller with a nationalist mission, to bind together the nation with a common language. He sought "to diffuse an uniformity and purity of language in America —to destroy the provincial prejudices that originate in the trifling differences of dialect, and produce reciprocal ridicule—to promote the interest of literature and harmony of the United States."[4]

Some of Webster's proposals to eliminate derogatory usage would be welcomed by today's reformers; his goal of a standard language probably would not. Yet Webster dedicated himself to a uniform language in the name of a peaceful and democratic society. He disliked localisms, because they threatened social peace. "Small causes, such as a nick-name, or a vulgar tone in speaking," he wrote in *Dissertations on the English Language* (1789), "have actually created a dissocial spirit between the inhabitants of the different states, which is often discoverable in private business and public deliberations. Our political harmony is therefore concerned in a uniformity of language."[5]

Webster observed that peculiarities of language rested on social and economic realities. "I should ascribe the manner of speaking among a people to the nature of their government and a distribution of their property." He drew a distinction between the cadences of New England and the South. The language of New England expressed the egalitarianism of small property owners; the language of the South registered the domination of slave owners. In the

South, people with large fortunes speak with boldness and certainty. "Those who are accustomed to command slaves, form a habit of expressing themselves with the tone of authority and decision." On the other hand:

> In New England, where there are few slaves and servants, and less family distinctions than in any other part of America, the people are accustomed to address each other with that diffidence, or attention to the opinion of others, which marks a state of equality. Instead of commanding, they advise; instead of saying, with an air of decision, *you must;* they ask with an air of doubtfulness, *is it not best?* or give their opinions with an indecisive tone: *you had better, I believe.*[6]

For a model of an American democratic language Webster tilted toward New England regionalisms, but he also raised a critical question. How could a standard be set? Where would it come from? "An attempt to fix a standard on the practice of any particular class of people is highly absurd," he stated. "As a friend of mine once observed, it is like fixing a light house on a floating island. It is an attempt to *fix* that which is in itself *variable*." To be sure, this hardly stopped Webster; he sought a standard not in local practice but in "the general practice of the nation."[7] This was his floating lighthouse.

Webster's efforts to reform spelling also emerged out of a democratic ethos. If spelling were simplified, all would spell with ease, eliminating invidious distinctions. "All persons, of every rank, would speak with some degree of precision and uniformity. Such a uniformity in these states is very desirable; it would remove prejudice, and conciliate mutual affection and respect."[8]

Another reason drove Webster to preach the virtues of a uniform language: sales. Like Benjamin Franklin before him, Webster kept his eye on the market; and like Franklin, who was a printer, Webster realized that a standard language simplified printing, facilitating the production and selling of books across the nation. To profit from his market Webster also relentlessly fought for copyright protection. "Without doubt," states a biographer, "Webster was the father of American copyright legislation, and for that American authors owe him a profound debt."[9]

The history of American language reform is a history of failure: at least that is the conclusion of one of its historians. The reformers of American English, writes Dennis E. Baron, "have left one common legacy for their twentieth-century counter-parts to ponder: an overwhelming lack of success."[10] This is a bit unfair. Even some of the spelling changes that Webster supported succeeded. The dropping of the final "k" (as in "musick" and "publick"); the replacement of "-or" for "-our" endings (as in "honour" and "favour"); the transposing of letters in words ending in "-re" (as in "theatre" and "centre"): these became accepted usage. "Webster gradually conquered the country," concluded H. L. Mencken, the Baltimore critic and student of American English. "Many, though certainly not most, of the reformed spelling he advocated . . . are the American standard today."[11]

What determines the success of linguistic reforms? Language unfolds in contested territories, and professorial recommendations do not often suffice to bring about changes. In England regular teachings of correct language little affect linguistic habits. Another approach is widely used throughout the globe to promote (or suppress) a language: force. A language, a historian quipped, is a dialect with a navy. Yet force, also, has its limits. The Soviet domination of language, backed by the state apparatus, enjoyed only limited success. "The manipulation of language," notes a scholar of Soviet idiom, "has not succeeded to the extent one might expect from reading *Nineteen Eighty-four*," with its portrayal of an official Newspeak. "The existence of vigorous counterlanguages in the Soviet Union after seventy years of steady indoctrination of the masses by the Communist Party is proof of that."[12]

Successful language reform may require popular assent, if not initiative. Webster's desire for a democratic language found its counterpart in a popular protest against elitist terminology. In the spirit of democracy, some of Webster's contemporaries protested a vocabulary of social hierarchy. They wanted a new idiom informed by American egalitarianism. The widespread resistance to terms marking subordination astounded eighteenth-century visitors to the United States.

"If you want to hire a maid servant," wrote a visitor "she will not allow you the title of *master,* or herself to be called *servant.*" Another visitor was disgusted by this egalitarianism. "If you call at the door of any man, and ask the servant if his master is at home, he will say, 'Master! I have no master: do you mean Mr. Such-a-one?' " One English traveler called upon a friend; the door was opened by a newly employed "servant-maid" he had never before seen. The visitor transcribed the dialogue that took place "word for word":

Q: Is your master at home?
A: I have no master.
Q: Don't you live here?
A: I *stay* here.
Q: And who are you then?
A: Why I am Mr. ——'s help. I'd have you to know, *man,* that I am no *sarvant.*

The repudiation of "master" and "servant" settled on "help" as the egalitarian formulation. A European visitor observed that when American youth "go to service," "they satisfy themselves that they are *helps,* not servants,—that they are going to work with (nor for) Mr. so and so, not going to service,—they call him and his wife their *employers,* not their master and mistress."[13]

One of the many who applauded the terminology was James Russell Lowell, the poet and writer. Lowell, an ardent abolitionist and sometime feminist, captured the moment when language and reality converged—and diverged.

I do not value much the antislavery feeling of a man who would not have been abolitionist even if no such abomination as American Slavery ever had existed. Such a one would come home from an antislavery meeting to be the unhired overseer of his wife and children and *help* (for I love our Yankee word, teaching as it does, the true relation, and its being equally binding on master and servant) . . . It is a very hard thing in society, as at present constituted, for a male human being . . . to avoid being a slaveholder. I never see Maria [his wife] mending my stockings, or Ellen [the maid] bringing water for my shower-bath in the morning, without hearing a faint tinkle of chains.[14]

Some critics objected to the democratic idiom of "help." It does not seem accidental that a cranky author, James Fenimore Cooper, challenged the euphemisms. Cooper, who distrusted democratic conformity, raised a problem that continues to stalk language improvers. What principles justify linguistic revisions? Do the new terms illuminate or mystify? Might an idiom be democratized, and not the reality? "Help" might be an example. Have the conditions of "help" improved with the obsolescence of the word "servant"? In her thoughts on law and life, the African-American lawyer Patricia J. Williams recently reflected on the black nanny, who tends the master's brood. Already described and bemoaned by W. E. B. Du Bois, "this exploitation persists today, in the familiar image of grossly underpaid but ever-so-loved black female 'help.' "[15]

"Some changes of the language are to be regretted," wrote Cooper in his 1838 *The American Democrat,* "as they lead to false inferences, and society is always a loser by mistaking names for things." He noted the origin of the democratic terms. "In consequence of the domestic servants of America having once been negro-slaves, a prejudice has arisen among the laboring classes of whites, who not only dislike the term servant, but have also rejected that of master."

Cooper protested the "subterfuge" that servants and masters do not exist. "He who employs laborers, with the right to command, is a master, and he who lets himself to work with an obligation to obey, a servant." For the same reason "help" should be used when an individual actually "helps," but not, as is usually the case, when an individual performs the task alone. "A man does not usually hire his cook to *help* him cook his dinner, but to cook it herself. Nothing is therefore gained, while something is lost in simplicity and clearness by the substitution of new and imperfect terms." Cooper lamented that "the love of turgid expressions is gaining ground." He extolled "simplicity in speech," the virtue of calling "a spade, a 'spade.' "[16]

Cooper may have put his finger on something. A human need for prettifying terms is hardly dangerous, but unchecked it may eviscerate language, which becomes less a flash of illumination than a feather in the cap. A desire for an elevating idiom converges with a love for euphemisms, telling things like they are not. To be sure, euphemisms are universal and are not inherently bad. Many euphemisms seek to make palatable the unpalatable. "We'll have to let you go" substitutes for "You're fired"; "senior citizens" replaces "old people"; "life insurance" supplants "insurance for when you are dead."[17]

Other euphemisms, however, are less benign. "The whole tendency of modern prose," wrote George Orwell, "is away from concreteness." Throughout his career Orwell savaged euphemisms and jargon that abandoned the tangible and the particular—words like "pacification" for bombing or "rectification of frontiers" for expelling peasants from their land. Political language, he wrote, consists largely of "euphemisms, question-begging and sheer cloudy vagueness." Orwell targeted official English, Parliamentary English as well as what he called "pamphletese." "Many of the expressions used in political literature are simply euphemisms or rhetorical tricks. 'Liquidate' for instance . ∹ . is a polite word for 'to kill,' while 'realism' normally means 'dishonesty.' "[18]

Orwell, who may be too revered to be appreciated, met his match in the earlier critic of euphemisms and jargon, H. L. Mencken. "The typical American of today," Mencken grumbled, "is led by cheer leaders, press agents, word-mongers, uplifters."[19] Mencken was far more than a grumbler, however, and his major and estimable work, *The American Language,* chronicled the rise of American English, including its strengths and foibles—such as its love of euphemisms. An "American aversion to designations indicating a servile or ignominious status goes back to the first days of the Republic." Mencken documented the obsession with grandiose labels, especially of occupations. "Gardeners posturing as *landscape architects* and laborers posturing as *gardeners* are too numerous to be remarked. So are lobbyists under the guise of *industrial consultants,* press-agents disguised as *publicity directors* . . . detectives as *investigators* . . . messenger boys as *communication carriers.*" The "hatching of bogus engineers," he commented, continues unabated —for instance, *"custodial engineer"* for "janitor" or *"recreation engineer"* for "coach."

Most of these terms did not spontaneously emerge, but were coined and promoted by professional groups. Nevertheless, some were resounding successes, while others disappeared. In 1915 a scandal about a real estate agent worried a Minneapolis member of the Real Estate Board, a trade group; he feared he and his colleagues would be tainted by the disgrace. How could the board members set themselves apart from ordinary agents who had no scruples? "Do not the members of our board deserve a distinctive title?" To mark their distance from everyday real estate agents, Charles N. Chadbourn coined a term for the classier licensed variety: "realtor."

Several other coinages enjoyed similar luck and were widely adopted. Of course, some occupations sought more actively than others to embellish their trade. At least since the Civil War, when business was popping, undertakers promoted an ethereal "casket" in place of an earthy "coffin." Like Cooper protesting "help," Nathaniel Hawthorne objected. When touring an English cathedral, he was pleased that the sexton referred to a burial vault and its coffins. "Thank heaven, the old man did not call them 'caskets'!—a vile modern phrase, which compels a person of sense and good taste to shrink more disgustedly than ever before from the idea of being buried at all."[20]

Inspired by "physician," undertakers also suggested "mortician," which was eventually embraced by the trade as a more dignified term. Other inventions, like "beautician" (along with "beauty parlors" and "beauty shops"), passed into general usage, but many never traveled far. Except as jokes, "shoetrician" for "shoemaker" or "mixologist" for "bartender" remained dead in the water. Others seem perched between acceptance and abandonment, for instance "canine control officer" for "dogcatcher."[21]

Occupations were only part of the story. The American love affair with euphemisms encompasses titles and names. I met a "president" of a company, observed an English novelist, W. L. George, visiting the United States seventy years ago, "whose staff consists of two typists. Many firms have four 'vice-presidents.' " When George returned to a Boston theater to retrieve a forgotten item, he was told he must apply to the "chief of the ushers."

> He was a mild little man . . . rather a come-down from the pomp and circumstance of his title. Growing interested, I examined my programme, with the following result: It is not a large theatre, but it has a press representative, a treasurer (box-office clerk), an assistant treasurer (box-office junior clerk), an advertising agent, our old friend the chief of the ushers, a stage manager, a head electrician, a master of properties (in England called "props"), a leader of the orchestra (pity this—why not president?), and a matron (occupation unknown).

"What does this mean in American psychology?" wondered George.[22]

If he had looked back, he would have found that nineteenth-century American high schools puffed themselves up as "colleges" and colleges as "universities." An Ohio nationalist enthused in 1870: "There are two universities in England, four in France, ten in Prussia, and thirty-seven in Ohio." Titles were also generously distributed. Many visitors found the country aflood with "captains," "colonels," and "judges." Colonel E. M. House, an adviser to President Wilson, never commanded a regiment. "Doctor" and "professor" were bestowed on dance teachers, magicians, phrenologists, and other worthy souls. This inflationary titling elicited a protest that proposed surrendering all titles. At the University of Virginia professors gathered to half-seriously encourage "the use of *mister* to all men, professional or otherwise."[23]

Like so many American radicals, today's language reformers imagine they are pioneers; their efforts, however, stand in an old tradition of democratizing and elevating American English. They want to strip language of hierarchical insignia and upgrade titles and descriptions. Their proposals are as honorable and salutatory—and sometimes as half-baked—as those of the past.

The general program is straightforward: purge language of sexual, racial, and ethnic bias. Many universities, publishing houses, writing centers, and feminist groups have produced guides to a "bias-free," "nonsexist," or "inclusive" vocabulary. These manuals instruct writers how to avoid all invidious distinctions. Language should be accurate, free of insult, and should not unnecessarily call attention to sex, race, religion, size, age, or physical features. These well-intentioned tracts assume that a less offensive speech eases human relations, a proposition that seems incontestable. A sentence like "I gave a final grade of B to that fat girl" sins in three regards: "girl" for anyone over twelve or thirteen is considered derogatory; "fat" is itself prejudicial; and the student's size is irrelevant.

The reformers occasionally offer goofy substitutions for what they denounce as biased or sexist idiom. Not simply does "fat" become "big-boned" or "generously sized," but "manhole" becomes "maintenance hole"; "freshmen" turns into "freshpeople"; "snowman" transmutes into "snow human"; and "man-eating shark" emerges as "person-eating shark."[24]

In its single-minded search for sexism in language *The Bias-Free Word Finder,* a fairly levelheaded dictionary, stumbles upon "kaiser roll." "Strictly speaking," the guide hesitantly concludes, this is a "sexist term," a roll named after the German kaiser. A nonsexist substitute would be "Vienna roll" or "hard roll." This guide also scratches "jack-o'-lantern" as sexist, proffering "carved pumpkin" as a substitute.[25] Another guide finds "straw man" unacceptable and substitutes "unreal issue" or "misrepresentation." A third manual offers some improbable symmetrical terms, recommending "people not of color" to balance "people of color."

Nuttiness, however, accompanies all reforms, and hardly suffices to damn a project. The real questions emerge not from the extraordinary but the ordinary, the central logic of the reform. Here some of the inane suggestions may still be revealing, less for the particulars than the implications. To replace "straw man" with "unreal issue" or "jack-o'-lantern" with "carved pumpkin" or even "landlady" and "landlord" with "owner" drains language of vigor. Reformers promote a bloodless classifying; abstractions supplant concreteness, as Orwell observed.

A university *Guide to Inclusive Language: Suggestions for Improved Communications* is a case in point. Many of its proposals are sensible. Don't always use male pronouns, as if the world were only male—or, conversely, don't automatically use female terms. Don't say "Mothers should ensure that their children eat a proper breakfast," but "Parents should ensure that their children . . ." Don't use derogatory labels and adjectives. Don't exclude people, and don't use unnecessary racial, social, or biological tags. Consider the identities of those around you.

This laudable goal carries with it the inherent danger of bringing about a neutral, almost scientistic language. All particulars are tainted; only the most general passes muster. "Good evening, ladies and gentlemen" is out. Why? While "ladies and gentlemen" is egalitarian "with respect to gender," it represents "only one social class." Correct usage would be: "Good evening, everyone."[26]

By embracing a neutral idiom many proposals of the language reformers exude a bureaucratic ethos; the word revisers champion an organizational vocabulary. *The Bias-Free Word Finder* rejects the slangy "adman" as sexist, and offers as substitutes "advertising executive" or "creative/art director," "acount executive," "advertising representative." For the prosaic "secretary" this dictionary recommends "executive secretary" as well as "executive assistant," "administrative assistant," "administrative coordinator," and "office administrator."[27]

The recommendations smack of public relations and plumped-up résumés; admen become advertising executives, secretaries become executive secretaries; copiers become assistant communication officers. The suggested terms and descriptions are hardly unfamiliar. On the contrary, they are the coin of the business realm. Oppositional language reformers ratify these euphemisms, instead of protesting them; they promote the language of bureaucracy as the language of liberation.

The bureaucratic spirit can be glimpsed even in the word "Ms." Today only the most inflexible traditionalist challenges its use. In its symmetry to "Mr." and its parallel refusal to register marital status, "Ms." marks a victory for egalitarianism and feminism. Ambrose Bierce, the writer who disappeared in 1913, did not think up "Ms.," but he did propose a male complement to "Miss." In his *Devil's Dictionary* the complete definition of "Hers" read: "pron. His." Under "Miss," Bierce had this to say:

> n. A title with which we brand unmarried women to indicate that they are in the market. Miss, Missis (Mrs.) and Mister (Mr.) are the three most distinctly disagreeable words in the language, in sound and sense. Two are corruptions of Mistress, the other of Master. In the general abolition of social titles in this our country they miraculously escaped to plague us. If we must have them let us be consistent and give one to the unmarried man. I venture to suggest Mush, abbreviated to Mh.[28]

While "Mh." vanished with Bierce himself, a widening use of "Miss" once denoted not an encroaching sexual market but a protest against it; lower- and working-class women objected to the false intimacy of first names. They wanted to be addressed more formally as "Miss." A visitor in the early nineteenth century noted with surprise that "servant girls in New York assume the title of 'Miss'; their male visiting friends invariably making use of this term in inquiring for them."[29] In her 1897 *Domestic Service,* Lucy Maynard Salmon recounted:

> An employer invited her Sunday-school class to her home to spend an evening. One of the members went into the kitchen to render some assistance, and found there the housemaid . . . The employer said, "Miss M, this is Kate." The maid, who never before had showed the slightest consciousness of occupying an inferior position, said, under her breath, "I am Miss, too."[30]

To the degree that history illuminates usage, the origins of "Ms." had less to do with egalitarian or feminist protest than bureaucratic ease. In the name of efficiency office management groups first advanced "Ms." in the early 1950s. The National Office Management Association ("Better Management through the Office") dedicated itself to streamlining office practices. To this end, it offered suggestions on simplifying the typing of business letters. The Association recommended that by dropping indentations in business letters—by moving dates, paragraphs, and closings to the left margin—typing strokes will be saved and office efficiency will be increased; a secretary (or "executive assistant") will no longer need to "tab" over to type a date, begin a paragraph, or close a letter. "A basic motion unit analysis of the typing alone on a 96-word letter proves a saving with the Simplified Letter of over 10.7%. A savings like that can't be ignored."

The group also suggested how to avoid stumbling or hesitating as to whether "Miss" or "Mrs." was appropriate. In the mid-fifties the Association urged that its members "use abbreviation Ms. if not sure whether to use Mrs. or Miss. This modern style solves an age-old problem." Lest this seem too bold, the group advised "Ms. Office Secretary" to "talk it over with your boss." And to the boss, it advised, "If you're like most people, you'll resist the change at first. . . . Use the Simplified Letter for 30 days. You'll like it after you've tried it."[31]

The origins of "Ms." hardly constitute a judgment on its undeniable merits. Moreover, "Ms." went nowhere until the sixties, when sanctioned by a feminist movement. In any event, neutral terms by themselves do not signify linguistic bureaucratization. Some words violate accuracy and egalitarianism and should be retired. No one regrets "Down's syndrome" supplanting "Mongolism."

The issue is not one, ten, or a hundred words, but a general approach and its consequences. Do some flagrantly objectionable terms justify abandoning "motherly" or "masterly" or "manhunt" as biased? Or "idiot"? The feminist "bias-free" dictionary tells us to avoid all these. "Idiot" is "unscientific" and "highly demeaning," replaceable by "someone with a mental impairment." Instead of "I'm an idiot! I forgot the tickets!" we would have "I'm someone with a mental impairment! I forgot the tickets!" The phrase "not a fit night for man or beast" sins against women and animals; this dictionary offers instead "not a fit night for two-legged creatures or four-legged ones."

The effort to strip language of bias is as old as modern science. Governments and professional groups have backed this project for decades. Outside of the hard sciences, however, the bill for surgical objectivity is often a crushing jargon, the familiar infirmity of academic prose. In the name of objectivity, scholars bury lucidity and, eventually, thought. Critics complain, for instance, that education professionals "abandon the simple value-laden terms like *lazy, idle, stupid, clever,* and *poor* and replace them with expressions like *educationally and socially disadvantaged groups, underachievers, those on the lower end of the ability scale, high verbal-ability subjects, disadvantaged home environments,* and *underprivileged children.*"[32] Today this bureaucratic language has spread far and wide; it hardly elicits comment. A parent received an invitation to a new school program, which read:

> Our school's Cross-Graded, Multi-Ethnic, Individualized Learning Program is designed to enhance the concept of an Open-Ended Learning Program with emphasis on a continuum of multi-ethnic academically enriched learning, using the identified intellectually gifted child as the agent or director of his own learning. Major emphasis is on a cross-graded, multi-ethnic learning with the main objective being to learn respect for the uniqueness of a person.[33]

Language reformers cannot be burdened with the primary responsibility of jargonizing language; they are only accessories. Many of their proposals are sensible; gratuitous or insulting references to race or sex can hardly be defended. However, an honorable rejection of an offensive vocabulary easily turns into a dishonorable flight from anything concrete. What is the gain when "nosy" is replaced by "curious" or "straw man" makes way for "diversionary tactic" or "starlet" for "star in the making"?[34] "Starlet" harbors skepticism of a Hollywood that "star in the making" celebrates. Too often leftist and feminist language rectification partakes willy-nilly of public relations and linguistic bureaucratization. Language reformers dream they protest society as they spread its word.

A therapeutic ethos gone amuck and a misplaced social analysis compromise language reforms. At a certain point euphemisms decay into mystification; the reasonable desire for equality or embellishment slides into a dogma of happy thoughts. The reformers envision a world where language serves triumphant individuals; weakness or failings are taboo. This approach revives with an individualist spin "socialist realism," once the official doctrine of Soviet art. "Socialist realism," which was neither socialist nor realistic, enjoined pictures of smiling peasants and powerful workers striding purposefully into the future; pessimism, doubt, or failure belonged to the bourgeoisie. Language reformers instinctively prescribe something similar; they champion a positive vocabulary portraying powerful women and men confidently taking command of their lives.

The *Guide to Inclusive Language* gives examples of incorrect and correct sentences. "Harriet Tubman helped slaves to escape" is disallowed, but "Harriet Tubman led slaves to freedom" is approved. Why? Is helping bad? Yes, because it suggests the helper is not the sole actor. "Leading" is better because it gives "women deserved credit." The early American republicans preferred "help" over "serve"; later republicans prefer "lead" over "help."

Other guides follow these same principles: everyone becomes a leader and hero. A teacher's manual on how to draw up examinations advises that "written materials can wrongly depict relations of status and power." The manual provides examples of misleading and corrected sentences that might be used in an examination. "Congress finally granted Blacks broad enforcement and protection of their right to vote in 1964" is dubbed "misleading." Why? Because in America individuals are first; they are not granted anything, they take and win. The preferred formulation: "Blacks finally won broad enforcement and protection of their right to vote in 1964." Or a teacher might use this sentence for some purpose: "Ms. Teodoro's husband disapproves of her job, although he allows her to pursue her own interests." This statement, however, distorts status and power. The corrected statement reads, "Ms. Teodoro is pursuing her interest in computers and has accepted a job in a major corporation."[35]

This example exudes the rosy assumptions of language reformers; the world rewards strong independent individuals. Ms. Teodoro does not simply have a job; she now works for a major corporation. Indeed, she is so desirable she has "accepted" this job, as if she were simply appointed by a high government commission. In the corrected formulation the ogre Mr. Teodoro disappears. In the first statement he is the subject. Where did he go? Is he watching television? Did he run out? Perhaps he continues to disapprove, even if his wife now has a cushy corporate job. Perhaps he dominates because he is larger, physically or emotionally, and "allows" —or forbids—his wife to work.

Shouldn't language bespeak the injustices of the world? Utopia has not yet arrived; should we pretend that it has? The new reformers seek to strip language of shadows, merging euphemisms and advertising. At the national conference of self-promotion they pass out linguistic smile buttons. They want language to radiate a positive world of egalitarian men and women, black and white, success-

ful and progressing. Language turns opaque, however, if punished
for the sins of a punishing world.

Compton College is located in one of Los Angeles' most beleaguered communities, largely black and Latino like the school itself.
To reach the college requires driving along boulevards lined with
scrap-metal yards, tire-recapping factories, burnt-out buildings, li-
quor stores, and taco shops. The landscape seems forbidding, but
Compton College pops up, not as temporary classrooms next to a
freeway, but as a series of low-slung brick buildings from the 1950s
spread across eighty green acres.

I chat with its affable African-American president, Warren A.
Washington, whose reception area is strewn with clippings of interviews he has given and news of community meetings he chaired. I
ask about racial and ethnic hostilities. He tells me there are virtually
none. Students come to Compton, a community college, single-
mindedly, for courses and credits they need for jobs. But wait. Just
the other day, a Latino student stopped him and claimed he was a
victim of discrimination. "A teacher looked at him funny."

The impulse to shrug should be resisted. We have entered the
world of gestures, words, and signs. Hostile looks, epithets, and
loaded comments fill much of daily life. "Verbal aggression," which
includes graffiti and printed flyers, is the most common form of
campus racism.[36] A defaced poster triggered a major racial conflict
at Stanford. The evening after an argument between black and
white students as to whether Beethoven had an African ancestor,
two intoxicated white students altered a poster of the composer by
drawing in "Afro" features and hair. They later apologized, claiming it was a joke, but the damage was done. It led to a series of
rallies, caucuses, an appearance by Jesse Jackson, and, apparently, a
deterioration of campus race relations.[37]

Few dispute that racial and ethnic relations on American campuses are worsening. The larger social racism; the increasingly diverse student populations; the manifestos of cultural identities; a
resentful backlash by white students; naïveté; and, especially, student drinking: all these figure into incidents of campus racism.[38] In
some schools these events spur calls for codes prohibiting hate
speech and insulting speech. Numerous campuses have considered
speech codes. Few have been adopted, and insofar as they have
fared poorly in the courts, their future remains in doubt.

The momentary fate of the codes may be less important than the individuals and arguments supporting them. Those advancing speech codes see themselves as liberals, leftists, feminists, and friends of civil liberties. If they have broken with a traditional liberal defense of the First Amendment, it is in the name of greater equality and freedom. "By now there is an experience of *déjà vu*," complained Charles R. Lawrence III, an African-American law professor, "each time I am asked to explain how a good civil libertarian like myself—a veteran of 1960s sit-ins and demonstrations, a liberal constitutional law professor, and a person who has made antiestablishment speech his vocation—could advocate censorship."[39]

Almost without exception those most vigorously advancing speech codes are law professors. To a cynic this is hardly surprising. Law professors like laws. This is what they do: study and rethink laws. They respond to an old or returning evil like racist speech by calling for legal codes. For English professors the world is a text; for law professors it is a statute. Virtually every campus with a speech code has a law school. This makes sense: law schools produce law professors who produce laws for schools. If you wander onto a community college and inquire about speech codes, or even a controversy about their merits, you will receive blank stares. Speech codes are for elite schools.

This is a bit unfair, but it does indicate a difficulty: why should speech be regulated on certain elite campuses but not elsewhere—and not outside the campus? Isn't this a new form of "in loco parentis" that schools have generally renounced over the last thirty years—and which liberals have pushed to dismantle? Administrators and professors no longer pretend to be parents guarding students. They no longer regulate the dating and sexual habits of their students; should they now presume to protect them from racial slurs? For exactly this reason some minority students have objected to speech codes as patronizing and condescending.

No one who reviews the contribution of those arguing for speech codes can fail to be impressed by their passion and thoughtfulness. Unlike conventional law professors, they write frequently in the first person, drawing upon experiences from their lives. Lawrence closes an essay recalling the humiliation when he was nine and playing ball with white friends; they chose the captain by reciting a racist ditty, "Eenie, meenie, miney, mo . . ." Mari J. Matsuda begins an essay referring to her fright as a Japanese-American professor; arriving in Australia, she was confronted by posters saying "Asians Out or Racial War."

In different ways these law professors argue that an "absolute" free speech must not be elevated above egalitarianism, the right of all to live and learn in a nonthreatening environment. Hate speech, insults, slurs, and verbal attacks should be proscribed to protect the rights of long-suffering minorities. "I am troubled," writes Lawrence, "that we have not listened to the real victims, that we have shown so little empathy or understanding for their injury." Protecting hate speech in the name of absolutist free speech, states Matsuda, unfairly burdens the minority victims, violating "the principle of equality."[40]

Of course, few want to defend racist speech as fundamental to the Republic. Leaving aside First Amendment issues, do the arguments for speech codes join in, perhaps accelerate, the fetish of words? Obviously they do; these law professors claim that racist speech is more than a string of words. It wounds individuals and should be outlawed. "Racist speech causes tangible injury, and it is the kind of injury for which the law commonly provides, even requires, redress."

The strength of speech code advocates is their weakness. To their credit, they honor words, hating hateful words. In exalting language, however, they slight reality; they risk misplacing their anger, targeting society's idiom, not the idiom's society. This engenders the central paradox of correct language and campus speech codes: language gets better as society gets worse. Almost everywhere the incidents of racism, shootings, and rapes register increases. Obviously this is not cause and effect, as if improved language causes social regression, but for professors and students it may be the reverse. A deteriorating society may accelerate efforts to reform language—not everywhere, but among a select group, campus liberals and leftists.

Stymied by vast social ills, academics can at least identify racist or sexist comments. If we cannot reform society, goes the implicit reasoning, we can at least clean up objectionable language. Racism seems intractable, but racist comments, jokes, and perhaps research might be eliminated. Moreover, professors and students feel at home with words, texts, and speech; unlike a wider reality, even ambiguous or complex writings can be examined, monitored—and censored. On the campus, people commend neutral terms like "significant other," referring to lovers or wives or husbands; they vigorously enforce proper terms for groups and individuals. They outlaw racial slurs; meanwhile racism and violence against women increase.

To indict language reformers for accelerating violence would be unfair. They may be guilty, however, of shifting attention from reality to its lingo. Distinguished urban universities are often a stone's throw from major ghettos: Columbia University, Boston University, the University of Chicago, the University of Southern California, and Yale University border on urban wastelands—and Harvard, MIT, UCLA, and UC Berkeley are not much farther. What does it mean if on the green campuses proper and respectful language fills the air, but blocks away poverty and violence mock this gentility? The Los Angeles riots burned up to the edge of the University of Southern California.

Other weaknesses riddle arguments for speech codes. In the name of hard-nosed political realism, these law professors argue that "free speech" is never neutral, and does not protect minorities. Matsuda begins from the premise of "the standard teaching of the street wisdom: law is essentially political." "Most blacks," writes Charles Lawrence approvingly, "unlike many white civil libertarians—do not have faith in free speech." "Free speech," affirms Richard Delgado, is "a powerful asset to the dominant group . . ." After they deride free speech as nothing more than a tool of an oppressive state, they turn around and suggest that the state will neatly adjudicate between free and racist speech on behalf of minorities.

Why do they suddenly have such confidence in the state? Here the free speech "absolutists" surely have the better argument: they distrust the state's ability to assess speech for good or bad. Several cases illustrate the dangers: After a campus speech code was passed, a student was charged with derogatory and insulting language. She opposed the Gulf War, comparing the American missiles to phalluses.

Speech codes frequently ensnare the minorities they were intended to protect. The University of Michigan disciplined a black female student for violating its code. According to an ACLU attorney, "In an argument with a white law student, she used the term 'white trash.' She was forced to write a humiliating letter of apology." Another student interrogated for homophobic and sexist expression was black. The student at the University of Connecticut penalized for an allegedly homophobic poster was an Asian-American.[41]

As in so many debates, a speeding reality leaves the disputants behind; society slips out of their racial categories. "Whenever we decide that racist hate speech must be tolerated," writes Lawrence, "we ask blacks and other subordinated groups to bear a burden . . . This amounts to white domination, pure and simple." Throughout their writings, these professors refer to hate speech and insults directed by "dominant" whites at blacks and other minorities. This fires their passion, the need to protect minorities from the slurs of the dominant majority.

Lawrence, Matsuda, and Delgado all aim to shield "members of racial minority groups traditionally victimized." Indeed they suggest that speech codes would not "protect people who were vilified on the basis of their membership in dominant majority groups." If a white student called a black student "a dumb nigger," this would be prohibited. If a black student called a white "a dumb honky" this would be acceptable. Matsuda's code would exempt hate speech directed at white women by Native Hawaiians. Inasmuch as this hate emerges out of a history of oppression, it is allowable. "If there is any legal limitation of racist hate speech," concludes Matsuda, "it should not apply to hate speech that comes from an experience of oppression." On the hate-speech floor of the department store of babel, oppression is a gold credit card.

Even as the law professors dwell on issues of ethnic hate speech they barely seem to realize that we live in an authentically multicultural society—with multicultural hatred and insults. Hate and hate speech are egalitarian. These academics operate with a simple conception of a white majority affronting minorities, who regard each other with warmth and consideration. "The mere experience of racial oppression," remarks Randall L. Kennedy in a criticism of Matsuda, does not "inoculate the victims of oppression against their own versions of prejudice and tyranny."[42] Indeed from Miami to New York and Los Angeles, not only white-black but Latino-black, Hasidic-black, and Korean-black racial insults and strife permeate our city streets. In Los Angeles high schools the hostility between Latinos and blacks is more explosive than between either of these groups and whites.

Anti-Korean racism marked the boycott of Korean merchants by black residents in Brooklyn. "One lesson is obvious though often forgotten," writes a Korean-American commentator. "People of color who have suffered racial discrimination are nonetheless able and willing to oppress other racial minorities."[43] At the session on the "racist speech controversy" that I attended at UCLA, a young Korean woman rose from the audience to talk haltingly, and passionately, about black-Korean hostilities. An uneasy silence settled upon the room.

Hate speech does not cease being hateful if directed by one minority at another. The analysis of these law professors, however, rests on gauging the impact of hate speech on the individual as a member of a victimized group; this means assessing "the experience of the victim's group over the course of time and space." They want laws and codes to protect minorities from the dominant majority. But if minorities are insulting minorities, what then? How could a judge or law calculate the impact? If an African-American insults a Korean-American, or a Chicano offends an African-American, who could calibrate the damage? We would enter the world, not of law, not even of sociology and history, but of mystical comparative therapy. Which group feels worse? Which group has suffered more? Nat Hentoff has called this the "sliding scale of free speech" doctrine. "Under this notion that some people deserve more free speech than others, punishment of bad speech is measured by which *groups* have been more discriminated against over time. Members of those groups get extra free speech."[44]

Campus anti-pornographers, notably Catherine A. MacKinnon, advance positions parallel to the speech coders; and their boats sink on the same rocks. Like Matsuda, Lawrence, Delgado, and other speech coders, MacKinnon is a law professor; like them, she sees evil and thinks law. Like them, she believes some speech—pornography—passes beyond speech to injure individuals. She proposes laws that would treat pornography as transgressing the rights of women. "Our law," she wrote, referring to an anti-pornography code she helped draw up, "defines pornography as the sexually explicit subordination of women through pictures or words." She also scorns the First Amendment, which she believes is a "sexual fetish." "Pornography is at the core of the First Amendment."[45]

The real issues for MacKinnon are power and sexual politics; the anti-pornography movement challenges the state, and its "ruling ideology," pornography. This is the same state she wants to enforce new anti-pornography codes. Of course, the American government, like many states, has not been idle in this field. From Flaubert's *Madame Bovary* in the 1850s to James Joyce's *Ulysses,* Edmund Wilson's *Memoirs of Hecate County,* and Vladimir Nabokov's *Lolita* governments have banned literature as obscene. For MacKinnon these familiar facts count for little. Her beef is with pornography, which she boldly cleaves from obscenity. They "represent two entirely different things." Men not only like obscenity; they also like to ban it.

What is the difference between obscenity and pornography? Although she tries, she cannot explain. Obscenity is an idea; pornography is not. "Pornography is more actlike than thoughtlike." However, pornography "furthers the idea of the sexual inferiority of women" through writing, speech, and pictures. To a skeptic, pornography looks very much like obscenity. As Ellen Willis indicates, the anti-pornographers like MacKinnon are motivated by a puritanical zeal and attack a symptom, "not a root cause," of sexual violence.[46]

Where MacKinnon's logic leads might be glimpsed in the laws she has sponsored, as well as events at her own law school. Both Minneapolis and Indianapolis passed anti-pornography laws "drafted" by MacKinnon and another feminist, Andrea Dworkin. These defined pornography as "the graphic sexually explicit subordination of women, whether in pictures or words." As critics pointed out, this covered a lot of ground; everything from Homer's *Iliad* to James Joyce's *Ulysses* could be banned. Both laws were struck down in the courts. The judge stated that the Indianapolis ordinance classified speech on the basis of its content. "Speech treating women in the approved way—in sexual encounters 'premised on equality'—is lawful . . . Speech treating women in the disapproved way . . . is unlawful . . . This is thought control."[47]

At the University of Michigan, law students dismantled an art exhibition on and partly by prostitutes; the students explained they were just protecting women's safety and equality. The action caused a small furor. Was this censorship? Not at all. Rather, according to MacKinnon, "First Amendment fundamentalists" are engaged in a "witchhunt," "persecuting and blacklisting" herself and others as "art censors." In fact the "fight" is "between those who wish to end male supremacy and those who wish to do better under it."[48] If your group credentials are in order, censorship is fine, even necessary: this is the wisdom of the new law professors.

For the law professors and the language reformers, words are the weapons and the cure. Yet an obsession with words may promote language breakdown. In personal interactions, a charged idiom causes language to stutter and stop. Doubt about proper terms occasionally lead to bold interventions, but usually to silence and withdrawal. "I was at a party," recounts a student, when an Asian woman student snapped, " 'Don't say Oriental. That offends me. The proper term is Asian.' " The accused student pondered this, and concluded that while an improvement over "Chink," "Oriental" really is outdated. "Yes, I agree 'Oriental' should be phased out, and in time, I believe it will be. But that does not give us the right to disregard all forms of social politeness while we go about it." It was a "strange encounter," he adds, "seeing that I am 100 percent Korean and really do not look like anything other than a 100 percent Korean, Asian boy."[49] He should have stated: Asian man.

The premium on correctness gives rise to a paradoxical impact: no language. Students do not know the appropriate words; to avoid embarrassment or giving offense they retreat to their own groups. These concerns can be belittled, but are widespread. A study of racism at Stanford found that many white students fear inadvertently insulting black students. "I'm scared to be called a racist. You've really got to be careful all the time." The charge of racism is so damning, the waters so treacherous, that many believe that the risk of trying to "bridge a cultural gap" is too high.[50]

Their misgivings are hardly unjustified. Even those abreast of the times may find it difficult to keep up with the proper terminology. Vocabulary responds to accelerating political and historical cycles. "Black" and "African," for instance, reemerged in the 1960s propelled by newly independent African states and the American civil rights movement. For two hundred years, one scholar noted,

preferences and arguments have swelled and swirled around a whole collection of labels: "blacks," "Africans," "negroes" with the small "n," "Negroes" with the capital "N," "Coloreds," "Colored People," "Colored Americans," "People of Color," "Ethiopians," "Racemen," "Negrosaxons," "African Americans," "Africo-Americans," "Afro-

Americans," "Aframericans," "American Negroes," "Negro Americans."[51]

No matter the quickening shifts, people should be addressed as they see fit. This is so obvious, however, that it bypasses a problem: it is not always certain what people want to be called: Latino? Chicano? Hispanic? Mexican? Mexican-American? Puerto Rican? American? El Salvadorian? When referring to another student or ethnic group, students hesitate, garble, swallow, and backtrack.

The uncertainty rests on good grounds. "Hispanic," states one author, is "a repulsive slave name." She demands Latino, but others reject this as irrelevant, a term recalling the Latin of the Roman Empire. One survey of Latino/Hispanics concludes that most care little for either label; they prefer to be identified by their country of origin. A director of the study remarked of the feud over "Latino" or "Hispanic": "The intelligentsia engaged in a political debate that has no resonance among the people."[52]

Perhaps. But the problem of how to address or refer to someone weighs on students and surely others. The uncertainty and fear of a humiliation leads to withdrawal. The revised, corrected, bias-free, hateless speech turns into its opposite: everyone becomes reluctant to talk to those who are different. Inasmuch as campus reformers are frequently leftists and liberals, these consequences are especially ironic. It is an irony, however, that points to a leftist and liberal mythology: the belief that conflicts can be resolved through communication. This is the religion of the twentieth century. American leftists and liberals are the first communicants.

Within a generally bleak period of race and ethnic relations, one note of optimism should be registered. The standard view of increasing incidents of racial violence and hate speech in higher education might be wrong or at least dangerously simplified. Few want to entertain this proposition, as if truth itself might be inopportune. "A few years ago," writes John Leo, a *U.S. News & World Report* columnist, "anyone who made wildly inaccurate charges about race on campus would have been challenged immediately. Now, race relations are so touchy that a lot of overblown rhetoric sails by."

To illustrate, he observed that a Wellesley College report on racism arrived at a pessimistic judgment about worsening conditions for minorities. What did the report, two years in the making, present as evidence? Five anonymous and offhand remarks, like "Black students are routinely late to class because they are not taught about time at home." Yet it concludes that the situation is grave. "Although these clear and direct expressions of racial prejudice are not numerous," the report stated, "stories about them are so often repeated that they are important because they generate widespread perception."[53]

Of course, this logic leads to report heaven, generating a pseudo-crisis and more reports about the crisis. Little is found, but that little—stray sentences of prejudice—circulates about, appearing more significant than it is. Instead of puncturing misconceptions, the report sanctions them, adds a Wellesley imprimatur, and circulates the materials further, abetting more misconceptions. The conclusion is cited in other reports, additional proof of the serious situation. The initial evidence gets befogged, inflated, and finally lost.

The findings of the Wellesley paper may be typical; within a highly charged situation insulting remarks and small incidents translate into major events. Another survey of campus racism offered examples: "A Chinese-American student sat down at the end of a library table. At the other end, a group of students . . . began telling ethnic jokes and directing anti-Asian slurs at her. She left." "A Native American activist was discouraged by her chairman in her pursuit of promotion and tenure." "A Black columnist on a student newspaper depicted White people as 'irredeemable racists' and called for Blacks to 'unite, organize and execute' Whites who pose a threat." Students reported events like these: "I was playing basketball and blocked a shot. I was called a nigger." (Black male.) "I was called a Jew because it was thought that I was cheap." (Jewish male.)[54]

A study of racism at Stanford found that 60 percent of the black students thought racism was a "very serious" issue on campus. They meant, however, "institutional racism" or the structure of power, which they believed was inherent in American society, and not unique to Stanford. Though half this number experienced racist behavior firsthand on campus, few could explain what happened. "Most of the black students who said they had personally encountered racist behavior at the University . . . were hard pressed to describe what it was like or how it worked . . . A black freshman said, 'There's nothing that's actually been done to me, but there are things that have been hurtful—like people who don't think black writers have anything to say.' "[55]

Within a tense environment even well-intentioned remarks may be received as insults. At another school an instructor told a black student that he could "excel" and "receive an A grade." The student interpreted this as a racist comment, meaning that despite being black he could receive an A. He registered a complaint.[56]

The question is not whether racism exists, which cannot be doubted, but whether campus racism has increased; and increasing campus racism must be set against another increase, the elementary facts of sharply augmented numbers of minority students throughout higher education, and especially in schools that had been almost completely white. Stanford itself has gone from a school with few minority students to a 1990 entering class 43 percent black, Latino, and Asian-American. In a seven-year period whites at UCLA have moved from the vast majority to a minority; in 1991 56 percent of the undergraduate population at UCLA was black, Latino, and Asian-American.

In higher education as a whole black enrollment grew from about 150,000 in 1960 to over a million today. Nor has this increase been evenly distributed. Since the late seventies, breaking with a historical pattern, more black students attended integrated schools than all-black schools; this new black presence includes sharp jumps in enrollment at elite and Ivy League schools.[57]

This is hardly a reason for national self-satisfaction. Crude numbers hide important divergences—for instance, troubling dropout rates for blacks and Latinos, and in recent years a disturbing decline in numbers of blacks in higher education (and an almost complete absence in certain fields). The rate of black high school graduates going on to college crested in 1977, when it almost matched the rate of whites. For the next ten years it declined, especially in comparison with white enrollment, which continued to increase; in the last few years, the black rate appears to be inching up again.[58] In any event, the face and faces of higher education have dramatically changed over three decades. To put this differently: when Stanford was a white school with just a few blacks, racism was not a campus issue. The charge of racism emerges as the racial composition shifts; it is almost backhanded evidence of progress.

Moreover, no one suggests reducing black or minority enrollment to prevent racism, a logical if unpalatable step. Virtually everyone argues the reverse, which suggests an advance. When the numbers of Jewish students began to creep up to 20 percent at Harvard in the 1920s, incidents of anti-Semitism also began increasing. President Lowell used this as a reason or excuse to limit Jewish enrollment. "The anti-Semitic feeling among the students is increasing," Lowell observed, "and it grows in proportion to the increase in the number of Jews. If their number should become 40 percent of the student body, the race feeling would become intense. When, on the other hand, the number of Jews was small, the race antagonism was small also."[59]

What does an "increase" of racial incidents actually mean, and what is the evidence? Again, the number of African-American students has grown enormously in higher education, especially in previously all-white institutions. In the early 1950s only 1 percent of the blacks in higher education attended predominantly white institutions; by the late 1970s this figure jumped to 50 percent. On many white campuses with previously only a handful of blacks, the African-Americans came to constitute 5 to 10 percent of the study body. A larger group not only acted differently but was perceived differently.[60]

An "increase" in racial incidents or deaths in a population or automobile accidents may mislead unless changes in the size of the pool are considered. For instance, to state that the number of automobile fatalities soared between 1920 and 1970 from 12,000 to 50,000 would be accurate, but not especially informative unless the additional automobiles, miles driven, and population were also considered. During this same period automobile registration climbed from 8 million to 90 million.[61] The increase in fatalities may hide the fact that the rate of accidents (per person, cars, miles driven) has not changed, or even has fallen.

In the same way "increasing" racial incidents may mislead unless figured on the basis of increased numbers of black students in white schools. This is always the problem of increasing (or decreasing) events; changes in the pool or population must be kept in view. Otherwise the numbers distort the situation. This is true of rates and percentages as well; the real numbers have to be ascertained. When restricting Jewish enrollment at Harvard, Lowell gave as a reason that 50 percent of the students caught stealing books from the library during the previous year were Jews. It sounded ominous.

Felix Frankfurter, later a Supreme Court Justice, inquired as to the total number of students caught. Lowell reported: "Two."[62]

Talk of a "rate" of racist incidents may be delusionary, impossible to figure out or even consider. As in automobile fatalities, numbers do not tell all: one fatal accident or one racial fight is too many. Yet any levelheaded discussion of a "crisis" of racism in higher education must attend to the vastly augmented numbers of blacks at previously all-white schools.

Moreover, the actual number of racial incidents is extraordinarily difficult to assess. According to one authority, over a two-and-a-half-year period several hundred racist incidents have taken place on American campuses. Again, this must be situated in the context of a student population of almost 14 million at several thousand schools. Perhaps more pertinent, what is an incident? Major acts of violence—arson, vandalism, shootings, brawls—call attention to themselves; they are fairly easy to monitor and count. The press wakes up and sends reporters. For instance, racial fights and strife have several times struck the University of Massachusetts at Amherst; these are reported in the national press.[63]

The vast majority of hate incidents on campus, however, consist of verbal aggression, meaning insults and taunts, and racial discrimination, meaning "minority students' perception of unfair treatment and racial insensitivity."[64] Both pass unnoticed by administrations, journalists, or sociologists unless the individuals involved come forward to report them. To measure and discuss these incidents is also to measure people's inclination to report them.

"Self-reporting" is subject to many variables, however. People do not automatically or naturally report racial incidents. An increase of ethnic slurs on campuses may reflect, not increased incidents, but an increase in students willing to register complaints and an increased willingness of administrations to record them. This is the conundrum of studies drawn from public records and newspapers, which always plague historians and sociologists. What do public statistics represent?

For instance, government figures show that serious crime increased in England in the first half of the nineteenth century. Yet the numbers might indicate, not more criminality, but a public more willing to report delinquency. The figures may also reflect improved statistics, an increasing ability of the state to collect national statistics; the numbers might mask actual decreases. "Crime rates," writes a historian of crime, "cannot tell us how much crime (as a discrete entity) is committed in society. They measure most directly the State's perception of and administrative ability to deal with the vast range of activity of which it disapproves—as well as the public's readiness to connive at the disciplining of those who break the law."[65]

Today a parallel with sex harassment cases might be drawn. Few would dispute that suits charging sexual harassment in the workplace are increasing. To conclude that this reflects greater workplace sexual harassment would not be merited. It may be that rates of harassment are stable or decreasing. The greater number of cases probably registers the fact that more women are willing to air and press charges. For the same reason the additional incidents of campus racial abuse may indirectly testify to a change in cultural climate that encourages individuals to protest affronts.

Language and psychology are difficult, even impossible, to separate. Campus reformers no longer even concede, however, that they are distinct. They promote the psychologizing of speech; the issue of free speech is not what threatens the social order but what makes individuals feel unwelcome or disliked. The Supreme Court declared unconstitutional the St. Paul "hate crime" ordinance, a model for campus speech codes; this law was cast in the idiom of psychology. A misdemeanor, the law had stated, will be charged against those who arouse "anger, alarm or resentment in others" because of race, color, creed, religion or gender.[66] The formulation is typical; defenders of speech codes eloquently justify them on the basis of how students feel when confronted by hate speech or graffiti. They feel hurt, wounded, unwelcome, or, as the St. Paul law put it, resentful.

The law professors who advocate these codes write articles with titles like "Words That Wound" or "Language as Violence." Matsuda offers a veritable encyclopedia of the personal impact of hate speech. Individuals attacked feel "emotional distress," including "fear in the gut, rapid pulse rate," and worse. "The effect on one's self-esteem" is "devastating." "To be hated, despised, and alone is the ultimate fear of all human beings. . . . Racist speech . . . hits right at the emotional place where we feel the most pain."[67] From feeling alone, it is a short hop, at least to Matsuda, to criminalizing hate speech.

This ideology of feelings and sensitivity dovetails with a religion of self-esteem preached from every platform. Educators, scholars, and legislators hammer away on the importance of self-esteem and self-respect. This is what all students need, and minority students especially do not have. The speech coders and revisers concur that words should reinforce, if not aggrandize, the individual. They subscribe to the therapeutic ethic as the answer to everything; words become a function of self and self-esteem.

No one can reasonably argue that students—or any individuals—should make others feel unwelcome or should themselves be depressed and lack self-confidence. This is hardly the point. To oppose the ideology of sensitivity does not entail prescribing brutality. Rather it suggests that the ideology of sensitivity partakes of the primal myth of American society, the illusion that a smile and robust self-confidence guarantee success. The standard recipe in the American cookbook of success offered nothing else. "Never admit defeat. Always feel powerful. Think success." This was the wisdom of Orison Swett Marden, vice president of the Success Company, editor of *Success* magazine, and author of *Every Man a King* and other popular books at the beginning of the century.[68]

In these success pitches, economic and social realities evaporate, and we are left with a pep rally of the self gazing in a mirror. "I feel great! I'm tops! I can do it!" Or we are left with a program of self-esteem that is completely insular: self-esteem is built by building self-esteem—and by joining self-esteem groups and purchasing self-esteem books. In the days when states had money to burn, California even established an official Task Force to Promote Self-Esteem, which did the usual things: hold conferences, publish a journal (*Esteem*), and issue a report. Before winding down as a state project, it devised an enviable three-point program: "Work on raising your own self-esteem . . . get our report, 'Toward a State of Self-Esteem' . . . join the National Council for Self-Esteem."[69]

"Self-esteem" as a research topic dribbles all over because of its vagueness. After all, what is an individual esteeming about himself or herself? Is it just a generalized self-confidence? Very little evidence suggests that self-esteem leads to better achievement, and this may be because of the hollowness of self-esteem.[70] A person might cherish family, country, athletic prowess, or designer clothes, but these feelings may not convert into being a superior student or better citizen.

In fact, the relationship between self-esteem and achievement might almost be inverse—"almost" because a serious lack of self-esteem leads nowhere. Yet insecurity and self-doubts also stoke achievement and hard work; and they place self-esteem on a real basis. The relationship between self-esteem and achievement may, at the very least, be reciprocal. The way to achieve self-esteem is through skills and accomplishments, not through self-esteem workshops and lectures.

Those very pleased with themselves and their possessions may do little else than flaunt themselves. Indeed, a vigorous sense of self marks the American character. Unfortunately it may have less and less to do with reality. A venerable *New Yorker* cartoon has a psychiatrist talking to his patient. "First the good news: your ego is in excellent shape. Now the bad: it has no relationship to reality."

The relatively poor showing of American students in standard tests compared with other students has become a commonplace. Less familiar (and fewer) are observations culled from studies correlating self-esteem and educational performance. Perhaps surprisingly, a simple relationship does not hold.[71] Those who think themselves top dogs are bottom feeders. Those who think themselves losers are winners. International studies of mathematical and science skills show that Americans are the most self-assured and self-confident—and do the worst. Asian students are more insecure and self-doubting—and finish on the top.

One study of children's mathematical proficiency in the United States, China, and Japan found that the American children regularly scored lower than comparable Chinese and Japanese children, but the American mothers were far more "positive" about their children's performance. "American parents, whose children generally score below Chinese and Japanese children," observe the researchers, "gave the most positive evaluations when asked about their children's schools and how their children were performing." The children themselves, even as they scored significantly lower in mathematics than the Chinese and Japanese, considered themselves to be "among the best."[72]

Another study, of thirteen-year-olds in five countries and four Canadian provinces found the American students at the bottom of the scale in mathematical proficiency, right below Irish students and French-speaking students of Ontario, with Koreans the highest scorers. When these students were asked whether they "are good at mathematics" the tables are turned upside down. The American students rise to the top, believing they are best, while the Koreans, who did the best, sink to the bottom. "Despite their poor overall performance, about two-thirds of the United States' thirteen-year-olds feel that 'they are good at mathematics.' Only 23 percent of their Korean counterparts, the best achievers, share the same attitude." A larger study with a different mix of countries found roughly the same results. The Americans scored near the bottom, after Spain but before Jordan, in mathematical skills, but when asked how well they thought they did, Americans floated to the top.[73]

David Halberstam's book on America's future closes with an allusion to a related study.

> A foundation tested thirteen and fourteen year olds from seven countries. Not surprisingly, the Japanese and Korean children recorded the highest scores. Again, not surprisingly, the American children were at the bottom. The children were also asked how well they *thought* they had done. The results showed that American children thought they had done the best of all.[74]

Deliberate efforts to reform language are probably as old as language itself. Almost everywhere, passion and politics saturate these endeavors. Which tongue should be used in which region fires conflicts on every continent. From Bangladesh to Canada language engenders disputes and sometimes wars. In many countries government officials and specialists standardize, purify, or simplify a language. In the name of modernization and nationalism reformers in China, Norway, and Israel have revised, recast, and reinvented languages.[75]

Today many scholars believe that language not simply dominates but defines a reality unknowable outside of its linguistic apprehension. Not only is the unconscious structured like a language but so is the conscious—and everything else. Reality is linguistic. Words, symbols, and images detach themselves from concrete references and become the references themselves. Television does not transmit reality; it is reality—or a reality. It refers as much to itself—old shows and situation comedies—as it does to anything else. The line separating language and reality grows faint.

"Sticks and stones will break my bones," goes the nursery rhyme we once recited, "but words will never hurt me." The ditty expressed a half-truth: the words hurt, but less than a beating. We recited it at a safe distance from a bully, near parents or teachers. We are not smarter, but perhaps we now attend to words both more and less. We heed them more because they are all we have. We heed them less because they stream at us from every direction; we become inured, indifferent, uncertain.

"I now begin to see land, after having wandered . . . in this vast sea of words," wrote Samuel Johnson in 1755, as he finished his *Dictionary of the English Language.* Johnson and other wordsmiths from Webster to Mencken knew where the sea ended and land began; they believed in a resolute and stout truth. "*Truth* is the end to which all learning should be directed," stated Webster. "We want *truth* in literature; we want *truth* in science; we want *truth* in politics; we want *truth* in religion; we want *truth* in everything."[76] Today few scholars subscribe to Webster's credo. We are less confident about truth or, at least, less confident about the boundary between land and sea.

The simpler truths and plainer realities are gone forever, dispatched by shifts in jobs, technologies, and scholarship. Without a sure sense of linguistic limits, we are tempted to heal social ills by correcting, revising, and prohibiting language. Reforming language is not new, but reforming society by reforming its language reflects a postmodern world; it also deflects from an unmodern world, old injustices and inequalities neither dispatched nor diminishing. In easing the pain, decorous talk may forget the disease.

4

FABULOUS, FOREIGN, AND DEAD

"WHEN I CAME UP TO BERKELEY for the entrance examinations at the University of California I failed in Greek, Latin, and enough other subjects to be put off for a year. My father was alarmed. . . . he thought . . . that my failure was his fault."[1] The year is 1884, and the student, the writer Lincoln Steffens. All was not lost, however. Father sent young Steffens to "the best private school in San Francisco," where he boned up on Greek and Latin; a year later he was admitted. Others were not so lucky. Of course, few applied. In Steffens's day college was still a limited affair. The University of California had opened its doors just fifteen years earlier with a handful of professors and about forty students. By the mid-1880s only several hundred attended.[2] As a freshman, Steffens "used to shoot quail . . . along the edges of the college grounds."

Over the next several decades, the situation turned around. Enrollments increased, colleges expanded, and entrance requirements and curriculum shifted. By 1910 Steffens could have ignored classieal languages. Most American colleges dropped Latin and Greek as requirements for entering or graduating.

The story of the transformation of American universities has been told from various perspectives: industrialization, professionalization, democratization. It can also be approached by examining the curriculum with its assumptions about Western culture, core studies, basic books, and a cultivated life. Although the terms were not used, the issues of relativism and multiculturalism informed the endless discussions. Hundreds of colleges during the late nineteenth and early twentieth centuries convened innumerable committees to study curriculum; these committees issued endless reports recommending that entering students know this; freshman or seniors study that. The reports specified changes in entrance or graduation requirements; they listed books to be known, sometimes even the chapters and pages. Little appears more tedious than these findings and recommendations.

This is not true, however. If the reports make for dreary reading, the issues spark interest. Curriculum is the turf where relativism and multiculturalism play out; here more abstract issues of what students should learn are presented. What is the role of Western classics? What is the place of modern languages, even modern history? Is there a single truth or many? These topics can be discussed in lofty terms, but they get mean and dirty when discussed in particular terms: what courses should be taken? what books should be studied?

The history of these disputes is not simply the story of old fogies defending traditional studies and idealistic reformers embracing the future. An unattractive nationalism and professionalism often inspired critics to challenge the classical curriculum, which they considered unpatriotic and amateurish. Some nineteenth-century reformers used the formidable stick of the capitalist free market to dispatch the old curriculum. They appealed to the model of the free consumer in a free market to unseat required courses.

The outcome was preordained. In his history of the rise of specialized literary studies, *Professing Literature*, Gerald Graff found surprising the weakness of the old guard, the "generalists," who resisted the new academic professionals. Their feebleness is hardly mysterious, however. In the same way and for the same reason that "mom and pop" retailing could not stand up to the modern department store, the traditional American college was either swept aside or turned into the departmentalized university offering innumerable items to student shoppers.[3]

Though hardly noticed by today's combatants, the victory by the professionalizers has been so complete a coherent curriculum has disappeared. The elective system, the academic corollary to the free market, triumphed virtually everywhere. This makes passionate arguments about the curriculum seem like shadowboxing; at least in higher education no punches can be landed, because the object, a liberal education, has vanished. Yet there is no going back. Traditionalists, who want to restore a standard curriculum with great works as its backbone, secretly know this. In their effort to promote the "Great Books" they exploited the very marketing forces that already sent them packing.

"A full and true account of the battle fought last Friday, between the Ancient and Modern Books in St. James's Library" dates from 1697.[4] Jonathan Swift's satire represented one chapter in an argument that has lasted centuries, the importance of the classics or ancients. For Swift the issues pivoted on the kind of knowledge and morality represented by the ancient and modern authors; he challenged the pretensions of modern writers.

While the quarrel goes back to the seventeenth century, it does not consist of hoary traditionalists defending the classics against youth championing new writings. Compared with the more recent medieval writings, the classics seemed like fresh air. Without their rediscovery and reappreciation the Renaissance is not conceivable. Obviously nothing is discovered or rediscovered by itself; books do not contain a will of their own. They must be met at least halfway. "We must insist upon it," wrote Jakob Burckhardt in *The Civilization of the Renaissance in Italy,* "that it was not the revival of antiquity alone, but its union with the genius of the Italian people" that constituted the Renaissance.[5]

Swift considered the advocates of modern writing deadly blowhards, a position captured in the insults traded by the spider as the modernist and the bee as the classicist. In "The Battle of the Books" the spider accused the bee of being "a vagabond without house or home." Your "livelihood" is "universal plunder," a "free-booter over fields and gardens." "Whereas I am a domestic animal, furnished with a native stock within myself." My "large castle" or web demonstrates the progress in mathematics, and "is all built with my own hands, and materials extracted altogether out of my own person." This is Swift's picture of the modern, vain, and self-sufficient author.

The bee agrees he visits "the flowers and blossoms of the field and garden," but only to enrich himself without injuring their beauty or scent. In short, the question comes down to this:

> Whether is the nobler being of the two, that which, by a lazy contemplation of four inches round, by an overweening pride, which feeding and engendering on itself, turns all into excrement and venom, produces nothing at last but flybane and cobweb; or that which, by an universal range, with long search, much study, true judgment, and distinction of things, brings home honey and wax.

Aesop, who hears the dispute, happily retains the bee as an advocate for the ancients. He sees an exact parallel between the spider and the bee on the one hand and the modern and the ancient books on the other. We are "content, with the bee, to pretend to nothing of our own beyond our wings and our voice, that is to say, our flights and our language." Instead of "dirt and poison," the byproduct of the modernists, we furnish "mankind with the two noblest of things, which are sweetness and light."

The classics never again found a spokesman with the bite and eloquence of Swift. Yet these talents would not have sufficed; the tide ran strongly against classical learning. "Rarely has so great a book been written in a lost cause," wrote one scholar of Swift's satire.[6] If the classics were once liberating, many now saw them as constraining. A myriad of reasons motivated the critics of the classics and a classical curriculum; the grounds ran from the desire to render learning more scientific and practical to that of making it more democratic and nationalistic.

A rising patriotism undermined a classical education that derided national histories and cultures. Classicists sometimes believed that knowledge of Greek and Roman writings sufficed for the educated individual. Aeneas Silvius (later Pope Pius II) outlined in 1450 a liberal education for the young king of Bohemia and Hungary. He lauded knowledge of history, especially the history of Rome and historical sections of the Old and New Testaments. "It is advantageous to know as many histories as possible," he wrote, yet he cautioned against "superfluous work." "I would not permit in any manner the histories of the Bohemians or of the Hungarians to be given a boy," he advised the guardian of the king of Bohemia and Hungary. "For they are written by the ignorant, containing many foolish things, many lies, no maxims, no ornaments of style."[7]

These sentiments could not survive the consolidation of the nation-state, a process not completed until the second half of the nineteenth century. On all levels of education, national governments sought to inculcate patriotism. "There were no better instruments of indoctrination and patriotic conditioning," writes the historian Eugen Weber in his study of French modernization, "than French history and geography, especially history."[8] In this vein, Chancellor Otto von Bismarck stated in 1889 that German schools "must incorporate contemporary and recent history into instruction and prove that state power alone can protect the individual, his family, his freedom, and his rights."[9]

Throughout the nineteenth century critics in the United States assailed the classical curriculum and its belittling of American history. President James A. Garfield, remembered for little except his death from an assassin's bullet after four months in office, protested the curriculum for this reason. Garfield, a former professor of Latin and Greek, maintained an interest in education; as a congressman he pushed through legislation establishing the federal Bureau of Education.[10]

Two years after its conclusion, Garfield attributed the Civil War to a faulty educational system. Students studied too much Latin, Greek, and classics, neglecting American government and history. Due to "our defective system of education" students lacked knowledge and appreciation of the United States that would have prevented the war. "Seven years ago there was scarcely an American college in which more than four weeks out of the four-years' course were devoted to studying the government and history of the United States. For this defect of our educational system I have neither respect nor tolerance."

Garfield surveyed college catalogs and found a woeful disregard of American history. "I have recently examined the catalogue of a leading New-England college, in which the geography and history of Greece and Rome are required to be studied five terms; but neither the history nor the geography of the United States is named in the college course, or required as a condition of admission." Harvard was no better. "We find, that, to earn a bachelor's diploma at Harvard, a young man, after leaving the district school, must devote four-sevenths of all his labor to Greece and Rome." The entire course of study contains little of American history, even of English literature.

> In the whole programme of study . . . no mention whatever is made of . . . the general history of the United States. A few weeks of the Senior year . . . furnish all that the graduate of Harvard is required to know of his own country and living nations of the earth . . . He must apply years of arduous labor to the history, oratory, and poetry of Greece and Rome; but he is not required to cull a single flower from the rich fields of our own literature . . .

Sounding very much like a contemporary educational radical, Garfield stated, "Our educational forces are so wielded as to teach our children to admire most that which is foreign and fabulous and dead."[11]

Garfield was hardly the first American educational reformer to protest an excessive focus on the classics. Benjamin Rush, a signer of the Declaration of Independence, had already charged that Latin and Greek were undemocratic, unfit for the new republic. "While Greek and Latin are the only avenues to science, education will always be confined to a few people. It is only by rendering knowledge universal, that a republican form of government can be preserved in our country."[12]

This became a regular note throughout the nineteenth century: Thomas Jefferson, George Ticknor, Francis Wayland, Charles W. Eliot, and others chipped away at the closed and antiquated curriculum. To be sure, two concerns drove these reformers. Some wanted to crack the domination of classical studies; others wanted to do this as well as to allow student choice in what to study. These motives fed into each other, but could diverge.

Rush's objections to Latin and Greek did not imply support for an open or free curriculum. His own program for a "Federal University" set out a detailed course of studies.[13] On the other hand, Jefferson wanted to give students more freedom to choose courses. He informed George Ticknor, a Harvard professor, that the new University of Virginia would break ranks; it would not follow Harvard and most American colleges in "holding the students all to one prescribed course of reading . . . We shall, on the contrary, allow them uncontrolled choice in the lectures they shall choose to attend."[14]

With little success, Ticknor sought to "open up" Harvard in the 1820s by paring course requirements, allowing increased choice for students and greater access for the community. Harvard "should open its doors to all; for, if its resources be properly and efficiently applied, it has means of instruction for all." In this way not only will Harvard serve the community; it will shed its elitist reputation.[15] Francis Wayland had more success in 1850 at Brown University. Arguing for greater student options, he put the issue bluntly:

> The objection that would arise to this plan, would probably be its effect upon the classics. It will be said, that we should thus diminish the amount of study bestowed on Latin and Greek. To this the reply is easy. If by placing Latin and Greek upon their own merits, they are unable to retain their present place in the education of civilized and Christianized man, then let them give place to something better . . . In our present system we devote some six or seven years to compulsory study of the classics . . . And what is the fruit? How many of these students read either classical Greek or Latin after they leave college?[16]

After the Civil War the pressures intensified to reform curriculum and to open wider the college gates. The Morrill Act, or Land-Grant Act, passed in the midst of the Civil War, accelerated the collapse of the classical curriculum. Inasmuch as it provided federal support for colleges that included agricultural and mechanical arts, it spurred the shifting of resources from classical studies to sciences and modern languages. It also facilitated the democratization of higher education. Ezra Cornell, who managed to obtain the New York State share of the Morrill Act for his new school, proclaimed that at Cornell "any person can find instruction in any subject."[17]

No one was more successful than Charles W. Eliot, Harvard University president for forty years, in shaking off the classical curriculum; Eliot championed the elective system, in which students chose the courses they wanted, as befitting a democratic age. Curriculum conservatives opposed his reforms in the name of the classics. Eliot noted the irony: once conservatives resisted the Renaissance return to classics in the name of Christian writings. Now they have reversed themselves.

> The revived classical literature was vigorously and sincerely opposed as frivolous, heterodox, and useless for discipline . . . Precisely the same arguments which were brought forward by the conservatives of that

day are brought forward by the conservatives of today, only they were used against classical literature then, while now they are used in its support.[18]

Like the other reformers Eliot protested a curriculum distorted by a heavy emphasis on Greek and Latin and by a virtual neglect of English. Until recently, "American colleges made no demand upon candidates for admission in regard to knowledge of English . . ." Moreover, Eliot charged that the traditional curriculum was undemocratic, authoritarian, and, perhaps worst of all, it rubbed against the grain of learning.

Eliot forcefully raised the issue of the freedoms and idiosyncrasies of learning. To follow one's own whims and needs belongs to the heart of education.

> There must be variety in education instead of uniform prescription. To ignorant or thoughtless people it seems that the wisdom and experience of the world ought to have produced by this time a uniform course of instruction . . . but there are two strong reasons for believing that this convenient result is unattainable: in the first place, the uniform boy is lacking; and, in the second place, it is altogether probable that the educational value of any established study, far from being permanently fixed, is constantly changing.[19]

The elective system in which students choose courses, which Eliot enacted, "takes account of the needs and capacities of the individual child and youth."[20]

In a 1906 lecture Eliot put it sharply: the elective system spelled freedom, which its critics opposed. "There has come upon us, right here in these grounds and among Harvard's constituents, and widespread over the country as well, a distrust of freedom for students, of freedom for citizens, of freedom for backward races of men. This is one of the striking phenomena of our day, a distrust of freedom."[21] In "The Freedom to Choose," Eliot declared:

> Is freedom dangerous? Yes! but it is necessary to the growth of human character . . . It is choice which makes the dignity of human nature . . . Do you want to be automata? Do you want to be cogs on a wheel driven by a pinion which revolves in obedience to a force outside itself? . . . Now, there are some clear objects for choice here in college, for real choice.

During the course of Eliot's presidency, Harvard's curriculum was transformed. In the 1860s an almost totally prescribed curriculum dominated, and learning usually consisted of class memorization and recitations. Henry James, the nephew of the novelist, wrote a biography of Eliot in which he observed that the classics at Harvard had degenerated into "grammatical disciplines." To illustrate, he reported that a student, "a product of the old order," complained about the changes to his father, the Harvard philosopher William James. Previously, this student maintained, philosophy was better and more understandable. Why? "We used to commit it to memory."[22]

In 1869, the year before Eliot became president, writes a historian of Harvard:

> All freshman studies (Latin, Greek, Mathematics, French, Elocution, Ethics and Duruy's *Histoire Grecque*) were prescribed. Sophomores had to take Physics and Chemistry, German, Elocution, and themes, and recite twenty chapters of Gibbon's 'Decline and Fall' and 'about 350 pages' of Dugald Stewart; for the rest, they must choose at least eight hours a week from four different classes of Latin (mostly in Cicero and Terence), two of Greek, four of Mathematics, one of Italian, and one of English (Child's Anglo-Saxon).[23]

Thirty years later, the elective system reached its "apex" with virtually no required courses.[24] To be sure, the dismantling of the prescribed curriculum did not mean that requirements for admittance to Harvard and other colleges shifted at the same rate.

Harold Stearns, a bit player in the expatriate generation of the 1920s, recalled his "nightmare of terror" of 1909 caused by the "stiff entrance examinations" at Harvard. "I intended to enroll for a Bachelor of Arts degree, which meant taking elementary *and* advanced Latin examinations . . . And I was nervous about my 'advanced' Latin—I had but three years of it, instead of the usual four; I was weak on Virgil especially." After getting into Harvard, it was a different story. "I was free to take any course I wanted—I could concentrate on one subject, or I could wander gaily from history to economics to medieval literature, as I chose . . ."[25]

The rigid entrance requirements eventually went the way of the standard college curriculum. All colleges dropped a Latin or Greek proficiency as a condition for entrance. Each began revising admission requirements, a process that continues to this day. By the turn of the century, the variations in college entrance requirements prompted the founding of the College Board, which would administer a standard Scholastic Aptitude Test to prospective freshmen. The first sentence of a history of the College Board puts it well: "The College Entrance Examination Board was in its origins an attempt to introduce law and order into an educational anarchy which towards the close of the nineteenth century had become exasperating, indeed almost intolerable."[26]

In the course of the twentieth century, with sporadic countermovements, anarchy triumphed over curriculum law and order in higher education. "Although they won some skirmishes," writes an education historian of the exponents of a standard curriculum, "in the twentieth century" they "essentially lost the war." The very term "curriculum," which once designated a shared set of books and subjects, has lost its meaning. Now it refers to a "sum of courses" picked out of catalog. "It had the same relation to the curriculum of the past that a cafeteria tray at the checkout counter bore to the fancy meal."[27]

For these reasons the battle over the curriculum is mainly beside the point. At the university level, there is no curriculum—and there has not been one for decades. The University of Wisconsin, for instance, has not had a core curriculum in this century. The efforts to require an Ethnic Studies course at Wisconsin or elsewhere hardly change the general situation. Even the requirement is misleading; at Wisconsin students must choose one course out of ninety that are dubbed equivalent courses in Ethnic Studies.[28]

While the heterogeneity of higher education undermines generalizations, here it supports generalization; curriculum varies not simply from state to state, but from school to school. Even within the same schools and the same department, the "same" course may be taught completely differently within a single year. A statement about "the" curriculum may be valid only for the extremely few schools with invariant courses.

No discussion of higher education should forget that half of America's youth never get to college. The formal learning obtained in elementary and high school must suffice to turn students into educated individuals. Town, city, and state governments have long recognized this truth, and since the first common schools in the nineteenth century, they have preoccupied themselves with improving primary and secondary education, which included establishing a common curriculum.

The structure of primary and secondary schooling reflects the government's concern. Public monies bankroll the schools; and with taxes come inspection and monitoring. In the 1880s a "free textbook" movement, which succeeded almost everywhere, enhanced the government's role. Its supporters convincingly argued that free textbooks must accompany free and compulsory schooling.[29] Consequently the state not only supervises public schools, but in funding the books, decides which books will be studied.

The decision making mirrors the financial structure; a government unit, either a school, a school district, or a state committee, makes the decisions about textbooks.[30] No single teacher chooses the books, except perhaps for a minor addition to the main texts. Inasmuch as the books are provided free to the students, are ordered through the school, and funded by the school district or state, they are approved for an entire grade in a school. All fifth grades in one school or in a school district or even in an entire state will use the same books.

Controversies about multicultural texts and offerings in primary and secondary schools pivot on this reality.[31] Twenty-odd states approve (and fund) textbooks on the state level; at issue is what books will be purchased for millions of students. California alone enrolls 3.7 million students in kindergarten through eighth grade, and pays about $30 per student for textbooks. The state does not require local school districts to second its decisions, but it subsidizes only approved books; for this reason almost every school district adopts books certified by the state. For parents, teachers, and publishers the state textbook selection process carries high stakes.[32]

Here higher education sharply diverges from primary and secondary schooling. Discussions of multiculturalism slide between secondary schools and universities, obscuring the differences. For higher education, not only has the common curriculum disappeared, there is neither the mechanism nor the will to establish it. No two schools have the same curriculum. "Admission and graduation requirements" in American universities, writes a historian of education, have "diversified to a point of near-meaninglessness."[33]

In college students purchase their own books. This marks a fundamental difference from primary and secondary schools. Government agencies or university committees do not pay for, approve, or even know the books used in courses. These books are ordered directly by the instructor and paid for directly by the students. The bookstore, not a school or a state committee, serves as the intermediary. Moreover, unlike primary or secondary school textbooks, books for college courses change regularly.

When an elementary school or its school system adopts a history text, the book, as property of the school, will be collected and handed out again each year. This redoubles the gravity of textbook adoptions inasmuch as the material endures, leaving its mark on almost a generation of students. Not so in college; the books are used once, and their student owners either prop up their beds or bookshelves with them or (try to) sell them back to the bookstore. The next year, indeed the next semester, students in the same course, perhaps with a different instructor, may purchase completely different books. The closer one looks, the more arguments about "the" university curriculum splinter into a zillion courses. There is no curriculum.

To be sure, the curriculum of American colleges and universities has not collapsed into complete randomness. Some courses and materials are still required, most commonly history and English composition. To graduate, other courses are necessary, but these are either "breadth," "distribution," or "general education" requirements that can be fulfilled by various courses. Again many variations exist, but to obtain a BA a student typically must take a certain number of courses in sciences, languages, humanities, and social studies.

Inasmuch as history and English composition are almost standard requirements, most controversies over the canon have involved these courses. What should be included or excluded? Again an illusion of a cohesive object undercuts discussion. For instance, triggered by the controversy at Stanford about adding non-Western readings to the basic course, scores of commentators have agonized over what should be included in a Western Civilization course. Should Western Civilization be revamped to include other civilizations? A good question, but almost without an object: most students do not take a Western Civilization course.

One of the few surveys of a higher education curriculum, drawing on over 500 schools, concluded that while 60 percent required students to take a history course, only 22 percent of four-year colleges required a Western Civilization course.[34] The percentages are lower at two-year schools. This puts new light on heated exchanges about adulterating a Western Civilization canon. What Western Civilization canon?

The Stanford controversy also assumes a coherent object. Many critics have decried the changes and lamented the introduction of trendy political writings. Yet the revised curriculum at Stanford parallels the main trends of curriculum revisions of the previous century. In the place of a single required course, Western Culture, Stanford introduced in 1989 a new requirement, Cultures, Ideas, and Values, designed so that its acronym, CIV, would sound like the usual term for the old course, (Western) Civ(ilization).

Freshmen must take a full year of CIV; but "the" new course is actually eight courses that are sponsored by eight different departments and programs. The student chooses one course out of eight possibilities; most involve familiar topics and books: Philosophy or Great Works or History or Humanities would hardly raise eyebrows. In fact, only one sequence, Europe and the Americas, explicitly offering an alternative to more conventional fare, has caused controversy.

It is easy to ridicule some titles from a yearlong course that seeks to engage students. D'Souza pulled out a single book from Europe and the Americas as the text which "best reveals the premises underlying the new Stanford curriculum." (Indeed, he named his chapter "Travels with Rigoberta" after this book, a Guatemalan oral autobiography, *I, Rigoberta Menchu;* its author later won a Nobel Prize.) It is just as reasonable, however, to reverse the argument: even this course that promises to be so different includes many standard works—Augustine, Shakespeare, Aristotle, Melville. In any event, this course is an elective. One book from one of the eight courses hardly reveals the underlying assumptions of the Stanford curriculum, as D'Souza supposes.

It is true that all the CIV courses are instructed to give substantial attention to "race, gender, and class," yet these are just recommendations, difficult to measure and monitor. Did a course fail to give "substantial" attention to these three topics or just one of them? How can one tell? It depends on the instructor. Beyond their differences all eight courses do share a short reading list. Yet this common reading also reflects typical curriculum reforms. The required readings are few, vague, and change annually; each year the faculty determines the common readings for the following year. For in-

stance, in 1909–90 it specified only Marx, Freud, the Bible, an early
Christian thinker, a classical Greek philosopher, a Renaissance
dramatist, an Enlightenment thinker. For the following year, the
faculty threw caution to the winds and offered the same list with a
single addition: "an epic."[35]

Unlike Western Civilization, English composition is required by
virtually every school; all schools demand writing proficiency to
graduate.[36] Very few schools, however, pay much attention to English composition. In fact, in most large universities, regular faculty
stay away from it, especially from courses designed to help those
deficient in writing. Mike Rose, a director of the writing program at
UCLA, recalls that during his years in a tutorial writing center "not
one [regular English] professor visited." He notes that "tutorial
centers don't produce research—the coin of the realm—but, rather,
provide a service . . . The work the center does is not considered a
contribution to a discipline . . . those who perform the work become an intellectual underclass."[37]

This is generally true of all writing composition courses. To teach
writing is judged a lowly task with few payoffs; it is shifted to a
special writing program, physically or intellectually separate from
an English Department; or it is delegated to graduate students. One
commentator bemoans the "widespread practice of having first-
year graduate students teach composition courses without having
had any experience teaching and, in some cases, without having any
desire to teach. Not only is this situation not seen as ridiculous, it is
seen as normal."[38]

Controversies about reforming English composition courses usually ignore these realities. George F. Will, the columnist, denounced
as "political indoctrination" the proposed course revisions of a University of Texas English course. "Politicized professors" from the
sixties, he wrote, were attempting "to give a uniform political topic
and text" to the English course.[39] Yet critics crying politics avoid
the nonpolitical problems English composition courses face.

"Every year, about 3,000 relatively inexperienced student writers
take expository writing classes from relatively inexperienced graduate student teachers," states Linda Brodkey, formerly director of
the Lower Division English program at UT Austin. These instructors "prefer to teach literature—which they are studying—rather
than writing—which they are not." Indeed, this situation prompted
the course revision at Texas. The several hundred graduate student

instructors felt "uncomfortable" with their tasks; and the course itself received "increasingly negative student evaluations."[40]

Adding to their doubts, the instructors were barred from using literature—novels, poems, short stories—which they knew best. This act itself bespeaks the fundamental hierarchy of teaching writings skills and teaching literature. Inasmuch as literature is judged superior to composition, regular faculty and courses claimed it as their monopoly. At a loss about how to proceed, the graduate students asked for a syllabus.[41]

The undertrained and underpaid graduate students previously taught by instinct. For the conservative critics, this is dandy. They object not to this situation, but to a new curriculum. Why? At first, they opposed as left-wing propaganda the proposed new text, an anthology entitled *Racism and Sexism*. This was quickly dropped, according to conservatives because of their protests, and according to the course architects because they could not "justify the expense" of a book which would be little used.

After this round, a newly proposed syllabus outlined a detailed fifteen-week course based on a standard writing textbook and a packet of essays and legal opinions on discrimination cases. As Brodkey explained, she chose legal writings for two reasons: the course was "forbidden" to use literature, and legal prose was accessible and pertinent. This new course could be criticized less for its political slant than for its details and ambition. It seeks to do too much and spells out too many precise assignments. The syllabus specified a complete list of questions, issues, and assignments for every single meeting.[42] Brodkey explained that the novice instructors needed an exact structure and assignments. For seasoned professors a detailed curriculum would not be necessary or even desirable.

The situation at Texas—the introduction of a standard course for some 3,000 students—was relatively rare; usually instructors make their own decisions about books and materials. Outside commentators rarely remark on this incoherence, since it defies summary; no pattern is visible. However, the effort to reform or give a structure to a course gives rise to controversy; all can participate in evaluating the curriculum. At Texas critics called the revised course "Marxism 306." Eventually, angry opponents convinced the dean to shelve it.

Curriculum is not as decisive as many suppose. People love to discuss it for simple reasons: a curriculum can be inspected, a list of books, perhaps assignments, topics, and subjects. It appears to be hard and firm; and unlike intractable issues like teaching or racism or government funding, curriculum seems like something that can be easily—and cheaply—altered by simply adding or subtracting a topic or reading. With a curriculum in hand, parents, commentators, and faculty can eloquently argue about education. They can complain and declaim.

Yet even on the primary and secondary level, curriculum can be diversionary, an argument about which books when there are no books, few teachers, and distracted students. "At a time when schools throughout the country have open holes instead of windows, heating systems that do not work . . . and inadequate numbers of antiquated textbooks," writes a reviewer of Jonathan Kozol's *Savage Inequalities*, "scholars debate whether or not children should learn Mayan mathematics . . . and they imagine that the achievements of black students would miraculously improve if only the curriculum they studied focused largely on the glories of the African past."[43]

Attention to college curricula may also mislead. A course may sharply diverge from its title or description. No one would study a Protestant religious sect by examining only the Bible; far more decisive would be the events and people that brought about the new group. The relation of an actual course to its outline or entry in a catalog is roughly parallel. Studies of changing curricula that use course descriptions as an index may end up with little. "The best way to misread or misunderstand a curriculum is from a catalogue."[44] The worry of commentators over what is left out or included in the syllabus of a Western Civilization course is usually misplaced.

If a department recommends that its Western Civilization course cover the topic of gender, outsiders might jeer (or cheer). They will read the catalog description—"This course will also consider the impact of gender in the French Enlightenment"—and denounce or celebrate the fact that feminists have seized control of the university. Yet such recommendations mean little. The content of the course itself depends much more on who is teaching and what materials are being used. These change from year to year, while the course description does not.

Inasmuch as specific books are not mandated, it is up to the instructor to decide how these topics will be pursued—or not pursued. When a teacher is handed—or chooses—a course like Western Civilization to teach, rarely is anything else specified besides the sketchiest description. It is up to the instructor to decide what books to order and what lectures to deliver. Nor does anyone especially care. If I want to emphasize European and American imperialism or the oppression of women through the centuries when I teach Western Civilization, I choose the books and lecture accordingly. The course may be listed as Western Civilization, but may dramatically differ from the same course at the same school taught a year earlier by another instructor.

A mechanism to supervise a course's content rarely exists. Few want to establish a monitoring system, since it looks like an infringement of academic freedom, which includes the right of an instructor to use any book he or she thinks appropriate. For higher education this right is rarely questioned. Americans idolized German universities during the nineteenth century, and they adopted its doctrine of "freedom of teaching," which gave the professor unregulated choice as to what to teach and what materials to use.[45] Challenges to assigned books take place in the United States almost exclusively in primary and secondary schools, where the "freedom of teaching" has weaker foundations.

One reason for departments to buck curricula anarchy and establish required courses should be mentioned: economic. A course in English or history or sociology for all undergraduates gives a department a bigger budget and staff. This is the economic secret which is rarely discussed: core requirements create economic monopolies and interest groups. "A core curriculum," writes a critic, "constructs protective tariffs around those disciplines in which enrollments are languishing."[46]

A larger departmental budget translates into hiring more faculty, and hiring is the name of the game. Whom to hire and whom to retain (or tenure) constitutes the real hot stuff of any department. From the wording of the job notice to the résumé, letters of recommendation, written work, interview, and demeanor of candidates everything is carefully weighed, discussed, and contested. On these matters departments expend gargantuan amounts of energy in meetings, telephoning, and bickering; often the process terminates in acrimonious departmental splits.

Compared to the intensity of hiring, the curriculum gives rise to blurred eyes and yawns. The disproportionate attention reflects the dominance of bread-and-butter issues, but it also rests on a basic truth: teachers dominate curricula, and not the reverse. The curriculum or course description matters less than the fitness, intelligence, and inclinations of the teacher. A brilliant curriculum with a feeble teacher is a feeble experience; a feeble curriculum with a brilliant teacher may be a brilliant experience. Or to put this more precisely: a feminist course taught by an anti-feminist is not a feminist course; conversely, a traditional course taught by a feminist is a feminist course. Realizing this, faculty fight passionately over who shall be hired, and less over what should be taught.

Many academics know, but do not admit, that detailed curricula are irrelevant for university education. Liberal arts colleges regularly beat their breasts, reflect, form committees, and recommit themselves to revising their basic required courses. They issue thoughtful reports, but very rarely are these translated into a specific curriculum and books. A blunt overview of curriculum reform concluded: "One of the great indoor sports of American faculties is fiddling with the curriculum. The faculty can engage in interminable arguments during years of committee meetings . . . They can fight almost without end about . . . providing useful or liberal knowledge. They can write learned books and articles . . . The harsh truth is that all this activity is generally a waste of time."[47]

Why? Especially at the elite universities which profess the most concern, faculty devote themselves to their fields, publications, and their own courses, but not to teaching general requirements. This puts in a new light the regular cycles of liberal education reform: very little changes. Lionel Trilling recalled the outcome when Columbia evaluated its general education in the mid-sixties. Daniel Bell wrote a "brilliant report for the college," *The Reforming of General Education*, examining the situation. What happened? "I wish," noted Trilling, "only to commemorate as a sad and significant event . . . the response of the Columbia College faculty to the questions the report raised and sought to answer. From my long experience of the College, I can recall no meetings on an educational topic that were so poorly attended and so lacking in vivacity . . . these meetings led to no action whatever, not even to the resolve to look further into the matter."[48]

This is roughly the scenario in most recent curriculum reforms: many reports, many recommendations, no response. The Harvard

Report of 1945, generally considered a key document in post-World War II undergraduate education, called for a widespread revamping of courses; nothing much was done. "The Harvard committee," explains an education historian, "had expected to follow its report with the development of three divisional core courses as requirements in general education . . . no core courses were developed."[49]

The same is true of other major efforts to reorganize curricula. The Yale Report of 1971 sought to bring order to an incoherent undergraduate education, but led to nothing. "Even Yale faculty," noted an observer, "would now be hard put to find a copy on their own campus."[50] The 1978 Harvard Report on reforming undergraduate education met with very modest success. "A new curriculum," wrote a critic, "does not yet exist. Four years and countless hours of committee work brought a faculty vote agreeing to the outline of the requirements for a core. 'Core' is, in truth, a misnomer since the faculty in the next several years will create or redesign no fewer than 80 and no more than 100 courses that students may take to fulfill the requirements." The real winners are committees. "The particular curricular proposals are less significant than the committee's recommendations that eight new committees be charged with implementing the new curriculum, which remains only the vaguest of paper designs."[51]

Run-of-the-mill curriculum reforms follow the same pattern: committees engender reports calling for committees that engender reports. Ernest L. Boyer's field investigation of American campuses recounts the usual tale. A large midwestern university, "troubled" by the incoherence of the undergraduate curriculum, appointed a committee to consider the matter. "After two years of study this committee, called the Commission on the Improvement of Undergraduate Education, submitted a report that began as follows: 'The university's undergraduate program has no common requirements. . . .' As a remedy the commission called for the creation of another blue-ribbon committee to define the core curriculum. Although this new group has met regularly since July 1982, progress has been glacial. When we were on the campus two years later, the only positive step that had been taken was a proposal to add requirements in English and mathematics . . ."[52]

Obviously some departments do design detailed courses that are required for all undergraduates. In these situations—for instance, at the University of Texas in English or at Stanford in history—controversy arises as to what to include or exclude. Yet these are rare efforts, and they generally illustrate, not dogmatic leftism, which exists, but how little the changes alter the general trends.

Most schools do not bother to establish even a modestly coherent curriculum; neither the faculty nor the administration has the energy or the desire to sit down and work out the details; nor do they have the economic incentive. The system of professional advancement pays little notice to good teaching and no notice to time spent planning and reforming a curriculum, an effort which must be collaborative. Again courses are considered the responsibility of individual instructors, and will alter from year to year and from instructor to instructor. The increasing fragmentation and choice in higher education have not changed for a century.

Conservatives regularly announce that abandoning the classical curriculum accelerates the demise of civilization. "Should the time ever come when Latin and Greek should be banished from our Universities," wrote an education observer, we would "regard mankind as fast sinking into absolute barbarism . . ."[53] This comment from the 1820s speaks to the present, and finds believers in every decade. Modifying the standard classical curriculum, to these observers, means embracing subjectivism, emotionalism, and anarchy.

"Our colleges . . . need to concentrate on a comparatively small number of standard subjects . . . Those who are for taking up with every new subject and untried fashion are . . . educational impressionists. As a result of this impressionism, our colleges . . . instead of doing thorough work in a few studies of approved worth, are falling into that 'encyclopaedic smattering and miscellaneous experiment.' " Allan Bloom in the 1980s? No, Irving Babbitt in his 1908 *Literature and the American College: Essays in Defense of the Humanities.*[54]

Today conservatives look for educational inspiration, not to Babbitt, but to a German-Jewish refugee, Leo Strauss, who taught at the University of Chicago. "The students of Leo Strauss," wrote D'Souza, "comprise an intellectual community, a school of thought, that can, without exaggeration, be described as the most rigorous conservative force in political theory, with increasing influence on public policy."[55] On this score, however, Strauss failed his conservative disciples: he was too much a scholar, too little a public thinker. "He could have become one of the celebrated men of the age," wrote Bloom in a eulogy, but he was intransigently opposed to "popularization." Only a "tiny number of men" were "profoundly affected by [Strauss's] books." "For those who admire gain or want to influence the world's events," Bloom lamented, "his career is a disappointment."[56]

Strauss idolized "great minds" and books. He asked, "What is liberal education?" He answered: It is culture, and cultivation of the mind. This requires teachers; and these teachers are themselves students who need teachers. Where does this "infinite regress" end? If all teachers are pupils, how do we learn? For Strauss, it stops with teachers who are not students. These are "the greatest minds," who are "extremely rare." "It is a piece of good luck if there is a single one alive in one's time." Since none are around now, and few have ever existed, liberal education consists in "studying with the proper care the great books which the greatest minds have left behind."[57]

Bloom took much from his teacher Strauss: an idiom, an elitism, a denunciation of relativism, and a passionate love for great thinkers. He followed Strauss both in condemning an incoherent education and in prescribing the cure. "Of course, the only serious solution is . . . the good old Great Books approach, in which a liberal education means reading certain generally recognized classic texts."[58] The phrase "of course, the only serious solution" suggests dogma. Bloom and others do not simply criticize the current educational confusions; they do not simply reflect on past failures and present inadequacies; they have an Answer, the Great Books or the standard curriculum.

The "good old Great Books" emerged at the University of Chicago, where Bloom studied and later taught until his death in 1992. To be sure, "great books" might refer to any collection of distinguished works; and in the past other sets of the "great works" have been published. The history of these sets reveals something of Great Works and Great Truths: they often emerge out of not so truthful advertising agencies and not so great public relations bureaus. They are hawked to an insecure public longing for time-tested verities, better education, and more impressive bookshelves.

Charles W. Eliot, who introduced the elective system at Harvard, had remarked in public lectures that a series of books, taking up no more than three feet of shelving, could provide anyone with a liberal education. This idea attracted a publisher, who asked Eliot to edit such a collection. After he retired from Harvard in 1909, Eliot began choosing selections for a fifty-volume set, now expanded to five feet of shelf space, known as the *Harvard Classics*. Like the later "Great Books," Eliot's *Harvard Classics* found an enthusiastic public. "Many more persons know Dr. Eliot through his 'five-foot shelf,' " commented a biographer, "than through his development of the theory of education."[59]

In print advertisements Eliot touted his "Five-Foot Shelf of Books" as a complete education, requiring only "fifteen minutes a day."[60] The set came with a "reading guide" that chopped the classics into fifteen-minute snippets for every day of the year. "Take a few minutes out of your busy day to commune with these great writers . . . That fifteen minutes will carry you on wings of romance and adventure to other lands, to the scenes of other days . . ." On July 22, following the guide's come-on ("Trapped in a Cave with a Frenzied Giant: Odysseus . . ."), a diligent reader would spend fifteen minutes on nine pages of the *Odyssey;* the next day he or she would turn to eight pages of Bacon's *Essays*. ("Friendship above Love? . . . Bacon knew the true test of a friend"), and so on till the end of the year.[61]

While intellectually more ambitious, Chicago's "Great Books" also sought a vast market. They derive from a course that John Erskine, a Columbia University English professor, gave after World War I in which students read a classic a week. "It would take two years of Wednesday evenings to discuss all the books on my list," Erskine explained. By then, all the students would share a remarkable store of information. "Here would be, I believed, the true scholarly and cultural basis for human understanding and communication."[62]

As the course expanded, it added instructors, including a Columbia graduate student, who eventually made the course his life's work. Mortimer Adler also had a knack for making enemies; his arrogance and nitpicking antagonized people. He ingenuously recalled of his undergraduate days: "I was an objectionable student, in some respects perhaps repulsive."[63] Adler took the Erskine course to Cooper Union, when he began teaching in its extension division. The enlarged and successful program generated conflicts among the instructors as to which books were properly classics. To resolve the dispute Adler worked up a "jumbo list of 176" titles subdivided into several categories, compared with Erskine's 52. Through discussion and "balloting" among the instructors, the list was reduced to 76 authors.[64] Most importantly, Erskine's course and the controversy it engendered sent Adler into a lifelong activity of tabulating the great books.

In 1929 the University of Chicago appointed as its president the youthful and debonair Robert Hutchins, the thirty-year-old dean of the Yale Law School. Hutchins, who had met Adler in New Haven when he came up to give a talk, had been much taken with the brash New Yorker, offering him a fellowship at the Law School. According to Adler, Chicago's new president, embarrassed since he had no particular views on education, turned to his friend for advice. Adler sang the praises of Erskine's course and proposed using the classics to revamp education at the University of Chicago. Hutchins became a believer. Adler had just wrapped up his dissertation at Columbia by turning out twenty-seven pages in twenty hours (Adler always read and wrote quickly); and in one of his first acts Hutchins foisted Adler on the Philosophy Department, which precipitated several resignations.[65]

For the next fifteen years Hutchins, Adler, and others battled to reconstruct the University of Chicago by establishing a Great Books curriculum required of all undergraduates. Their success was mixed, although it regularly brought national publicity to Hutchins and the University of Chicago. They had more luck in establishing a Great Books program in the university's extension division. First aimed at wealthy executives, by the later 1940s the Great Books courses found a larger public. Great Books courses, seminars, and lectures popped up everywhere. Adler even took it on the road. In 1948 the Chicago mayor declared "Great Books Week." Adler recalled:

> During Great Books Week, I delivered a number of addresses, one entitled "The Great Books in Today's World" to a large audience in the auditorium of the Fair Department Store on State Street; and Bob Hutchins and I conducted a discussion of Plato's dialogue on the trial of Socrates before a capacity crowd of 3,000; an additional 1,500 were turned away . . . Clare Luce and I took the stage of large packed auditorium in Los Angeles to demonstrate a Great Books seminar . . .[66]

As one historian dryly notes: "The Great Books idea was no longer just a prescription for academic and cultural reform; it was show business."[67] It was also business. A Chicago advertising executive, who enrolled in a Great Books course, had trouble locating the necessary books. William Benton had persuaded Sears, Roebuck, the giant Chicago retailer, to transfer to the University of Chicago rights to the Encyclopaedia Britannica, which Sears owned uneasily; after all, Sears was neither British nor a publisher. Benton needled the Sears chief: "Don't you think it's rather unsuitable for a mail-order house to own the Encyclopaedia Britannica . . . ?"[68]

The Encyclopaedia Britannica (EB), which dates back to eighteenth-century Edinburgh, had originally boasted a new arrangement for an encyclopedia, a mix of long general articles, short technical pieces, and many cross-references. The full entry for "Woman" in the first edition (1771) read as follows: "*Woman:* the female of man. See *Homo.*" By the end of the nineteenth century, the EB had attained great critical acclaim, but little financial success in England.

An American businessman, Horace Hooper, purchased control of the British company and introduced American advertising techniques, including personal testimonials by eminent public figures and "Absolutely Final Day" prices repeated for months. He also introduced installment buying, new to the British book world. To encourage payments, Hooper imported a 300-pound, six-foot-six New York ex-policeman and provided him with a van brightly painted "Debt Collection Agency."[69]

After he shifted publication to the United States (and oversaw its most famous edition, the eleventh edition of 1910–11), Hooper persuaded his friend Julius Rosenwald to market through his company, Sears, Roebuck, a cheaper and smaller edition of the set, known as the "Handy Volume" EB. But World War I wrecked sales of all editions; facing bankruptcy, Hooper convinced Rosenwald to buy the company. Sears was never comfortable running the EB, however, and by the late thirties wanted to unload it. In 1943 the mail-order house handed the set over to the University of Chicago.[70]

Benton suggested that the university might issue a Great Books set in tandem with the Encyclopaedia Britannica, resolving the difficulty of locating the classic texts. The idea struck home, but Hutchins, Adler, and Benton himself agreed they needed a gimmick to successfully peddle the set door to door, which is how the Encyclopaedia Britannica was sold. In fact, for some years the University of Chicago spurned sponsorship of the Britannica. The trustees expressed doubts about associating with a publishing venture "whose sales methods were distasteful to many members of the University community."[71] These doubts never bothered Adler, who hit on the come-on for the Great Books: a complete index of the Great Ideas. "It will save the student and the scholar unnecessary drudgery . . . A man won't have to read through all the books to find what he wants . . ."[72]

The project was set in motion, and the title *Great Books of the Western World* copyrighted. Adler jumped into what he loved best: listing and categorizing great books. He frankly admitted to an "anal-erotic compulsion—the need to order and arrange things and keep them rigidly fixed in the order I have imposed on them."[73] This time the committee headed by Adler came up with 443 great books by 74 great authors.

The pièce de résistance, however, was the comprehensive index of ideas, dubbed the "Syntopicon." The "Great Books" would not simply be another set of great works; it would be a set with a master key to unlock its mysteries. Adler's project dwarfed the paltry index to the *Harvard Classics,* which cost "$50,000 and a year of expert work." Adler took over a three-story building, hired seventy-five people, and worked for seven years sifting through the great texts, classifying nuggets of great ideas.[74]

They produced two fat volumes organized around 102 Great Ideas. Why 102? No special reason. Alphabetically, the first three Great Ideas are: Angel, Animal, and Aristocracy. (Even Benton was startled. "Why did you begin with [Angel]?" he asked Adler. Because it is first alphabetically, answered Adler. "But where is Adultery?" wondered Benton.[75]) The "Syntopicon" subdivides the 102 Great Ideas into exactly 2,987 Topics, which are in turn treated by precisely 1,798 Terms.[76] The index refers readers to the pages of the great texts in which the topics of the Great Ideas have been mentioned. To the uninitiated the "Syntopicon" looks like a footnote that went berserk for two thousand pages.

The Great Books were marketed like the Encyclopaedia Britannica, on a time-share basis, door to door, mainly to lower-middle-class customers. Inasmuch as the University of Chicago assumed publication, it also assumed the other critical component of installment buying: collection.[77] Yet Benton was worried that the "Syntopicon" might not do the trick; and he suggested the addition of "applied courses" highlighting suitable texts for Christmas or Thanksgiving. "After all, I want to read the Great Books in order to be popular and successful—and what are the applications I would like to make of these Great Books that will help me and my child to become popular and successful?"[78]

An enthusiast of the set was Walter Paepcke, the highly successful founder of the Container Corporation of America. Paepcke had an eye for cash and culture. He hired Adler for a new Container Corporation advertising campaign, Great Ideas of Western Man. Adler leafed through his endless files of Great Ideas and provided the quotes; an advertising agency worked them up into a Container Corporation Great Ideas pitch. Later this became a Container Corporation of America traveling exhibition, "Great Ideas of Western Man."[79]

In the 1940s Paepcke and his wife happened upon an old boom mining town in a spectacular mountain setting. Down to 1,000 people and a decaying hotel, the place had seen better days. Paepcke envisioned Aspen, Colorado, as a winter and skiing resort; he also realized it needed culture. "Instead of traveling or buying yachts or collecting art as their peers did," wrote an Aspen resident, the Paepckes "chose to turn a shattered town into a kind of national treasure of arts and ideas."[80]

Paepcke did two things: he purchased large chunks of the town; and imported culture. He convinced Hutchins to stage an event celebrating Goethe's 200th birthday in Aspen, perhaps the first and maybe the last time an advertising agency was enlisted to advance Goethe's name. (To add allure to the event, Albert Schweitzer was persuaded to come to Aspen—his single visit to the United States.) Paepcke also established the Aspen Institute for Humanistic Studies, with Adler and the Great Books as its guide.[81]

Leaving aside the commercialism and the bureaucratic mania to count, index, and rank the Western tradition, even a sympathetic discussion of the Great Books enterprise would find serious flaws with its execution. The editors themselves mention that "except for Freud's later writings, the set of great books contains no works published in the twentieth century."[82] No Joyce or Kafka or Einstein. This is tradition with a vengeance.

The choice of authors is sometimes bizarre. One volume collects three scientific texts from the eighteenth and nineteenth centuries, but is all 600 pages of Michael Faraday's *Experimental Researches in Electricity* central to a Western tradition? Or must a reader tackle "Equations of the Uniform Movement of Heat in a Solid Prism of Infinite Length" from Joseph Fourier's *Theory of Heat?* There is no way to know, for in keeping with their notion of great thinkers as transmitters of eternal truths, the editors added only brief biographical information, but nothing to explain why these writings may be important or should be read. In forty years, Volume 45, which includes Faraday and Fourier, has never been checked out of my local public library.

After its publication in 1952, the University of Chicago published regular updates. In *The Great Ideas Today 1968* the editors observed with some awkwardness the omission of "the idea of Equality" from the Great Ideas. They found room for Prudence and Habit and Angel, but not Equality. To be sure, they explained, Equality received a "double entry" in the "Inventory of Terms" but it did not rank with the real greats. It is "a strange and difficult idea"; and it may be just too new. It is "an idea that was late in coming to have an impact on human history and for that reason also late in becoming a subject of major discussion."[83]

Late in its impact and discussion? Rousseau's *Origin of Inequality* dates from 1754; the "all men are created equal" of the Declaration of Independence dates from 1776. The enlightenment, the American Revolution, the French Revolution, socialism, trade unionism, abolitionism, the Civil War: over two centuries few ideas have done more to shape the world than Equality. The editors found room for Induction and Opposition but could not squeeze in Equality.

In a scathing attack on the Great Books, Dwight Macdonald objected to the selections, the organization, and above all the assumptions. Adler and Hutchins, the creators of the Great Books, write "as if the Truth were an easy thing to come by." Their "fetish for Great Writers" and their belief that "major cultural achievements are of timeless, absolute value" lead them to compile texts with no introductions, but no modern reader can simply pick up Aquinas or Hippocrates and join in a Great Conversation. The "Syntopicon," Adler's prize, is both useless and cracked: useless because its vast list of references direct the reader to irrelevant discussions; and cracked because it assumes ideas are like marbles or stamps, easily classifiable, counted, and listed. "The true reasons for this set of Great Books becomes apparent," wrote Macdonald.

Its aim is . . . to fix the canon of the Sacred Texts by printing them in a special edition . . . In its massiveness, its technological elaboration, its fetish of The Great and its attempt to treat systematically and with scientific precision materials for which the method is not appropriate, Dr. Adler's set of books is a typical expression of the religion of culture that appeals to the American academic mentality.

Macdonald cited Hutchins: "This is more than a set of books. It is a liberal education . . . The fate of our country, and hence of the world, depends on the degree to which American people achieve liberal education." Macdonald's rejoinder? "Poppycock."[84]

5

THREE RINGS: RELATIVISM, RELATIVES, AND WANDERING YAMS

ANYONE WHO HAS TAUGHT—anyone who has lived in American society—will recognize a truth in the widespread charge of student "relativism." Confronted with unfamiliar stances, outlandish positions, and even inhumane practices, students often shrug their shoulders, unwilling to approve or condemn. "It all depends" comes the irresolute comment, the motto of the relativist. Is footbinding good or bad? Watching ten hours of television a day? "It all depends." Depends on what? On everything: on who and what and where.

This is what might be called relativism or an unwillingness to judge. Everyone and everything is right, a variant of "I'm OK; you're OK." I think this; you think that. All have equally valid opinions. It is not necessary to resolve, even pursue questions very far, because all is relative to the individual and to circumstances. Faced with the resistance to judge, a high school teacher of mine put it well some thirty years ago. "You're so open-minded," he would say, "your brains are falling out."

Philosophers, theologians, educators, and citizens are troubled by this relativism; it poisons thinking, values, Western culture itself. Individuals and society no longer stand for anything. The individual grows pliant and insubstantial, indifferent and cynical. Like other conservatives, Allan Bloom in *The Closing of the American Mind* was troubled by it. He bemoaned the relativism of American culture.

Students arrive at college as relativists. Cultural differences are simply differences; everything is equal; nothing is superior. Shakespeare is no better than comics, nor is Bach superior to rap. Higher education confirms this relativism. Anything can be studied and everything is; students take courses like Native American Herbal Medicine or Black Hair as Culture and History.[1] It makes no difference. Students graduate as impassive souls, accepting of everything, defending nothing. As Bloom put it, the openness leads to closure, "the closing of the American mind."

As with many issues, conservatives take the offensive, liberals and radicals take cover. Moreover, the conservative cause seems just. Nobody wants intellectually slothful students indifferent to right and wrong, or individuals unwilling to make judgments and commitments. We want ourselves and others to stand up for certain beliefs and values, not to mumble, "It all depends." We respect decisiveness, not passivity. We want college graduates to know something of the world, to draw conclusions and to act.

Yet are the charges true of students—and Americans generally? And if true, have the critics identified the causes of this relativism? If students are relativists, is this due to an incoherent curriculum? Faddish faculty? Deafening rock 'n' roll? Moreover, relativism seems a half-step from tolerance and multiculturalism. Are they guilty of the same sins? Are they forms of intellectual indifference parading as liberalism? Has the university become a vast cafeteria for bored diners?

At the first glance, a paradox leaps out; those denounced as relativists are also damned as dogmatists. On the one hand, they supposedly believe in nothing; on the other, they are passionate ideologues. Students and faculty approve of everything; they also censor or intimidate anyone who differs from them. But how can people be both relativists and dogmatists? Both indifferent and committed? Too tolerant and too censorious? How can they be both passive relativists and ardent champions of Latino or African-American Studies?

Of course, no one is completely logical and campus ideologues may succumb to vast inconsistencies. On occasion they are indifferent; at other times, intolerant. Conservatives can justly accuse them of both relativism and intolerance. It is also possible that an assortment of individuals are being treated as a single group. Some are dogmatists, others are relativists, but few individuals may be both.

More likely, the contradiction is an illusion or invention. Critics seek to score points, not nurture insight. They toss out labels that sound ominous. When students and faculty ignore favored precepts, they are attacked as mindless relativists. "They don't believe in anything!" This means: they don't subscribe to conservative beliefs about the ills of rock 'n' roll or the virtues of a standard curriculum. When they sharply differ from conservatives, they are branded as dogmatists and totalitarians. "Why, the campuses are full of ideological dictators!" This means campus activists advance passionate beliefs about equality.

This may be true, but insufficient. Beliefs can transmute into their opposite, by virtue not of fractured thinking but of mechanical thinking: a thoughtless unfolding of a single idea. Superficially nothing seems further apart than relativism and despotism. Yet a relativism may slip into absolutism by flatly rejecting any idea as superior to any other. It is also possible that tolerance evolves or devolves into intolerance, a contempt for those unwilling to affirm the complete equality of all positions.

The fluidity of concepts like relativism precludes any simpleminded criticism. If relativism and tolerance turn into their opposites, it is not easy to state how and when. Few contest that within certain limits relativism, diversity, and tolerance should be promoted and blessed. No one believes that one flavor of ice cream represents truth. In the freezer section of the supermarket tolerance, diversity, and relativism should reign. They play a different role in education and culture: that is the rub.

What is the threat of relativism and multiculturalism? Some view relativism as a twentieth-century disease ravaging civilization. The opening chapter of *Modern Times* by the conservative historian Paul Johnson is titled "A Relativist World." Johnson begins with Einstein and throws in Freud, Dada, Stravinsky, Proust, Joyce, and World War I; this ensemble yields relativism by undermining "a settled and objectively true moral code, which was at the centre of nineteenth-century European civilization." For instance, "the impression people derived from Einstein, of a universe in which all measurements of value were relative, served to confirm this vision—which both dismayed and exhilarated—of true moral anarchy."[2]

Historians have busied themselves with similar arguments, viewing early-twentieth-century cultural events as dispatching intellectual absolutes. These accounts are partially true, but the parts do not add up. Did the world become more relativistic because of Einstein or Freud or even World War I? To be sure, journalistic opinion interpreted Einstein's theory, itself named relativity theory, as positing a relativist universe. When the solar eclipse expeditions of 1919 confirmed a piece of Einstein's theory, *The Times* of London editorialized that certainty had abandoned the world. "The ideals of Aristotle and Euclid and Newton which are the basis of all our present conceptions proved in fact not to correspond with what can be observed . . . Space is merely a relation . . . Here and there, past and present, are relative, not absolute, and change according to the ordinates and coordinates selected."[3]

These opinions inspire historians and commentators, who run on about a corrosive relativism. Yet is this relativism and is it dangerous? Einstein did not cause or hasten "moral anarchy." Einstein's theory pertains to objects as their speed approaches the velocity of light. "For all practical purposes—namely, in the realm of ordinary, everyday things—Newtonian physics is completely valid."[4] Moreover, few understood Einstein's theory; and what people understood of its implications or applications—the atomic bomb—was not relativistic.

As a public figure Einstein himself was hardly a relativist; he was passionate about world government, pacifism, and socialism. He joked that national hostilities cause newspapers to describe him in relativistic terms. "By an application of the theory of relativity to the taste of readers, today in Germany I am called a German man of science, and in England I am represented as a Swiss Jew."[5]

The same could be said of Freud. The originator of psychoanalysis explored sexuality and the unconscious, but neither in theory nor in person was he a relativist. He preached acceptance of the ill and the neurotic, but he barely challenged conventional behavior or values. The standard feminist criticism of Freud as patriarchal is closer to the mark. Freud objected, for instance, to a nebulous universal love. "A love that does not discriminate seems to me to for-

feit a part of its own value . . . all men are not worthy of love."[6]
One study of Freud is subtitled *The Mind of the Moralist.*[7]

But didn't World War I subvert moral codes and authority, intensifying aesthetic and cultural confusion? Again, historians like this theme, and surely it has validity. "The fads and madcap behavior of the younger generation of the twenties," writes a historian, were largely motivated by "cynicism" about the "moralistic idealism that kept busy the slaughterhouse that was the Western Front." Modris Eksteins, in his well-regarded *Rites of Spring: The Great War and the Birth of the Modern Age,* continues:

> When Josephine Baker made her Paris debut in 1925 at the Théâtre des Champs-Elysées, her waist ringed in bananas, carried onstage upside down doing splits, she was symbolizing the extravagance not just of urban bohemianism but of a western culture that as a whole had lost its moorings.[8]

Perhaps. But Josephine Baker had been hired by an ailing French theater that sought to cash in on the popularity in France of things African; nothing madcap there. "Two specific elements had been established," wrote the *New Yorker* Paris correspondent of Baker's debut. "Her magnificent dark body, a new model . . . to the French . . . and the acute response of the white masculine public in the capital of hedonism of all Europe—Paris."[9] Both suggest less a world unhinged than unchanged.

If World War I really "caused" anything, the Russian Revolution would head the list, followed by a defective peace treaty and economic dislocation, the backdrops to Italian fascism and German Nazism. In outlining the ills that came out of World War I almost every category has a place, yet it is farfetched to view either Soviet Communism or German Nazism through the lens of relativism. The Communists believed in Truth with a capital T; the Nazis in "Nordic" or Aryan culture. The Nazis banned "Negro art" and jazz; they incinerated millions of Jews and others. They were hardly relativists.

In a speech opening the House of German Art, Hitler damned the relativist idea that art changed as history changed. "True art is and remains eternal." The standards of art do not vary for "yesterday and today" and "modern and unmodern." Only a single eternal measuring rod exists. He indicted the Jews for the "discovery" that "art was just the affair of a period." Why do people advance these relativist ideas? "Those who do not create for eternity do not readily talk of eternities."[10]

If several categories must be selected to capture a twentieth-century experience, racism, nationalism, militarism, absolutism, or intolerance would be more appropriate than relativism. The anti-Semitism of the Dreyfus Affair better symbolizes a dangerous age than the eroticism of Josephine Baker, which was neither relativist nor ominous. World War I, wrote a scholar in the thirties, "marks the beginning of strong accentuation of militant intolerance."[11] In more recent years, this has hardly changed. A survey of the globe that simply names places—Northern Ireland, Sri Lanka, Bosnia, India—evokes a world suffering from fratricide, not relativism.

"I have no doubt whatever that Cambyses was completely out of his mind." Cambyses was a Persian king in the sixth century B.C.; and the judgment was that of Herodotus, who is often dubbed the "father of history." What was his evidence? Cambyses trampled on the rituals of the Egyptians, his allies. He broke open ancient tombs; he jeered at sacred statues; he made fun of holy images. Only insanity, Herodotus observed, could drive Cambyses to mock Egyptian customs.

Cambyses's acts provoked additional reflections by Herodotus on the role of customs. If anyone were given "the opportunity of choosing from amongst all the nations of the world the set of beliefs which he thought best, he would inevitably, after careful consideration, . . . choose that of his own country," commented the Greek historian. "Everyone without exception believes his own native customs, and the religion he was brought up in, to be the best . . . There is abundant evidence that this is the universal feeling about the ancient custom of one's country." Referring to the Greek poet Pindar, Herodotus concluded that custom was "king of all."[12]

These pages of Herodotus go some way toward countering the frequent charges by conservatives that a corrosive relativism promoted by academic leftists undermines education. The idea that beliefs and truths vary by culture is not a recent insight. Moreover, this relativism is not mentioned only by Herodotus; as a teaching it is as old as the Greek sophists and is discussed in Plato. If relativism shows up extensively in Greek thought, how could it be inimical to Western civilization? It is part of Western civilization.

What is relativism? Of course, it resists a simple definition. Very crudely, relativism posits that perceptions, customs, and morality, and perhaps truth, depend on the individual and environment. As critics have argued, relativism may be logically inconsistent. How does relativism avoid relativism? The principle that all perceptions and values are relative is offered as a universal truth, but how does this truth escape the spell of relativism? Apart from the conundrum, in various forms relativism appears in the pre-Socratic sophists and skeptics.

Protagoras, the leading sophist, was known—in Plato's somewhat ironic words—as "the wisest man now living."[13] The sophists have not fared well in history, however; a reputation for dishonesty or deceptiveness has always dogged them, a suspicion that extends to their very name. Today "sophistry" is a term of abuse, indicating empty if clever reasoning. Originally "sophistry" meant wisdom; the "sophists" were sages and wise men.[14] In "sophistication" or "sophisticated" both meanings of wisdom and deception still echo. The sophisticated are superior in knowledge; they may also be fraudulent and superficial.

What comes down to us of the sophist doctrine is familiar, perhaps too familiar. Protagoras's most famous sentence—"Man is the measure of all things"—is modern, almost self-evident. It implies a complete relativism; all judgments depend on the individual. As the individual changes, so does truth. I see things one way, you see them another, and we're both right.

An even earlier formulation of this skepticism is attributed to Xenophanes, who may have influenced Pindar, whom Herodotus cited. Xenophanes questioned the prevalent anthropomorphism, the penchant of attributing to the gods the qualities of mankind. He carried his criticism a step further, however. Not only do men see the gods like themselves with human voices, clothes, and emotions, but the gods of different men register human differences. Each group imagines the gods to be like themselves. "The Ethiopians say that their gods are snub-nosed and black, the Thracians that theirs have light blue eyes and red hair." Even lions and horses, if they could, would view the deities as themselves. "Horses would draw the forms of gods like horses, and cattle like cattle."[15]

Socrates challenged the relativism of Protagoras, who believed that "any given thing 'is to me such as it appears to me, and is to you such as it appears to you.'" Socrates employed an example. "Sometimes, when the same wind is blowing, one of us feels chilly, the other does not . . . Well, in that case are we to say that wind in itself is cold or not cold? Or shall we agree with Protagoras that it is cold to the one who feels chilly, and not to the other?" For Plato, this relativism sabotages truth; it means that "nothing is *one* thing just by itself, nor can you rightly call it by some definite name, nor even say it is of any definite sort. On the contrary, if you call it 'large,' it will be found to be also small, if 'heavy,' to be also light."[16]

Over two thousand years later, Hegel complained that the relativism of the sophists remained quite common. Educated individuals use relativist arguments to dismiss philosophy. "There are, they say, various philosophies, various opinions, and this is contrary to the one Truth." They conclude that reason is weak and truth is relative; what matters are feelings and heart. For Hegel, as for current critics, this leads to the relativistic swamp. "The right and the true" become products of opinion and personal conviction, not rational thought.[17] Everything becomes arbitrary, subjective, and relative.

Yet a relativism that undermines fixed beliefs is not all bad. Inasmuch as it recognizes diversity, a version of relativism is probably inseparable from civilization; it acknowledges that one's own family, town, religion, country, culture do not fill the globe. It admits that other customs and beliefs exist. The process is hardly complex. Through trade, travel, or war one culture comes across different practices and values.

If an immediate response to cultural encounters is hostility, another, more reflective reaction ponders the meaning of one's customs. Augmented contacts with other cultures gave rise to the relativism of the sophists. A historian of Greek philosophy explains that the multiplying encounters

> made it increasingly obvious that customs and standards of behavior which had earlier been accepted as absolute and universal, and of divine institution, were in fact local and relative. Habits that to the Greeks were wicked and disgusting, like marriage between brother and sister, might among the Egyptians or elsewhere be regarded as normal and even enjoined by religion.[18]

This is a regular story of history: expanded contacts lead to a reconsideration of habits and customs. Sextus Empiricus, a Greek skeptic, listed opposing customs to show that it was impossible to arrive at what is true. "Some of the Ethiopians tattoo their children, but we do not; and while the Persians think it seemly to wear a brightly dyed dress reaching to the feet, we think it unseemly." He continued with cases of law and belief and sexual behavior. "Among the Romans the man who renounces his father's property does not pay his father's debts, but among the Rhodians he always pays them." "Amongst the Persians it is the habit to indulge in intercourse with males, but amongst the Romans it is forbidden by law to do so." For Sextus Empiricus "so much divergency" demonstrates the impossibility of determining the "real essence" of something, and he is led to suspend judgment.[19]

By the seventeenth century and the early Enlightenment, spurred by travel and voyages of discovery, the recognition of cultural divergency had become a ram to batter down traditional beliefs and politics. The first chapter of Paul Hazard's classic account, *The European Mind 1680–1715*, is titled "The Ferment Begins." He explained that information (and misinformation) about distant cultures led to the reexamination of concepts like Freedom and Justice.

> Perspectives changed. Concepts which had occupied the lofty sphere of the transcendental were brought down to the level of things governed by circumstance. Practices deemed to be based on reason were found to be mere matters of custom . . . We let our hair grow and shave our faces. The Turks shave their heads and grow beards on their faces. We offer our *right* hand to a friend; a Turk his *left* . . . Who is right? Who wrong?

Hazard cited a traveler to China who concluded that only "prejudices of our childhood" prevented us from realizing that differences in customs are arbitrary. Maxims such as these, summarized Hazard, "take us a long way, take us, indeed, to nothing short of universal relativity."[20]

A recognition of diversity leads to relativism, but the *philosophes* of the Enlightenment were hardly relativists—at least in the modern sense; they did not believe that ideas and beliefs and customs were equal. If anything, they maintained the opposite; they passionately believed in justice and truth and equality. Recognizing diversity led to questioning certain practices, not embracing all of them. Though they regularly referred to customs elsewhere, no one would state that Voltaire and Bayle and Rousseau were relativists.[21]

They did, however, believe in tolerance. They marshaled reports of foreign customs to set against intolerance. Montesquieu's popular *Persian Letters* from the eighteenth century used the contrivance of two Persian visitors to Europe to comment on French practices. "Transported" to France, the Persian visitors found "another universe"; its "strangeness" allowed them to wonder and criticize. They noted the diversity of practices, and argued for tolerance. "It seems to me," writes one Persian traveler to another, echoing Xenophanes, "that all our judgments are made with references covertly to ourselves. I do not find it surprising that the negroes paint the devil sparkling white, and their gods black as coal . . . If triangles had a god, they would give him three sides."

The traveler also noted that "the spirit of intolerance" had abated. "It did no good to chase the Jews out of Spain, or, in France, to molest some Christians whose beliefs differed slightly from the king's. It has been realized . . . that in order to love and conform to one's religion it is not necessary to hate and persecute those who do not conform to it." This traveler later stated that "a multiplicity of religions" benefits all.[22] But what is tolerance and its relation to diversity and relativism? Is tolerance good and relativism bad? Where and why? The conceptual map grows confused.

On the evening of October 13, 1761, in the French city of Toulouse, authorities were urgently summoned to the house of a tradesman. They found the Calas family in an uproar and their twenty-nine-year-old son, Marc-Antoine, dead on the floor. With rope marks on his neck, he had either been strangled or hanged. Within a day, the five occupants of the house—Marc-Antoine's parents, his brother, a visitor, and the servant—were charged with murder. The Calases were Calvinists, a Protestant minority that had been persecuted in Catholic France on and off for two centuries. They were accused of killing Marc-Antoine to prevent his conversion to Catholicism.

M. Calas was found guilty; punishment of the others awaited the results of torture. He was condemned to make a public apology to God and king at a Toulouse cathedral and be conducted to the main town square for execution and burning. In early March 1762, before a sizable crowd, the sentence was carried out. On the rack and wheel the arms and legs of M. Calas were gradually pulled apart; his limbs were broken, and he was compelled to swallow enormous quantities of water. During the ordeal, M. Calas maintained the innocence of himself and his family.

Through the efforts of Voltaire the "Calas Case" became a cause célèbre, and a code word signifying religious intolerance in eighteenth-century Europe. No evidence for the guilt of M. Calas or even of the son's desire to convert to Catholicism ever surfaced, but some facts remain uncertain. Marc-Antoine may have committed suicide. Initially the family claimed they found him on the floor, not hanging, for a simple reason: the disgrace of suicide. French law dictated that confirmed suicides would be dragged facedown through the streets and deposited in the town dump and that the state would confiscate their property. To avoid this fate, the family probably lied about where they found him.[23]

The killing of Calas signaled the end of the juridical murder of French Calvinists, yet not the end of religious persecution, which sometimes targeted deviant Catholics. For singing blasphemous songs about God and the Virgin Mary, uttering "impure" words about the benediction, and other minor transgressions, in 1766 a young chevalier, La Barre, was sentenced to publicly repent at the town church in a "loud and clear voice"; he was then to have his tongue cut out, and to be transported to the town square for a beheading and burning.[24] These and other cases infuriated Voltaire; he sought to stop (unsuccessfully) the sentences, to preach (unsuccessfully) tolerance.[25]

From Locke to Lessing, Enlightenment thinkers fought for tolerance against a backdrop of religious wars and fanaticism. "It is not the diversity of opinions, which cannot be avoided," wrote Locke in his *Letter on Toleration* (1689), "but the refusal of toleration to people of diverse opinions . . . that has produced most of the disputes and wars that have arisen in the Christian world on account of religion.[26] Voltaire's entry "Toleration" in his *Philosophical Dictionary* closed this way:

> We should tolerate each other because we are all weak, inconsistent, subject to mutability and to error. Would a reed laid into the mud by the wind say to a neighboring reed bent in the opposite direction, "Creep in my fashion, wretch, or I shall petition to have you torn up and burned?"

Arguments for modern tolerance reach back to the sixteenth century.[27] At first only marginal thinkers and occasional state officials defended tolerance. A few governments recognized that religious diversity did not threaten the state, their main concern. A few theologians argued that persuasion, not violence, should be used to convince heretics. A few philosophers argued that truth could not be known with certainty or that it took many forms. These arguments diverged, crossed, and paralleled each other.

A classic text of Enlightenment tolerance, Lessing's *Nathan the Wise* (1779), took up the hostilities among Muslims, Christians, and Jews.[28] In medieval Jerusalem, the legendary Muslim Sultan Saladin summons Nathan, a Jew, known for his wisdom. The Sultan does not ask for a loan, which Nathan expected, but for wisdom. Saladin reflects that "only one" of the three religions—Islam, Judaism, or Christianity—"can be the true one." "A man like you does not remain where chance / Of birth has cast him: if he so remains, / It's out of insight, reasons, better choice." Saladin demands "instruction" and "insight" as to which religion is the true one. Nonplussed, Nathan begs leave, and returns to recount the tale of the three rings.

In antiquity lived a man who received from his beloved a wondrous ring; whoever wore and trusted it "found grace with God and man." He treasured the ring, and bequeathed it to his dearest son; and so it was passed along from father to favorite son. The ring came to a father with three sons, all of whom he loved and all of whom seemed worthy. He vacillated as to who was most deserving. Unwilling to wound two of his sons, as his death drew near he commanded a master craftsman to make two identical copies. On his deathbed, he called in each son separately, blessed each, and gave each a ring. Impatiently, the Sultan asked Nathan to conclude his story.

> The tale is finished.
> For what still follows, any man may guess.
> Scarce was the father dead, but each one comes
> And shows his ring, and each one claims to be
> True prince o' the house. Vainly they search, strive, argue,
> The true ring was not proved or provable—
> Almost as hard to prove as to us now
> What the true creed is.[29]

The tale of the three rings did not originate with Lessing; he borrowed it from Boccaccio's fourteenth-century *Decameron;* and with different accents and conclusions, the story is even older.[30] In almost all versions, a question is put to a Jew; and the Jews may have originated the story—for good reason. As a vulnerable minority, the Jews had the most to gain from a message of religious tolerance.[31]

Perhaps a Spanish Jew who witnessed a pogrom in Lisbon set down the earliest variant. In the spring of 1506, when Lisbon was suffering from drought and hunger, a miracle inspired the faithful; a light emanated from a crucifix in the Convento de São Domingos, a Dominican convent in Lisbon. Throngs gathered in the convent to view the wonder. On April 19 the group included several "New Christians," or Jews who had been expelled from Spain the day before Columbus departed for the New World. Some settled in Portugal, where in 1497 they were forced to convert to Christianity. Suspicions remained, however, as to the sincerity of their new beliefs; and some Dominicans preached that the false Christians caused the misfortunes of Lisbon. A few days earlier, several New Christians had been discovered celebrating a Passover Seder.

As he gazed upon the miracle, a New Christian expressed doubts. "How can a piece of wood work wonders?" he supposedly asked. He suggested that the light might derive from a candle behind the crucifix. The faithful did not appreciate these comments; they dragged the skeptic out of the convent, beat him, killed him, and, for good measure, dismembered him.

His brother arrived to inquire what was happening. He too was killed and both bodies were burned in a fire in the square. Several friars urged the crowd on with cries of "Heresy! Heresy . . . ! Destroy this abominable people!" Running in the streets holding crosses, they yelled, "Death to the Jews!" Mobs ranged throughout the city, dragging Jewish New Christians to the convent square for incineration. So many were rounded up that contributions were required to purchase additional kindling. At one point, four hundred bodies were thrown on the pyre. Within twenty-four hours six hundred Jews had been hunted down and killed; after three days, when the pogrom ended, over a thousand New Christians had perished.[32]

Solomon Ibn Verga was a Spanish Jew who had fled Spain for Portugal, and sometime after the Lisbon massacre, he left Portugal. Around 1508 he published a collection of reports and dialogues called *Shebet Yehudah*. This included not simply a description of the Lisbon events but accounts and discussions of Jewish suffering through the ages. He judged that anti-Semitic Dominicans largely provoked the Lisbon massacre, and that the "miracle" was a ruse. The Dominicans "made a hollow crucifix with an aperture in the rear, and its front of glass, and they would pass through there a lit candle . . . while the people would prostrate themselves and cry: 'See the great miracle!' "

Inasmuch as it drew upon older material, the *Shebet Yehudah* presented what may be the purest and oldest version of the rings.[33] In Ibn Verga's text the King of Aragon asks a wise Jew which is the better religion. The Jew first tries to deflect the question by stating that the King's Christianity is best for the King and the Jew's Judaism is best for the Jew. The King insists: Which is the better religion?

The Jew requests three days to respond. He returns, but offers no comment. Why is he silent? He explains he had been unjustly treated. A jeweler, leaving on a long trip, gave a gem to each of his sons. The sons brought the gems to the wise Jew, and demanded that he compare their value and beauty. The Jew observed that they should address this inquiry to their father, who as a jeweler could expertly judge the stones. This counsel angered the sons, and they beat the Jew. The King interjects that the sons have misbehaved and should be punished. Listen to your own words, concludes the wise Jew. Esau and Jacob were brothers who also received valuable stones. If you want to learn who has the more precious gems, send a messenger to the Father in Heaven; he is the master jeweler who knows the differences between stones. The King is delighted with this response, and commands his minister not to use violence against the Jews, although the minister is not convinced.[34]

With various twists and sometimes with just a hint of tolerance the story shows up throughout the centuries. A version of the three rings appears in a collection of Italian stories, *Il Novellino,* from the thirteenth century as well as in the *Decameron* from the fourteenth.[35] The tale is not as innocuous as it appears. The sixteenth-century censors of the Counter-Reformation regularly clipped out the story from the *Decameron;* they realized it preached a heretical tolerance.

They were not wrong. The historian Carlo Ginzburg in his reconstruction of the apostasy of a sixteenth-century miller, Menocchio, found one source in the *Decameron.* Menocchio had been denounced to the Holy Office for spreading blasphemous religious doctrines. The local Inquisitor summoned and questioned him. He demanded to know whether Menocchio had ever said that since he was born a Christian, he desired to be a Christian, but if he had been born a Turk, he would want to remain a Turk.

To answer this, Menocchio recounted the tale of the three rings. "I beg you, sir, listen to me." He concluded that each of the three sons judges himself to be in the right, just as each of the three religions sees itself in the right. "God the Father has various children whom he loves, such as Christians, Turks, and Jews, and to each of them he has given the will to live by his own law, and we do not know which is the right one." To this story, the Inquisitor demanded, "Do you believe then that we do not know which is the right law?" Menocchio answers, "Yes, sir, I believe that each person holds his faith to be right, but we do not know which is the right one." As Ginzburg comments, this is an "extraordinary moment" in the trial, where the heretic, forcefully seizing the initiative, speaks for a humanistic tolerance against the authoritarian Church. Not for long. In 1599, "by order of His Holiness, Our Lord," the Inquisition burned Mennochio at the stake.[36]

It is tempting to chart the spread of tolerance from the sixteenth to the twentieth century, yet it may be an illusory project. Intolerance always seems retrograde, always obsolete. Voltaire, in recounting the sentence of La Barre, stated that "this adventure did not occur in the thirteenth or fourteenth century, but in the eighteenth."[37] Variants of this statement could be repeated up through the present. Nazi genocide did not occur in the fifteenth or sixteenth century, but in the twentieth. Nor do the murderous conflicts in Bosnia or the Sudan belong to the past; they belong to today and tomorrow.

Always judged obsolete, intolerance is a growth industry with a promising future. "If the war in Lebanon," writes Jean Said Makdisi in her memoir of Beirut, "has come to mean anything to me, it is the putting out of lights; it is the corruption of cause after cause . . . For in the end, a killing is a killing, and one bullet looks very much like another." It is often said, she writes,

> that the genius of the Middle East is a religious one and that it found expression in Judaism, Christianity, and Islam. But of the wide and noble heights of the human spirit that these embody there is little trace to be found in the narrow and militaristic interpretations of the moment.[38]

A fat anthology could be collected of testimonies to a worldwide intolerance that seems if anything to be intensifying. The surprise of recent years is not simply the collapse of Communist nations but the rise of fratricidal regimes in their wake. The demise of Communist Yugoslavia alone, and the Serbian effort to rid Bosnia of Muslims, has filled many cemeteries. These are only the most recent victims of global ethnic killing. Harold R. Isaacs calculated that in the period 1945–75 by a "conservative reckoning" ethnic wars killed some 10 million, including 2 million Hindus and Muslims in the partition of India and Pakistan; 2 million in the civil war in Biafra; a half million in the war in Bangladesh.

> It is a somber catalogue: mutual massacring of Hindus and Muslims in India; tribal civil wars in Nigeria, the Congo, Chad, Sudan; Indians killing Nagas in northeastern Assam; Malays killing Chinese in Malaysia; Indonesians killing Chinese in Indonesia; Chinese killing Tibetans in Tibet; Tutsis and Hutus killing each other in Burundi; Catholics and Protestants killing each other in Ulster; Turks and Greeks in Cyprus; Kurds and Iraquis in Iraq; Papuans fighting Indonesians in New Guinea; Israelis and Arabs . . . and so on and on and on.[39]

Near the Croatia-Bosnia border, writes Christopher Hitchens, I found "an immaculate contingent of Jordanian U.N. soldiers," who were "politely concealing its shock at the tribal and atavistic brutality of this war between the whites. . . . Here came six busloads of Bosnian Muslim refugees, many of them injured, who had taken the worst that Christian Europe could throw at them and who were bewildered to find themselves under the care of a scrupulous Hashemite chivalry." To complete this mosaic of intolerance, later in a press conference under shellfire in Sarajevo, Hitchens asked the Bosnian President "what he thought of the *fatwa* condemning Salman Rushdie." He said "he did not like the book but could not agree to violence against the author."[40]

The point here is simple: to the degree that relativism is engendered by diversity, and to the degree that relativism fosters tolerance, it is hardly a threat. The reverse is closer to the truth: intolerance and the denial of diversity bloodies the past, present, and future. The wisdom of the tale of the three rings is hardly obsolete. We are witnessing a worldwide revival of a fundamentalism that was never spent.

———

"In the center of the stage and taking up about half of the entire area was an immense caldron across which was painted the sign 'Ford English School Melting Pot.' . . . Across the back of the stage was . . . the hull and deck of an ocean steamship." The 1916 article from the *Ford Times,* the newspaper of the Ford Motor Company, was describing a theatrical ritual regularly performed at the company school. From the gangway of the ship a "picturesque" figure emerged.

> Dressed in a foreign costume and carrying his cherished possessions wrapped in a bundle suspended from a cane, he . . . slowly descended the ladder into the "Melting Pot," holding aloft a sign indicating the country from which he had come. Another figure followed, and then another—"Syria," "Greece," "Italy," "Austria," "India," read the cards, as the representatives . . . filed down the gangway into the "Melting Pot." From it they emerged dressed in American clothes . . . Every man carried a small American flag in his hand.

A description of another performance reported that the several thousand spectators cheered as the Americans emerged from the melting pot. "They were American in looks. And ask any one of them what nationality he is, and the reply will come quickly: 'American!' 'Polish-American?' you might ask. 'No, American,' would be the answer. For they are taught in the Ford school that the hyphen is a minus sign."[41]

A third account tells of a huge "wooden and canvas pot" situated at second base on a baseball field. A master of ceremonies dressed up as Uncle Sam led the foreign workers into the pot. "They wore their native costumes, they were singing their national songs; they danced their folk-dances"; and they popped out "dressed in derby hats, coats, pants, vests, stiff collar and polka-dot tie . . . and all singing the Star-Spangled Banner."[42] Another witness recalls a "giant melting pot" erected outside the Ford factory. "Into this marched a great line of immigrants, clad in their colorful native costumes, singing their folk songs . . . They emerged on the other side, scrubbed to a point of uncomfortable perfection, dressed alike in the approved American way" and singing the Star-Spangled Banner.[43]

The ritual at the Ford school symbolized a repressive "Americanization." In the midst of World War I the Ford Motor Company demonstrated the loyalties of its foreign-speaking employees. That

Ford himself promoted anti-Semitism only added to the negative luster of Americanization, but Ford was hardly alone. A series of organizations embraced Americanization.

The National Americanization Day Committee dedicated itself to turning the Fourth of July 1915 into a new holiday, "Americanization Day." "Every effort," stated one its leaders, "should be bent toward an Americanization which will mean that there will be no 'German-Americans,' no 'Italian quarter,' no 'East Side Jew,' no 'Up-town Ghetto,' no 'Slav movement in America,' but that we are one people." After 1915, the committee dropped "Day" from its name, and moved on to bigger things, ferreting out foreign and subversive influences. The group also changed slogans. The committee shelved "Many Peoples, But One Nation" for "English Language First" and "America First." The "English First" campaign initially targeted Detroit with its population 75 percent foreign-born.[44]

Both the number of immigrants and their differences from earlier arrivals fueled the Americanization drive. Unlike the earlier generations of Germans, Finns, and Swedes, turn-of-the-century immigrants came largely from Eastern and Southern Europe. For some worried observers they threatened America's unity and vitality. "These southern and eastern Europeans," wrote a professor of education and former school superintendent in 1909, "are of a very different type from the north Europeans who preceded them. Illiterate, docile, lacking in self-reliance and initiative, and not possessing the Anglo-Teutonic conceptions of law, order, and government, their coming has served to dilute tremendously our national stock, and to corrupt our civic life."

Moreover, the immigrants settle in groups and "set up here their national manners, customs and observances." What is to be done? "Our task is to break up these groups or settlements, to assimilate and amalgamate these people as part of our American race, and to implant in their children, so far as can be done, the Anglo-Saxon conception of righteousness, law and order . . ."[45] Others worried not only about foreign tongues but about foreign food. The General Federation of Women's Clubs committed itself to "ventilating the houses" of immigrant women, showing them how to prepare "American vegetables, instead of the inevitable cabbage." A company official discovered peeling wallpaper in the homes of its Polish employees. The cause? "The continual flow of steam" from boiling cabbage soup. The cure? Cook American.[46]

Both friends and foes of immigrants echoed these sentiments. Henry Pratt Fairchild in *The Melting-Pot Mistake* presented what he considered the "harsh" truth: immigrants must be completely stripped of their foreign mannerisms, behavior, and ideas. "The traits of foreign nationality which the immigrant brings with him are not to be mixed or interwoven. They are to be *abandoned*." A popular guide for immigrant Jews advised, "Forget your past, your customs, and your ideals."[47]

Against these developments, many sought to articulate a different conception of American identity. Critics challenged the monochromatic vision of America and the fear that diversity undermined the nation. The most forceful critics—among them Randolph Bourne, Horace Kallen, and Alain Locke—were themselves outsiders. Bourne was physically disfigured; Kallen was an immigrant Jew; Locke was gay and black.

Bourne, seriously crippled by birth and by childhood disease, moved about—to use his own words—with "a crooked back and an unsightly face." One of his earliest published pieces, which appeared anonymously in 1911, dealt with his appearance. "One cannot carry one's special chair everywhere," he wrote in "The Handicapped—By One of Them." "This sounds trivial, I know, but I mention it because it furnishes a real, even though usually dim, 'background of consciousness,' which one has to reckon with . . . No one but the deformed man can realize what the mere fact of sitting a foot lower than the normal means."[48]

By reason of his limpid prose and the brevity of his life—he died in 1918 at the age of thirty-two—Bourne became a favorite of critics and historians; all could speculate on his future. Would he have become the greatest twentieth-century American critic and essayist? Where would he have stood on the Russian Revolution, the Great Depression, and the growth of American Marxism? No doubt exists on where he stood on the idea of a homogeneous melting pot. In 1916, the same year as the Americanization ritual at the Ford school, Bourne contrasted a cosmopolitan "trans-national America" to "the failure of the 'melting pot.' "

It is time, he wrote, "to assert a higher ideal than the 'melting-pot.' " This has not only been unworkable, it has proceeded only under one aegis, "English snobberies, English religion, English literary styles, English literary reverences and canons, English ethics, English superiorities." "The truth is that no more tenacious cultural allegiance to the mother country has been shown by any alien nation than by the ruling class of Anglo-Saxon descendants in these American states." Americans of Anglo-Saxon descent, which Bourne acknowledges includes himself, have been "guilty" of "the imposition of its own culture upon the minority peoples."

Moreover, the melting pot means that "distinctive qualities should be washed out into a tasteless, colorless fluid of uniformity." Rather, we need new peoples "to save us from our own stagnation." Bourne pointed to the American South as a truly Anglo-Saxon region. "The South, in fact, while this vast Northern development has gone on, still remains an English colony, stagnant and complacent . . . It is culturally sterile because it has no advantage of cross-fertilization like the Northern states." Bourne called for the building of the "first international nation," a "cosmopolitan federation of national colonies, of foreign cultures."[49]

Bourne stated that his ideas about a new kind of nationalism had been inspired by Horace Kallen, a rabbi's son; and that the "Jewish ideal of Zionism" represented a model for him. He used to think, he confessed, that the "dual allegiance" of Zionists to Israel and the United States was contradictory, but he came to realize it indicated a solution, not a problem; it incarnated "a new spiritual internationalism." It is the way to avoid the militarist and chauvinist conception of America.

> What I mean by co-operative Americanism—that is, an ideal of a freely mingling society of peoples of very different racial and cultural antecedents, with a common political allegiance and common social ends but with free and distinctive cultural allegiances which may be placed any place in the world they like—is simply a generalization of the practical effect of the Zionist ideal.[50]

Unlike Bourne, Kallen was an immigrant. As a small child Kallen moved with his family from Germany to Boston, where his father became rabbi of an Orthodox congregation. The proud and strict father expected that Kallen, the oldest of eight, would follow his path, but his iron orthodoxy troubled his son. "It was a poor household," Kallen recalled, "and the rules" were always "more important than the members of the family." Young Kallen ran away from home several times. His father was "too powerful, too demanding . . . to be anything but feared and dodged and hated."

Kallen's refusal to follow his father into the rabbinate caused a break between them. For years they did not talk, only partially reconciling as the elder Kallen lay dying. "He is among the last of the old school of Jews," Kallen wrote, "who would make absolutely no concession to their environment, but made their environment wherever they went."[51]

In a long and productive life, Kallen sought to balance the imperatives of the environment and cultural identity. At a time of rising panic about immigration and immigrants, before and during World War I, Kallen wrote a series of articles in which he virtually copyrighted the term "cultural pluralism." In "Democracy *versus* the Melting-Pot," he wrote that the United States is "at the parting of the ways. Two genuine social alternatives are before Americans." One leads to subjugation of national groups, following the lead of Germany in Poland, Russia in the Jewish Pale, Austria among the Slavs, and Turks over the Arabs, Armenians, and Greeks. It would require "the enforced, exclusive use of the English language and English and American history in the schools and in the daily life." This "melting-pot by law" would achieve little.

The other model takes for "its point of departure the existing ethnic and cultural groups," and seeks "to provide conditions under which each might attain the cultural perfection that is *proper to its kind*." European exemplars exist, for instance Switzerland, where diverse nationalities live harmoniously with a superior educational and economic system. This model recognizes a fundamental truth:

> What is inalienable in the life of mankind is its intrinsic positive quality —its psycho-physical inheritance. Men may change their clothes, their politics, their wives, their religions, their philosophies, to a greater or lesser extent: they cannot change their grandfathers. Jews or Poles or Anglo-Saxons, in order to cease being Jews or Poles or Anglo-Saxons, would have to cease to be.[52]

When he collected his essays in 1924 Kallen called his standpoint "cultural pluralism," which he stated is "popular nowhere in the United States." He contrasted it to the cultural politics of the Ku Klux Klan with its hatred for all differences and all minorities. The Klan requires blind conformity to the mores of the American villages as interpreted by the Klan itself. Its persistence and power threaten America. Fortunately, a different cultural principle opposes the Klan.

> It is founded upon variation of racial groups and individual character; upon spontaneous differences of social heritage, institutional habit, mental attitude and emotional tone; upon the continuous, free and fruitful cross-fertilization of these by one another.[53]

This does not simply lead to antagonistic diversity, but to a harmonious unity. Cultural pluralism, Kallen concluded, is possible only in a democratic society which encourages "individuality in groups, in persons, in temperaments," leading to "a fellowship of freedom and cooperation." "The alternative before Americans is Kultur Klux Klan or Cultural Pluralism."

Kallen studied at Harvard and worked as an assistant to William James; he attended James's lectures at Oxford, which were published as *A Pluralistic Universe*. James's ideas on pluralism made their way into Kallen's formulation on cultural pluralism.[54] Another individual played a role both in Kallen's development and in furthering cultural pluralism, a black philosophy student, who became a leading interpreter of the Harlem Renaissance. Kallen explained:

> It was in 1906 that I began to formulate the notion of cultural pluralism . . . I was assisting both Mr. James and Mr. Santayana at the time and I had a Negro student named Alain Locke, a very remarkable young man, intelligent, poetic, very sensitive, who insisted that he was a human being and that his color ought not to make any difference. So we had to argue out the question of how the differences did make differences, and in arguing out those questions the formulae, the phrases developed—"cultural pluralism," "the right to be different."[55]

Several years later, Kallen bumped into Locke at Oxford, where Locke was a Rhodes scholar. According to one account, Kallen came to Locke's defense when Rhodes scholars from the American South refused to invite the black man to Thanksgiving dinner. This incident spurred further discussion about cultural differences and pluralism.[56]

Like Kallen, Locke had a long and productive career. He came from an old family of free and educated Philadelphia blacks. His grandfather had taught at the Institute for Colored Youth, founded by Quakers in the 1850s, from which emerged many doctors and professionals. Both his parents, graduates of the Institute, became teachers. His father, who also earned a law degree, died when Locke was five; his mother, with whom Locke was always close, undoubtedly played a key role in his life. A biographer calls her his "mentor, confidante and spiritual guide."[57]

His mother also became a follower of Felix Adler, whose life roughly paralleled Kallen's. Adler came to the United States as a small child when his father was appointed rabbi of a New York congregation. He attended Columbia, where he felt out of place as a German Jew "among typically American boys of the wealthy class." He shocked his father and family in turning from the rabbinical path. His father, a biographer reports, "was almost heartbroken: the long-standing rabbinic tradition in the Adler family was broken."[58]

Adler went on to found the secular Ethical Culture Society, which stressed education and ethical conduct, not religious dogma. "Deed, not Creed" was his motto for Ethical Culture. Like Kallen, issues of immigration and pluralism were close to Adler's heart.[59] In following the genesis of Locke's pluralism, one path leads back to his mother and Adler's Ethical Culture.

Educated at Harvard, Oxford, and Berlin, Locke taught at Howard for much of his life, always active in adult education and black causes and culture. By most accounts Locke was an impressive and cosmopolitan individual. In 1925 he published a collection, *The New Negro,* a key document in a cultural surge that became known as the Harlem Renaissance. He praised the diversity of Harlem. "It has attracted the African, the West Indian, the Negro American; has brought together the Negro of the North and the Negro of the South." Harlem is fostering a new culture. "In Harlem, Negro life is seizing upon its first chances for group expression and self-determination . . . Harlem has the same role to play for the New Negro as Dublin has had for the New Ireland or Prague for the New Czechoslovakia." It is the home of "the Negro's 'Zionism.' "[60]

In his 1932 roman à clef of the Harlem Renaissance, Wallace Thurman presented Locke as a "mother hen clucking at her chicks. Small, dapper, with sensitive features, graying hair, a dominating head, and restless hands and feet, he smiled benevolently at his brood." In the novel Locke tries to establish a salon of black artists and writers; he wants them to be respectable and productive. "You must not, like your paleface contemporaries, wallow in the mire of post-Victorian license." He also wants them to pursue beauty and ideals, as well as to mine their African past. "Let me suggest your going back to your racial roots, and cultivating a healthy paganism based on African traditions."

The salon lasts one meeting, breaking up into acrimonious discord between skeptics, Marxists, and aesthetes. Eliciting gasps, one participant asks, "What old black pagan heritage?" "Your African ones, of course," comes the retort. "What about the rest? . . . My German, English and Indian ancestors . . ." Another interjects, "Is there really any reason *all* Negro artists should consciously and deliberately dig into African soil for inspiration . . . ?" "What we ought to do," offered another, "is to join hands with the workers." "What does it matter," inquires a third, "so long as you remain true to yourself?" Before the barrage, Locke wilts.[61]

By reason of upbringing, inclination, and his philosophical training at Harvard, ideas of relativism and pluralism attracted Locke. In an autobiographical note to an essay published by Kallen, he explained the lure of pluralism by "the badge of circumstance." Beginning with his birth as a "doubting" American—a Negro—in a provincial Philadelphia flavored by urbanity, a series of paradoxes marked his life. At Harvard he clung to the genteel and academic philosophy but was attracted to the "radical protest" of William James. At Oxford he was

> socially Anglophile, but because of race loyalty, strenuously antiimperialist; universalist in religion, internationalist and pacifist in world-view, but forced by a sense of simple justice to approve of the militant counter-nationalism of Zionism, Young Turkey, Young Egypt, Young India, and with reservations even Garveyism and current-day "Nippon over Asia." Finally a cultural cosmopolitan, but perforce an advocate of cultural racialism as a defense counter-move for the American Negro . . . Small wonder . . . I project my personal history into its inevitable rationalization as cultural pluralism and value relativism, with a not too orthodox reaction to the American way of life.[62]

Alluding to the fact that he was gay as well, Locke once stated, "I belong to so many minorities that I've never known which one to grieve about."[63]

In a series of essays on pluralism Locke made a persuasive case for cultural relativism as "an antiauthoritarian principle." Only a "value pluralism" and "cultural pluralism" will facilitate widespread peace; these pluralisms imply mutual respect and noninterference and sustain democracy. "There seems to be an affinity, historical and ideological, between pluralism and democracy." Unfortunately few give up the absolutism that leads to intolerance. "How slowly does this ancient obsession retreat from the concept of an absolute God to that of an absolute reason, to that of an absolute morality, to linger on entrenched in the last-stand theories of an absolute state and an absolute culture!"[64]

Locke occasionally set off his position from "cynical indifference," "value anarchy," or "anarchic pluralism." Yet the brunt of his essays promoted a thoroughgoing pluralism founded on respect and tolerance. In the midst of World War II he called for "pluralism" as "our handiest intellectual weapon against the totalitarian challenge." The war and the cold war led to the rediscovery of the ideas of Locke, Kallen, and Bourne, if not their names. Critics and scholars contrasted democratic pluralism and diversity to monolithic Nazism and Soviet Communism. Postwar fears of a new conformist mass society gave another boost to cultural pluralism.[65]

Today everyone is a pluralist. In principle no one opposes tolerance, diversity, and multiculturalism. Heated adversaries challenge its exact dimensions, but not the pluralistic framework. The widespread concurrence should stir a suspicion that the words "diversity" and "pluralism" have surrendered all precision. A general agreement rests on a general confusion.

Even academic leftists commend pluralism, which is a striking change from the recent past. Not long ago radicals regularly denounced "pluralism" as the ideology of the status quo. "Traditional liberals continue to celebrate 'our pluralistic society,' " wrote the historian John Higham in a 1975 survey of the term. "Those radicals who pay heed to the theory of pluralism denounce it." A case in point might be Michael Paul Rogin, a left-leaning political scientist. He began his 1967 book on McCarthyism this way: "Modern pluralism emerged as American intellectuals, mainly ex-radical, responded to the events of their youth and the pressures of the 1950's . . . The pluralists . . . sought values in the traditions of mainstream America with which they could identify."[66]

Perhaps these words still ring true. Do radicals become pluralists as they join the mainstream? Or has the mainstream never really been pluralistic? Leftists bless pluralism everywhere, the more the better. The cult of plenitude may not be incidental. Americans love quantity. The days when ice cream came only in chocolate, vanilla, and strawberry are a distant memory. We want ice cream in fifty flavors, toothpaste in ten sizes and tastes, and paper diapers in many colors. The "multi" of multiculturalism promises more identities for everyone.

From here it is only a short hop to a new form of self-description, a listing of groups and affiliations. A feminist professor identifies herself "as a woman, a teacher, a daughter, a mother, a feminist (should I add a heterosexual, a Jew, an immigrant, middle class, an only child, a mother of sons?), within the institutions of patriarchy, of motherhood, of literary studies, of feminist studies, of the university in the United States (should I add of marriage, of divorce, of the Ivy League, of Comparative Literature and French Studies, of the development of Women's Studies?)."[67] A person becomes a series of groups, less an individual than twenty agendas.

Group affiliations can be amusing, benign, or laudatory. Increasingly, however, cultural pluralism abets questionable elements of group identification; the individual becomes simply a representative of the group—a Latino or African-American or woman; the individual counts for little, the group for everything. Is this an outcome of cultural pluralism or its distortion? The problem or the cure?

Already in 1920 a sharp-eyed criticism of Kallen's pluralism raised the issue of group domination. Isaac B. Berkson headed the Central Jewish Institute, a New York organization dedicated to preserving a vital Jewish life in the United States. Berkson did not follow the familiar route of defending the melting pot or Americanization. His own institution had been established in 1915 by Russian Jews who feared that their children were becoming thoroughly Americanized, New Yorkers who knew musical comedies but nothing of their parents' culture and traditions. "Gum chewing is their distinguishing characteristic," observed Berkson.[68]

Berkson repudiated an Americanization or assimilation that erased the past. He cited a New York school superintendent who stated that "broadly speaking" by Americanization "we mean . . . absolute forgetfulness of all obligations or connections with other countries because of descent or birth." Yet Berkson also distanced himself from the pluralism of Kallen and Bourne. He sensed its weakness, the virtual biologism or belief that ethnicity or race de-

termines the individual. "The theory is based on the assumption of
the ineradicable and central influence of race." It posits that "race
in the sense of ethnic affixation is the all-important and predestinat-
ing fact in the life of the individual, or that it ought to be."

What does it mean for an individual to belong to a racial or
ethnic group inasmuch as all studies have shown that race is extraordinarily plastic? Differences within one race are so great that
"one can prophesy nothing with any degree of certainty about the
original endowment of an individual from the one fact of his ethnic
origin." Much more important than race are environment, vocation, political institutions, zeitgeist, and social atmosphere. For
these reasons Berkson challenged Kallen's famous sentence that
"we cannot change our grandfathers."

> When a man forgets who his grandfathers were and neglects their tradi-
> tions . . . and adopts other models, to all intents and purposes he
> "changes his grandfather." Our grandfathers are psychological as well
> as physical. What we are depends not only on our original nature but
> also upon its interaction with the environment.

Changing beliefs, traditions, and social life is tantamount to
changing grandfathers; moreover, they can be changed through intermarriage. "Any individual who marries outside of his group is
thereby changing the ancestry of his children."[69]

Kallen himself indirectly confirmed Berkson's criticisms: he married a Methodist minister's daughter, who converted to Judaism. As
one historian commented, "Kallen did not change his grandfathers,
but where did it leave Mrs. Kallen?" Or the next generations? Their
daughter married a Quaker. Despite Quaker and Methodist forebears, however, the Kallens' grandson was raised Jewish.[70]

Berkson discerned a danger in cultural pluralism, its subordination of the individual to a static racial and ethnic identity. "To
regard every individual of an ethnic group as having primarily the
characteristics of that group" undermines individuality. "Undoubtedly an individual may be influenced by the character of his remote
ancestry," stated Berkson, "but before governmental organization
can be permitted to make ethnic origin the central consideration,
there must be overwhelming proof of its importance. Otherwise
such a scheme of government cannot help but artificially make race
a greater factor than it deserves to be, leading to the repression of
the individual."

Berkson suggested that democracies should resist, not promote groups.

Democracy does not oppose (as indeed it cannot) the influence of heredity, or church, or economic class; but it asserts that these must not have undue influence made possible by artificial organization of society. Since life is wider than any one of these factors, the rights of the individual must not be altogether determined by any one of these. So, too, when we would segregate our children in schools on the basis of nationality, we would tend to make one factor in the complex situation determine all other relationships . . .[71]

Berkson's questions have become, if anything, more pressing. Does cultural pluralism encourage group domination of the individual? Does it invite racial ideas positing the primacy of blood and ancestry? These questions lead to others. Do assertions of group identity exacerbate hostilities among groups? Does the idea of cultural pluralism, invented to promote tolerance, turn into its opposite, feeding group enmities?

It may be unfair to allude to hospitals and morgues in Bosnia or India as a retort to American cultural pluralists. It is fair, however, to inquire whether the ideology intensifies ethnic and group hostilities in America. The ethnic pluralism of many American campuses pleases visitors; at the same time, students stick together, socially and intellectually. African-Americans study African-Americans; Latinos study Latinos; women study women. This may be progress in knowledge and self-identity; it may also be a new parochialism, and perhaps a new hostility. Groups become defensive, aggressive, prickly. "It's a Black Thing. You wouldn't understand," reads a sweatshirt worn by African-Americans. The slogan compresses the problem: is there a point where cultural pluralism engenders group chauvinism with blood tests and passports?

Group thought and approaches spill out across society and education. If it is legal, and reasonable, to inquire how many women or African-Americans or Latinos work in certain jobs, the same inquiries transferred to culture hint of repression and cultural police; tags replacing thought. The issue becomes not what was said, a difficult proposition, but who said it, a simple proposition.

Edward W. Said, an English professor, recounts an incident from a talk he delivered. After the lecture, which, like his book *Orientalism,* dealt with cultural imperialism, a black woman professor stood up and asked what she labeled a "very hostile question." She passed no judgment on his presentation, but demanded why in the first thirteen pages of his paper Said, himself a Palestinian-American, cited only white European males? "How could you do such a thing?"[72]

The inference here as elsewhere is clear: pay obeisance to the group—and soon. Page fourteen is too late. The caliber of thought hardly matters. This might be called intellectual affirmative action. Randall L. Kennedy has challenged kindred arguments about "citation practice" in legal writings. Several critics have objected to the dearth of references to black and minority law professors in legal articles. Yet these critics, law professors themselves, make their case not by highlighting excellent work that might be ignored, but by counting references to minority scholars. As Kennedy remarks, this leads to a new stereotyping and group conformity; the race or sex of a scholar, not a scholarly contribution, warrants an acknowledgment.[73]

Many are happy to cooperate, especially since counting references and citations simplifies thinking. How many blacks or women or Jews were cited and how prominently? Paul Lauter, a leftist literary critic, applies "what I like to call the 'index test' to the works of the leading theoretical critics." This entails going through the index of a book counting the number of references to women. For instance, Lauter discovered that Hartman's *The Fate of Reading* mentions 232 men and 11 women.[74] The possibilities are exciting, especially if Lauter's "index test" expands to include racial, religious, ethnic, and sexual orientation—and if indexes begin to include this information.

Does affirmative action apply to thought itself? Does the prudent scholar carefully cite a proper mix of women and minorities? Is cultural pluralism, originally advanced to promote harmony and tolerance, encouraging group separation and hostilities? "By emphasizing ethnicity, by encouraging its development, pluralist thinkers are emphasizing the very set of developments which will prevent communication between individual members of different groups," wrote Orlando Patterson in his *Ethnic Chauvinism*. "In the end— and sadly, we seem already to have reached this point . . . the only kind of communication possible will be the formalized interaction of ethnic spokesmen who meet like ambassadors from warring camps . . ."[75]

The choice is not between a counterfeit universality (we are equal members of one species) and forced particularism (we are only members of ethnic or racial groups). We are both, but today the wider connections have become suspect. Everywhere barriers go up and ethnic or sexual résumés are checked. "Conservatives want to teach the canon, critics want to teach multiculturalism," states Benjamin R. Barber. "Who wants to teach democracy? Private agendas abound: Who will teach the public agenda?"[76]

Can a white Swede teach African-American history? Or an African-American give courses in Jewish or Chinese history? Or a male lecture on Feminist Studies? Few object in principle, but almost everyone objects in fact. "Last year," notes Henry Louis Gates, Jr., "I wrote *forty-nine* letters of recommendation for one talented white job candidate in African literature; all forty-nine applications were unsuccessful."[77] Even those who resist finally get the message: stick to your own kind. Numerous cases have arisen where minority scholars are nudged out of the fields they want to study into areas supposedly appropriate for their race or ethnicity. African-Americans should study Africa and black America; Chinese-Americans should study China and Chinese-Americans.

I know a student, Ukrainian on his father's side, Mexican on his mother's, who completed a doctorate in English history. In a tough job market, he added his mother's Latino surname to his own and now teaches Chicano history. The story is typical, but for a liberal education damning. The damage may be greatest not in hiring but in learning and teaching. At the end of cultural pluralism, a new provincialism looms; students study themselves and their group as taught by certified representatives.

"Dear Madame: Will you please let this nigger boy—I used the word 'nigger' to make the librarian feel that I could not possibly be the author of the note—*have some books by H. L. Mencken?* I forged the white man's name." "That night in my rented room," Richard Wright continues in his autobiography, *Black Boy,* "I opened [Mencken's] *A Book of Prefaces* and began to read. I was jarred and shocked by the style, the clear, clean, sweeping sentences." Few books present more forcefully the pain of racism; and few reveal more sharply the danger of dividing up literature by racial categories. Education must explode racial and ethnic approaches, not simply cultivate them. If in the current climate, Rich-

ard Wright has become a black author for black students and H. L. Mencken a white author for white students, we are all losers.[78]

Social and political events prompt public discussions that frequently take on a life of their own, ignoring the happenings that gave rise to them. A heated quarrel might proceed, while society answers the argument or renders the old terms obsolete. New immigration, ethnic hostilities, and bold declarations of ethnic identity propel the debate about pluralism and multiculturalism. Yet immigration does not automatically translate into cultural identity; American society may undermine, not sustain, distinct cultures.

The truism that the United States is a land of diverse immigrants does not tell the whole truth. Few of the "founders" were immigrants; Washington, Jefferson, Adams, and Franklin were native-born. Ninety-five percent of the leaders of the Revolution, signers of the Declaration of Independence, and authors of the Constitution claimed English Protestant backgrounds. In the first decades of the new Republic immigration was slight, probably 250,000 for the period 1776–1820.[79]

Beginning in the 1840s this changed. Driven by American prosperity and European suffering, immigrants arrived in waves: 1850s, 1880s, 1900s; and each wave spurred xenophobic sentiment from the "Know-Nothings" of the 1850s to the American Protection League of the 1890s and the "hundred-percenters" of the 1910s. American economic contraction intensified anti-immigration attitudes. In the 1850s the rate of crime and poverty among new immigrants angered many citizens. "No American could read the daily press," commented a historian of the Know-Nothings, "and escape the conviction that immigration must be checked if his country and its institutions were to survive." The plain numbers of immigrant voters added to the panic. Between 1850 and 1855 native-born voters in Boston increased about 15 percent; foreign-born, 200 percent. "The rapid increase of foreign voters made it appear inevitable that they would eventually rule the land."[80] From the wider view of American immigration, recent anxiety about the status of English and Western civilization might be seen as a typical, and passing, American response to the latest wave of arrivals.

The recent immigration is comparatively smaller than that reached before World War I, which provoked the most hysteria over Americanization. Of course, numbers do not tell the whole story, but size is pertinent. How big is the recent immigration? How much does it differ from past immigrations? These are hardly arcane questions, and many scholars are equipped to answer them, but for some reason this information barely enters public discussions.

More immigrants entered the United States in the period 1900–10 than in any decade before or since, approximately 8.8 million. In the peak year of 1907, 1.3 million arrived. "I visited Ellis Island yesterday," wrote H. G. Wells, who was touring the United States. "It was choked" with ten ocean liners backed up to unload "crude Americans from Ireland and Poland and Italy and Syria and Finland and Albania." " 'Look there!' said the Commissioner, taking me by the arm and pointing, and I saw a monster steamship far away. . . . 'It's the *Kaiser Wilhelm der Grosse*. She's got . . . eight hundred and fifty-three more for us. She'll have to keep them until Friday at the earliest. And there's more behind her, and more strung out all across the Atlantic.' " "In one record day this month," commented Wells, "21,000 immigrants came into the port of New York alone . . . This year the total will be 1,200,000 souls . . . Just think of the dimensions of it!"[81]

Immigration in the 1980s was smaller, about 7.3 million. This figure includes about 2 million illegal aliens, not technically immigrants, who were given legal permanent residence; the figure does not include an incalculable number of illegal immigrants. Nevertheless, in 1980 the American population was about three times its 1900 size (225 million compared with 75 million). Obviously the impact of even roughly similar numbers of immigrants on a population that differs by a factor of three will be sharply different. For instance, the percentage of foreign-born reached 15 percent in 1910. In recent years it is closer to 6 percent.[82] In many cities at the turn of the century the "foreign stock," meaning both immigrants and their children, constituted well over half the population. In Boston, "foreign stock" accounted for 69 percent of the population; in Milwaukee, 86 percent; in San Francisco, 78 percent.[83]

Numbers do not easily translate into experience and impact. An immigration that was relatively three times larger in the first years of the century, however, made its presence felt. For instance, to some observers foreign languages now threaten English, but in the early decades of the century, these languages seemed far more imposing. One index might be the foreign-language press in the United States.

Robert E. Park has estimated that in the early 1920s there were 1,300 foreign-language newspapers in the United States. Of course, many of these newspapers were quite small, but the total circulation and language spectrum were large. Park calculated their circulation around 7 to 10 million. In 1920 the list of foreign-language *dailies* included Ukrainian, Spanish, Russian, Albanian, Bulgarian, Serbian, Romanian, Finnish, Arabic, Croatian, Chinese, Greek, Japanese, Slovenian, Lithuanian, and Hungarian—probably 200, with 29 dailies in German alone![84]

More recent studies register sharp declines in the foreign-language press, a 57 percent drop between 1930 and 1960. A survey in 1958 found the foreign-language press dramatically down with only 73 dailies. An impressionistic survey in 1960 noted the further eclipse. In 1959 alone, commented the author, six dailies disappeared, two Chinese, two Finnish, a Spanish, and a Serbian. "The attrition in this field is unrelenting." A more complete study from 1976 tabulated a further drop with only 35 dailies remaining. The Norwegians no longer had a daily press; the Germans were down to 3; the Italians fell from 11 to 1. Reflecting recent immigration, however, some observers register a "fourth stage" of renewed publications.[85]

The demise of the foreign-language dailies illuminates the future of non-English in America. With the possible exception of Spanish, recent languages will probably not be able to maintain themselves. The spectrum of languages spoken in schools by new immigrants may present a serious pedagogical problem, but the monopoly, indeed the expansion of English is hardly threatened. The fate of German or Yiddish in America anticipates the fate of other languages. The United States, observes a historian, is "significantly less multilingual than many other multiethnic countries. Today as in the past few Americans beyond the second generation speak or even know the language of their immigrant forebears."[86] James Crawford in *Hold Your Tongue* notes that children of Hispanic immigrants acquire English at a faster rate than previous immigrants. He also believes that without continued immigration or "heroic efforts" "all minority languages would gradually die out in this country, with the possible exception of Navajo."[87]

Something else undercuts persisting ethnic identity. In the endless talk of multiculturalism, little notice is given to a multiculturalism that undercuts multiculturalism: the increasing numbers of marriages between ethnic and racial groups, as well as increasing numbers of multinational adoptions. The children of parents who are Japanese and Jewish or Latino and Thai or black and white move beyond the expanding categories and labels. They raise questions as to what *is* an ethnic identity. Is it simply a choice or option?

Intermarriage between ethnic groups is increasingly common. "Only one-fifth of husbands and wives born after 1950 came from the same single ethnic ancestry (outside of the South, only 15 percent)"; and interracial marriages jumped 100 percent in the 1970s. Immigration, intermarriage, and cross-ethnic adoptions render ideas of multiculturalism hopelessly retrograde. Lawrence H. Fuchs in his *American Kaleidoscope* reports that older Cuban-Chinese in New York—Chinese who fled from Cuba after Castro—maintained an affinity for Chinese culture and Buddhism. However, their children tended to identify with Cubans, attend a Roman Catholic church and marry outside the Asian community. "I am Cuban, Chinese and American," explained one immigrant. "I speak Spanish . . . but was raised in the Chinese way of thinking." She married an American of Italian descent. Their children will be—should be?—what? Chinese-Cuban-Italian-Americans?[88]

A sociologist, Mary Waters, has emphasized the role of choice in ethnic identity. She interviewed Slovenians in a San Francisco suburb, assessing their ethnic identity. One woman, a third-generation Slovenian—her four grandparents had emigrated to a Colorado mining town—retained a partiality for some Slovenian foods, rituals, and music. The interviewer asked about the woman's adopted son. Since the parents met the birth mother, they know he was half Irish.

> Q: Will you bring him up with special knowledge of his ancestry? A: I don't know. My husband and I were just talking about this . . . my husband said . . . "You know, James is half Irish," and I said, "Oh, God, I really feel like I should celebrate Saint Patrick's Day more than I have." . . . Q: What about your husband's ethnicity? A: He would have answered Russian Jew and English and Scottish on the census form. He really likes his Russian Jew part. We have a mezuzah on the front door. He converted to Catholicism when he married me. He grew up with his mother and she was Baptist . . . Oh, also I should mention that my son is one quarter Native American.[89]

This case may be extreme, but the general pattern is not. Of course, this very situation inspired the original announcement of a new American nationality freed from past loyalties. In *Letters from an American Farmer,* the 1782 ode to America, J. Hector St. John Crèvecoeur suggested "that strange mix of blood" in the United States constituted a new American type. "I could point out to you a family whose grandfather was an Englishman, whose wife was Dutch, whose son married a French woman, and whose present four sons have now four wives of different nations."[90] Not simply has the spectrum widened today but the ideology has altered. People choose among their various identities or simply adopt new ones. The issue of what *is* an African-American or Jew or Latino may lose meaning.

One incident may illuminate the tangle of ethnic choice and reality. From the 1940s through the present, Johnny Otis has figured prominently in the Los Angeles black rhythm-and-blues community; originally a drummer, he promoted shows, formed a band, and in the 1950s founded a small record label and recording studio. Otis, however, is white, the son of Greek immigrants, but his world and identity are "black by persuasion." In 1956 his label had one of his first hits, "Lonely, Lonely Nights," a doo-wop ballad by Los Angeles' first successful Chicano rock 'n' roller, Li'l Julian Herrera. "Li'l Julian came to me as a kid," Otis explained, "a young Mexican-American, and sang . . . I put him on stage and the little Mexican girls loved him . . . our Chicano audience was a big part of our audience in those days. I put him in the band and then he lived in my house."

As George Lipsitz comments in *Time Passages,* "Lonely, Lonely Nights" "presented a Chicano's rendition of a black vocal style on a record produced by a white man who thought of himself as black." But the story gets more tangled, a veritable multicultural paradigm. As Lipsitz recounts, some time later,

a juvenile officer walked into Otis's record company in search of Ron Gregory, a run-away youth from the east. When the officer showed Otis a picture, he realized that Ron Gregory was Li'l Julian Herrera. "He ran away from home, hitchhiked out here, and this Mexican lady in Boyle Heights takes him in and raises him as her son," Otis relates. It turned out that Los Angeles' first Chicano rock-and-roll star was born a Hungarian Jew.[91]

The truism of ethnic differences must reckon with its opposite, their attenuation. In the current celebration of cultural identity, few entertain the thought that real diversity might be diminishing. The original Americanizers and assimilationists tainted forever the suggestion of a single national society dominating smaller immigrant cultures. This is undesirable, hence unthinkable. Yet the undesirable also requires thinking; it demands reflecting on the possibility that cultural homogeneity, not heterogeneity, is the future.

Since the turn of the century, many sociologists and historians have argued that in the long run immigrant groups and minority cultures will be absorbed by the mainstream. Against this view, others have registered either the persistence or revival of ethnic differences. Using a generational approach, a midwestern historian, Marcus Lee Hansen, offered a compelling theory of revitalized cultural identities.

Hansen observed that the first-generation immigrant was too busy and hardworking to care about the old culture; an insecure second generation was caught between two worlds, foreign and American, and abandoned the father's language, customs, and religion. The "third generation," however, economically and culturally secure in America, rediscovered the old culture. This was what Hansen called "the principle of the third generation interest." "It explains the recurrence of movements that seemingly are dead . . . The theory is derived from the almost universal phenomenon that what the son wished to forget the grandson wishes to remember."[92]

This idea seemed plausible, and was used with great success by Will Herberg in his popular 1955 *Protestant Catholic Jew*, which posited a "third generation" revival of religion. Yet as critics noted, Hansen never offered much evidence for a "movement" of ethnic renaissance. Moreover, its vehicle, the third generation, was itself assimilated and Americanized. Hansen's theory can almost be turned against itself. The secure and Americanized third generation returned to its cultural past, but what could be retrieved? "The 'third generation,' " stated Hansen, "have no reason to feel any inferiority . . . They are American born. Their speech is the same as that of those with whom they associate. Their material wealth is the average . . ."[93]

This weakness or contradiction plagues exponents of cultural revivalism and diversity: the cultural differences are assumed, vague, or unconvincing. The classic 1963 work on ethnic differences by

Nathan Glazer and Daniel P. Moynihan, *Beyond the Melting Pot,* stated baldly, "The point about the melting pot . . . is that it did not happen." Yet Glazer and Moynihan were too savvy to believe that nothing happened. Did generations of Italians and Poles simply retain their languages, customs, and dress? Far from it. "Ethnic groups then, even after distinctive language, customs, and culture are lost, as they largely were in the second generation, and even more fully in the third generation, are continually recreated by new experiences in America." But what remains to be "recreated" after surrendering "language, customs, and culture"? Not much. The New York City ethnics have become "interest groups," identifiable by social associations and political attitudes.[94]

The language concedes more than it admits; cultural diversity translates into interest groups. This may be exactly right. The literature of ethnic revival coincides with ethnic decline or, at least, its conversion into ordinary urban politics, a series of beliefs about education, welfare, and religion. It is difficult to maintain, for instance, that today Polish-Americans and Italian-Americans and Irish-Americans represent distinct cultures, although they may represent distinct voting blocs.

Chicago Polish-American leaders pushed for recognition of Polish culture; and a Chicago congressman, Roman Pucinski, sponsored the Ethnic Heritage Studies Programs Act signed by President Nixon. As one historian commented, the official recognition did not lead to any real revival. Polish history and studies remained marginal to Poles; and even where Polish-Americans attended high school, Polish was dropped as an elective "for want of student (and parental) interest." Arthur Mann adds, "No more than the Poles and Italians did the mass of rank-and-file Irish-Americans show signs of being swept into a cultural renaissance."[95]

While the spectrum of cultural diversity today includes much more than the Irish, Italians, and Poles, their experience may be prototypical. Yet discussions typically ignore the American steamroller that has flattened immigrant cultures. The persistence of unique cultures within American society is increasingly questionable, but the debate assumes "culture" is sacred, almost beyond discussion; the argument proceeds without noticing, much less addressing, that multiculturalism may be a station en route to monoculturalism. A degraded definition of "culture," introduced by liberal anthropologists, feeds the ideology of multiculturalism.

Ruth Benedict's 1934 *Patterns of Culture,* the classic work of cultural relativity, studied three cultures: the native inhabitants of an island off New Guinea (the Dobus), and Native Americans of the southwestern pueblos and of the northwestern coastal waters. In the manner they worked and lived these groups undeniably differed from each other and from contemporary Americans. No one would confuse the Dobuan growing practices with those of present-day farmers or suburban gardeners.

"Yams are conceived as persons," Benedict wrote of Dobu ideas of gardening, "and are believed to wander nightly from garden to garden . . . Incantations lure the roaming yams to remain in one's own garden at the expense of the garden in which they were planted." As the harvest approaches, the Dobuans guard their plots, using charms to attract neighboring yams and to ward off the charms of neighbors. "These counter-charms root the yam tuber firmly in the earth where it was planted and safeguard it for the owner's harvesting."[96]

In the name of liberal tolerance Benedict argued for the fundamental equivalence of cultures. The supreme task for the present, she wrote, is "the recognition of cultural relativity." This anthropological relativism has carried the day. It facilitates the flattening out and multiplication of "cultures," a word which comes to mean little more than "lifestyles." A culture becomes not a unique structure of work, sexuality, and beliefs, which the Dobus exemplified, but a slight variation of of a similar life.

By virtue of choice or history, cultures proliferate within a single society, but they share essentials. We have "cultures" of suburbia, juvenile delinquency, sports, and dog fanciers. To talk of these cultures or that of African-Americans or Asian-Americans or Chicanos or gays or Italian-Americans means something very different than to talk of the culture of the Dobus. The American cultures partake of a larger American industrial society; they carry its signature in their souls and wallets. Even when locked outside the main event, they bear its marks and scars, and only want to be admitted.

The point is hardly that African-Americans or Latinos lack a culture; nor is it that they have not suffered—or triumphed; nor is it that serious economic and ethnic fissures and hostilities do not remain; nor is it that we should not study their histories and contributions. The issue is how different these "cultures" are from each other and the dominant American culture. Do they constitute distinct structures of work, living, and beliefs?

In their dress, activities, religion, and desires these cultures are becoming more alike. Only in the current ideological climate is this news or heresy. Earlier social thinkers may have exaggerated the American domination of immigrant cultures; however, those notions need to be qualified, not junked. America's multiple cultures exist within a single consumer society. Professional sports, Hollywood movies, automobiles, designer clothes, name-brand sneakers, television and videos, commercial music and CDs: these pervade America's multiculturalism. This is not a moral judgment, but a statement about the texture of American life. The multiple cultures define themselves by their preferences within a consumer society, not by a rejection of it. Only rare exceptions, like the Amish, carve out a life beyond and against the structure of advanced capitalism.

The most radical Afrocentric ideologue in the United States is culturally an American citizen of Western civilization. In discussions with campus black nationalists and Afrocentrists, Nicholas Lemann, an *Atlantic* magazine columnist, discovered that the students want to join the American mainstream—and are joining it. "Very few nationalists ask their followers not to join the mainstream economy." Lemann queried Molefi Asante, a leading advocate of Afrocentrism, about its social and cultural implications. "I asked Molefi Asante if you could be an Afrocentrist and work for IBM and live in the suburbs, and he unhesitatingly said yes." "From a distance," Lemann concluded, "it would be easy to worry that the black middle class wants to opt out of national life and create a psychologically separate black principality . . . But up close it's almost impossible to maintain."[97]

These observations tally with those of Gerald Early, the director of Afro-American Studies at Washington University. He reflected on his own identity as a successful black professor living in the affluent suburbs; and he pondered the anger of his black students over the failure of the "dream" of integration. As largely middle-class blacks attending a prestigious university they feel torn and threatened; they see that the price of success is the loss of black identity, and they gravitate to African or Afro-American Studies or to Malcolm X's espousal of all-blackness. "Yet in many ways these black students share fundamentally the same values—a belief in upward mobility and the rewards of hard work—as the whites who surround them," Early notes.[98]

How can strident affirmations of cultural identity be squared with its implacable weakening? No single reason explains this, but the relationship may be less paradoxical than inverse. Inexorable loss calls forth proud declarations of identity. Especially at elite universities cultural identity is most touchy because the surrender is most striking. On the one hand, African-American or Latino students enter the classic institution of upward mobility, the path enabling them to become full members of the dominant consumer culture. On the other hand, they bridle at the cultural costs, and demand courses, centers, and recognition of an identity they are leaving behind.

The search for "roots" and for distinct histories and cultural identities may be evidence less of real diversity than its opposite: as people feel threatened by standardization, they search out and cultivate differences. This should not be disparaged, as if individual choice and commitment were irrelevant. Nor should it be fetishized, as if it were possible to create or salvage a historical identity by willpower and daily exercise.

6

JOURNALISTS, CYNICS,
AND CHEERLEADERS

AN ACQUAINTANCE, writing a newspaper article about a forth-coming university conference on postmodernism, interviewed a number of academics. What did they think about Derrida? Post-structuralism? Fredric Jameson? Recent French theorists? The flap about Paul de Man? They had thoughts, but did not want to be quoted by name. Why? They were, well, nervous. Perhaps a colleague might discover what they actually thought. Maybe professional opinion had shifted. Possibly it would not look good to be airing opinions in the press. Play it safe; stay anonymous.[1] In 1990 tenured professors of the left with no fear of persecution or unemployment backed away from public statements on subjects most people have never heard of. This is the group conservatives think is destroying Western civilization.

Apart from the conservatives, few are aware of academic subversion. This needs immediate qualification. While acrimonious debates over structuralism or deconstructionism or postmodernism barely touch the public, other university findings shape far-ranging discussions. New academic research drives arguments about multiculturalism, and spurs the rewriting and reteaching of American history. The controversy over the 500th anniversary of Columbus's arrival in America would be inconceivable without a scholarly infrastructure. New university scholarship informs, and sometimes engenders, public discussions about museum exhibitions, welfare, poverty, the legacy of slavery, women in the workforce, learning processes, and other urgent subjects.

This should not be minimized; nor is it surprising. At least since the turn of the century, professors, especially social scientists, have addressed matters of community well-being, often joining government commissions that urge new laws and policies. Today the size alone of American higher education ensures that it produces lucid and original thinkers. By including more women, African-Americans, Latinos, and other groups, higher education is less than ever an isolated tower pursuing traditional subjects in a familiar manner; now colleges and universities reflect and partake of public life and its discontents.

What is surprising, however, is not the vigor of the general scholarly contribution, but its weakness, especially on its own turf, education. A case in point is the controversy about campus politics and curriculum. For all the ballyhooing about "culture wars," the war has been one-sided. Conservatives roll out big and sometimes incisive books, from *The Closing of the American Mind* to *Illiberal Education,* and a thousand academics respond with hoots, boos, and occasional essays, but nothing substantial. Where is the sweeping response to the conservative critics by our major leftist academics? Do they have better things to do? Are they unconcerned?

The situation may be changing, the replies now appearing. Yet this does not explain the long delay; nor a crippling ambiguity in the retorts. Some reasons for the silence I may have anticipated in *The Last Intellectuals.* Unlike past American intellectuals, the recent generation never left the campus; they went from being undergraduates and graduates to faculty members. This is not a moral judgment, but a statement of the facts of cultural activity and their consequences. A life passed exclusively on campuses affects how individuals think and write. The newer intellectuals never needed to write for a larger public; colleagues, departments, and professional conferences constituted their world—and bread and butter. After a while, either the ability or the desire to reach a nonprofessional public atrophies. When conservative books for this public appeared, the professors hardly answered, and perhaps cannot.

Yet facts can be resisted or celebrated. To a startling degree, American left professors embrace their professional roles. They are not radicals who are professors, but professors who are radicals. They encounter the world as secure employees of mainstream institutions. This recasts the topology of the "culture wars," for the leftists are not outsiders blasting society, but insiders enjoying society. Despite the academic fetish of "the other," "the boundary," "the margin," these categories hardly apply to university leftists, who frequently crow of their campus prowess and successes, denigrating the unaccredited and unaccomplished.

"It is all but impossible, I am told," writes Paul Lauter, a left literary professor, "to convince a congressperson of the importance of studying Zora [Neale Hurston, the black writer] together with, God forbid in place of, Ernest [Hemingway]." The mock surprise expresses the insider's real smugness. No need to worry about the evil senators. "That is no defeat; it says to me, that while the advocates of a broad, multicultural canon have consolidated our position within most educational institutions, the Bennetts and Blooms have been hard at work in the public arenas."[2] A recent summing-up of the academic culture wars confirms that the conservative rumblings stayed "outside the university"; inside things proceeded apace with "little negative effect . . . Race studies, queer theory, colonial and postcolonial studies, and others didn't miss a beat."[3]

At the very least, this is odd. Once upon a time, radicals subsisted as marginal writers, agitators, and labor organizers indicting society. Now left professors attack hegemony and conservatism from within hegemonic and conservative institutions. The standard conservative plaint that sixties radicals have taken over the university is twice wrong. Even on the most generous accounting, leftists assume a presence, hardly a majority, in few departments; and they behave like good employees: they give their courses, attend committee meetings, and hobnob at conferences. As David Bromwich, a Yale professor, observes, "True, some of the sixties people are still around; and true, sometimes now they have tenure. These facts say nothing about how they conduct themselves . . . One may say as a rule that their bureaucratic manners are impeccable."[4]

Sociological observations about today's radicals have their limits, however. Whether they are chaired professors at major universities or unemployed textile workers may be irrelevant; thought must be judged on its own merits. Conservatives love to mention the big salaries of (some) academic critics, as if money invalidates ideas; this may be the conservatives' own brand of Marxism. Just as Marxists once denounced philosophers as tools of power because of their state employment, conservatives denounce radicals because of their university wages. For each, pay stubs replace thinking.

Sociological remarks are not irrelevant inasmuch as they serve to illuminate, not dismiss. Who picks up the tab might be gossip, but also may be suggestive. The Internal Revenue Service interpretation of ideas, however, cannot stop with leftists. Those who heatedly denounce "tenured radicals" may be "tenured conservatives" elegantly dining at corporate expense. For instance, the Olin Foundation, perhaps the most savvy of the conservative foundations, dispenses many millions directly to conservative scholars who uphold private enterprise and the "American heritage."

These sums are not paltry. Samuel P. Huntington, long identified with cold war ideology, received close to $1.4 million to set up a center at Harvard; Allan Bloom walked away with almost $2 million to direct "seminars, publications, and fellowships" at the University of Chicago; Irving Kristol had to make ends meet with only $400,000. Olin money handsomely supported the three major critiques of American higher education: Bloom's *The Closing of the American Mind,* Kimball's *Tenured Radicals,* and D'Souza's *Illiberal Education.* Olin even earmarked funds just to promote D'Souza's book.[5] And this only begins the list of conservatives bankrolled by Olin and other foundations. Are coddled conservatives superior to "tenured radicals"?

The radical professors who indignantly report this are themselves beneficiaries of other foundations or well-endowed universities. Less monies are available to left-of-center than to conservative scholars, yet this assertion depends on how foundations are politically classified. "It is important not to lose perspective on the impact and extent of conservative funding," writes Paul Gottfried, a scholar of conservativism. "The big conservative foundations are dwarfs both in comparison to giants like Ford and Rockefeller and when measured against the vast sums available to conventional liberals and leftists."[6]

Marxist or post-Marxist professors, however, turn irritable when historical materialism comes home to roost. Conservatives are called servants of power, but leftist academics live on air. Inasmuch as they justify academia, however, the professors are not only radicals but ideologues, apologists for themselves and their institutions. In the "culture wars" little is more striking than the ease with which the new professors defend professional reputations and language, sophisticated theories and distinguished friends, heaping contempt on journalists and critics as backward outsiders. A left supposedly lives and thinks in the name of a larger public; among the new academics the democratic spirit flags.

In a response to conservative critics Michael Berubé, an English professor, protests that newspaper book reviewers do not stay abreast of academic writings; journalists ignore "new historicism" and "reception theory" and no longer read the new scholars. "The result so far is that recent literary theory is so rarely accorded the privilege of representing itself in nonacademic forums that journalists, disgruntled professors, embittered ex-graduate students and their families and friends now feel entitled to say anything at all about the academy without fear of contradiction by general readers. The field is wide open, and there's no penalty for charlatanism." Berubé's wording reveals the mental furnishings of the new academic; the world is divided between insiders, the true scholars, and outsiders, who are journalists, bitter professors, and charlatans.

Berubé is floored that a journalist failed to pay obeisance to the new academic honchos. Writing about "political correctness," this journalist did not cite Michel Foucault or Henry Louis Gates, Jr., or "*any* currently influential academic critic and theorist." Rather, he quoted a New York Board of Education task force, a Tulane draft report on race and gender, and a University of Pennsylvania administrator. Beat that! Not a single influential critic! No Foucault! Where has this rube been? "Whatever else they may be," Berubé huffs, "these are not the texts we academic critics normally rely upon in writing scholarly articles, book reviews, tenure evaluations, or course descriptions."[7]

This is the language of an academic establishment defending its trade from upstarts. "We" professors refer to "influential" thinkers like ourselves; we don't ask administrators or—gads!—New York Board of Education dumbbells. Nor are Berubé's sentiments unusual. A recent collection, *Messages from American Universities*, cites Berubé's wisdom, and the editor adds his own. The "academy

bashers," whom the editor also calls "opportunists," have "failed
to learn the new critical languages." "All the commotion," this
editor states, "is coming from a few splinter groups of academic
malcontents." Joan Wallach Scott, a professor at the Institute for
Advanced Study at Princeton, calls the critics of university practices
"disaffected scholars" and "marginal intellectuals."[8] Once this language—"splinter groups," "marginal intellectuals," "malcontents"
—was used by an establishment against a left; now it used by a left
establishment against its critics.

Barbara Herrnstein Smith, in her introduction to *The Politics of
Liberal Education,* a collection responding to conservative critics,
complains of "media exploitation" and "misrepresentation." The
reports of academic malpractice have "obviously" been "produced
by and for persons remote from the scenes of the alleged crimes."
She offers a lighter version of dumb journalists who cannot fathom
influential academic thinkers. The problem is that journalists and
professors use different "messages." The "messages" that professors typically send to each other "in specialized journals and at
professional conferences" are "long on new, challenging ideas,
short on familiar, confirming ones." Smith, who obviously peruses
few academic periodicals, writes that journalists, on the other hand,
send vivid, dramatic, and familiar messages. Unfortunately journalists do not understand their own simplicity; they make the "conceptual, abstract, challenging, unfamiliar" messages of academics
sound like their rudimentary communiqués.[9]

In 1987, a researcher discovered scores of articles in an anti-
Semitic and pro-Nazi newspaper penned by Paul de Man, a leading
American literary critic, who had died several years earlier. De
Man, who immigrated to the United States after World War II,
wrote a series of highly compromising pieces in the early 1940s in
his native Belgium—one recommended "the creation of a Jewish
colony isolated from Europe." As a prominent Yale professor of
literature, he had methodically masked his past life, alluding to a
fictitious career in the Resistance. News of his past and his lifelong
effort to bury it put academics in a dither.

Yet for many who rushed to defend their fallen idol it was simply
"news," the stuff of journalists and commentators too pigheaded to
understand the subtleties of high academic theory. David Lehman,
who covered the story for *Newsweek* and later wrote a book on the
affair, was taken aback by the journalist bashing. "Nothing quite

prepared one for the virtual declaration of war on journalism that soon issued from deconstructionist quarters." Many professors refused to talk with Lehman. Some denounced the "collaboration between the university and the mass media"; others attacked the "dismaying ignorance" of the "academic journalists," who were "shrill, strident, violent, (male) hysterical." As Lehman noted, these critics "retreated to a position of mystification. They, and they alone, were qualified to discuss the matter; all others, keep out."[10]

The disdain for a public prose should stick in the craw of left professors. It doesn't. It goes down smoothly, facilitated by a widely accepted proposition: clear language undermines critical thought. While the position can easily be ridiculed, it rests on some undeniable truths. Language is more than an empty vessel; not every argument can be made accessible to a general audience. Certain insights, information, and subjects require a specialized vocabulary. This is the justification for a technical idiom. No one picks up a pilot's training book or a report by a structural engineer and complains that they are not written in lucid and accessible English. They are not intended to be, and perhaps could not be; the subject matter necessitates a complex vocabulary.

In the exact sciences the proposition seems incontestable; papers by biomathematicians use a special vocabulary that limits a general readership. Yet transferring the point to the humanities and social sciences is dicey. Literature, history, and philosophy belong to the common stock of humanity; their importance resides partly in their openness to an educated reader. Thoughtful citizens can acquaint themselves with Western philosophy and literature from Plato to William James or from Sophocles to Kafka. Of course, this same citizen might well stumble on Kant or Wittgenstein. Nevertheless, the humanities as a whole resist becoming a technical discipline with a technical audience, an impulse that hardly marks Western science. An educated individual who could read Plato or Kafka would be stymied by Archimedes or Einstein. These require interpretations, introductions, and translations for even the well-educated.

Many, if not most, scholars in the humanities and social sciences challenge this reasoning or, at least, its implications. It seems to suggest that their work is inferior to scientific research because it is less complex and more accessible. They draw direct parallels between their studies and those in the physical and biological sciences;

their research is just as specialized and complex, and needs as much training to grasp. For this reason, for well over a century scholars have sought to yoke their endeavors more closely to science; they want to bask in its glow. The study of politics became "political science"; the study of society became "the science of society" or sociology. New disciplines pop up like "library science" and "information science." These tags mean: Stop. Do Not Enter. We are scientists. You need credits, degrees, and training to judge our work. It also means: we use a special vocabulary.

Left academics resuscitate an additional argument to justify their vocabulary. Not only do specialized fields employ a specialized idiom, but society, especially Anglo-American society, resists subversive truths by demanding a simple language. A "clear" sentence structure represses critical thinking that requires a counter-logic and vocabulary.

Again, this belief can be easily ridiculed; and again, it rests on some valid ideas from an honorable, and mainly Hegelian, pedigree. German idealism protested the domination of simple clarity as simplemindedness. Hegel ridiculed $2 \times 2 = 4$ logic and "healthy common sense." "To questions like 'When was Caesar born?' 'How many feet make a furlong?' etc., a straight answer ought to be given . . . But the nature of a so-called truth of that sort is different from the nature of philosophical truth."[11] Philosophical truths require surmounting common truisms and familiar categories; they necessitate an uncommon language or what Hegel once half-apologetically called an "obscure style."[12] These ideas passed into German and French philosophic thought, including Marxist varieties.

American poststructuralist, post-Marxist, and post-everything thinkers appeal to these ideas in justifying their language. We are highly trained specialists, using a complex prose, they say; and we are dedicated subversives, using an idiom that resists a repressive clarity. For instance, Judith Frank, a feminist professor, complains that a journalist critic "seems to expect the humanities to be utterly transparent to the general population, when the truth is that for those of us who have gone through graduate training, the humanities are a profession, and that the people who practice a particular profession are trained in its language."[13] This might be called pulling rank, showing the unaccredited to the door.

Fredric Jameson, a dean of Marxist cultural criticism, offers a similar justification; literary and cultural theory is as complex as molecular biology. It is "surprising" how many people take a "bel-letristic view," Jameson commented, making "the assumption, which they would never make in the area of nuclear physics, lin-guistics, symbolic logic, or urbanism, that such [cultural] problems can still be laid out with all the leisurely elegance of a coffee-table magazine." Cultural theory is no "less complex" than biochemis-try, and resists coffee-table elegance. An admirer, who quotes these sentences, continues:

> The intricacies of Jameson's sentences are a sign not only of the difficul-ties of the problems he analyzes but also of the seriousness of his ap-proach. His technical prose bears witness that cultural theory . . . is as valid as those "other disciplines."[14]

The reasoning is slick: complex sentences spell profundity, and profundity spells professionalization, which demonstrates cultural theory's parity with biophysics. The only piece missing is the politi-cal justification, which Jameson set forth in *Marxism and Form;* he defended the writing of the German critical Marxists from the charges of obscurity. "It can be admitted that it does not conform to the canons of clear and fluid journalistic writing taught in schools. But what if those ideas of clarity and simplicity have come to serve a very different ideological purpose . . . ?" What if trans-parency facilitates clichés, but avoids "real thought" requiring ef-fort and time? For Jameson the density of T. W. Adorno's writing exemplified a break with repressive clarity. His "bristling mass of abstractions and cross-references is precisely intended to be read in situation, against the cheap facility of what surrounds it, as a warn-ing to the reader of the price he has to pay for genuine thinking."[15]

The point is well taken; it is also misleading, and not only be-cause the characterization of Adorno's writings as a "bristling mass of abstractions and cross-references" misses the mark; this de-scribes academic writing, not Adorno's. The issue is not the diffi-culty of writing, but the fetish of difficulty, the belief that fractured English, name dropping, and abstractions guarantee profundity, professionalization, and subversion. With this belief comes the counter-belief: lucidity implies banality, amateurism, and conserva-tism.

These tenets are the new coin of the realm. New academics in-variably note that clarity is repressive, which becomes the standard alibi for half-written and sometimes unwritten prose. Gayatri Spivak, a feminist literary critic and translator of Derrida, broke new ground by publishing in a scholarly book her rough notes for a lecture and a transcription of a telephone conversation with the book's editor.[16] Why not? If clarity is repressive, incoherence is subversive, sloppiness is craft.

Whatever the truth of a repressive clarity, it requires specific demonstrations, not pronouncements. The new academics gripe that newspaper critics fail to master the technical prose, but where have they shown mastery of a newspaper prose? Or where have they established its inability to express their thoughts? After all, Hegel did not simply denounce common sense and philosophy: he labored to establish the insufficiency of everyday thinking and language. This remains a significant task, but the new academics avoid it, hurrying directly to metatheory and metalanguage.

Has American academic writing suffered from a surfeit of repressive clarity? A reasonable observer might find the opposite proposition more persuasive: an excess of clotted language and concepts distort its prose. In the late 1950s C. Wright Mills attacked the sociologist Talcott Parsons for employing academic jargon. "In many academic circles today," observed Mills, "anyone who tries to write in a widely intelligible way is liable to be condemned as a 'mere literary man' or, worse still, 'a mere journalist.' "

As an experiment, Mills "translated" Parsons's prose into ordinary English. For instance he "translated" a passage from Parsons that began this way: "Attachment to common values means, motivationally considered, that the actors have common 'sentiments' in support of the value patterns, which may be defined as meaning that conformity with the relevant expectations is treated as a 'good thing' relatively independently of any specific instrumental 'advantage' to be gained from such conformity, e.g. in the avoidance of negative sanctions." Mills's "translation" began: *"Or in other words:* When people share the same values, they tend to behave in accordance with the way they expect one another to behave."[17]

Mills's efforts on behalf of plain English disappeared without a trace. Everywhere a denunciation of repressive clarity leads to an embrace of obscurity in the name of revolutionary profundity. If clarity marks the idiom of capitalism, the vocabulary of subversion is opaque. The gate swings open, and planeloads of academics hustle through, carrying laptop computers with hard disks crammed with unreadable prose. These writings invariably nod toward

Adorno or Derrida or Jameson or include a pronouncement justifying muddy language and obscure abstractions.

For instance, in a book on postmodern education, two professors condemn clarity and defend complex or "bad" writing. "It seems to us that those who call themselves progressive educators, whether feminists, Marxists or otherwise, . . . have missed the role that the 'language of clarity' plays in a dominant culture that cleverly and powerfully uses 'clear' and 'simplistic' language to systematically undermine and prevent . . . complex and critical thinking." Oppositional languages, they state, "are generally unfamiliar, provoking questions and pointing to social relations that will often appear alien and strange . . . What is at stake is not the issue of 'bad' writing, as if writing that is difficult to grapple with has nothing important to say."[18]

Richard Wolff, a Marxist economics professor, offers a more ringing defense of "bad" writing. Poststructuralist and postmodernist writing is "difficult to read" because "major shifts in ways of thinking usually interact complexly with related shifts in ways of speaking and writing. Early in the process, the new ways of writing will often be convoluted and opaque." Not only is opaque language required for complex thinking, but a brainwashed American public prizes clarity; as long as the public does not wake up, we post-Marxists will appear to be "bad" writers. What this public rejects as incomprehensible proves its value, believes Professor Wolff. "To uphold radical and Marxist ideas and to develop them in new directions would quite predictably produce writings out of tune with the prevalent presumptions and desire of the postwar public: 'bad' writings in the eyes of many."[19]

The justifications for "bad" prose show up everywhere. An English professor begins his book stating that to analyze literature is a task "no less demanding of a specialized language, than the study of sub-atomic particles or mammalian respiratory systems."[20] In other words, he will avoid the vernacular for an arcane and specialized vocabulary. These pronouncements are not idle threats. The professors are as good as their word: they spread "bad" writing, dreaming it challenges capitalism, as they collect their paychecks, enroll their children in private schools, and invest in real estate.

The clumsy language has been widely pilloried by conservatives and other critics. Those attacked rightly object to a method that simply pulls out stray sentences from essays and books and holds them up for ridicule. A sentence here or there proves nothing. The issue, however, is not isolated sentences, but entire essays, books, and series that move from computers to university libraries unread and unreadable. This is not simply bad writing, but bad writing elevated to a principle. To show this, of course, requires examples, even if they remain vulnerable to the reply that they are unrepresentative.

A University of Massachusetts "cultural studies" professor, writing about "effective" intellectuals, states that "the question of the status of subjugated knowledge cannot be sufficiently probed unless we also simultaneously raise the question of the intellectual/mass relationship and the underlying ideology of the individual/society paradigm. The challenge that Foucauldian thought has to take up is that of postrepresentational politics and of accounting for the politics of intellectuality in a different way." This continues for some twenty pages, when the author is inspired to clarify his argument by citing two other lucid thinkers, Ernesto Laclau and Chantal Mouffe. "Since I found Laclau and Mouffe particularly convincing on this point, I will quote from them extensively." The quote begins:

> For, whereas political leadership can be grounded upon a conjunctural coincidence of interests in which the participating sectors retain their separate identity, moral and intellectual leadership requires that an ensemble of "ideas" and "values" be shared by a number of sectors—or, to use our own terminology, that certain subject positions traverse a number of class sectors.

Our intrepid professor, who selected this passage as especially illuminating, raises the obvious question: "I am aware that there is a problem with this reading: is this a Gramscian reading of Gramsci, or is it a poststructuralist extension or adaption of Gramsci?"[21]

A book on "recoding" history, which makes the obligatory nod toward semiotics, Baudrillard, and other French thinkers, explains why the analysis appears incomprehensible. "At the outset I acknowledge that my use of interpretants . . . is radically unfamiliar. But I argue this must be so: in the present cultural-economic conjunctions, academic discourse, in its presumed everydayness . . . leads the intellectual evasion . . . I . . . resort to a discourse that slows reading, that refuses to convince a reader by its cadence or even rightness."

Again, the author is as good as his word: in some three hundred pages from beginning to end little is lucid. "If transcendence is a permanent possibility of semiotic-intellectual destruction," runs a typical sentence, "because its minimal function is to make unthinkable the negation of that 'which ties one to reality' and holds one in place, this superfunction today is perfected in contexts where language is hypervalorized as the 'indispensable,' 'needed,' 'necessary,' 'required,' and so on, basis of enculturation."

The book is so opaque it comes with a glossary, which unfortunately could itself use a glossary. For instance, under the "A's" is an explanation of *"Actantial/actant"* This "refers to the complex exchange between what a 'historical' narration allows to be the subject of doing (for example, capitalism treated as the actant of innovation or capitalism presented as the subject of dialectical transformations) and the reader's ability (generally) to acknowledge primary roles of action as necessary to a culture."[22] With that explained, a reader returns to the text.

The first sentence of a new book on education by an English professor reads as follows: "This book was instigated by the publication of the Harvard Core Curriculum Report in 1978 and was intended to respond to what I took to be an ominous educational reform initiative that, without naming it, would delegitimate the decisive, if spontaneous, disclosure of the complicity of liberal American institutions of higher learning with the state's brutal conduct of the war in Vietnam and the consequent call for opening the university to meet the demands by hitherto marginalized constituencies of American society for enfranchisement."

This book, which deserves honorable mention in any competition for the worst-written book of 1993, continues in this vein for over two hundred pages. A sentence from the conclusion reads: "If the decentering of the anthropologos informing Occidental cultural practices points to the priority of difference over identity rather than the other way around, then the projective phase of a destructive pedagogy also requires a pedagogical comportment toward the curriculum that reverses the binary terms of the principle of identity that has historically determined canon formation and knowledge production (what it is permissible to publish)." This volume is not only titled *The End of Education,* it exemplifies the end.[23]

David Lehman in his book on Paul de Man and the blight of

deconstructionism paraphrases a cynical suggestion about how to make any academic essay publishable.

> The first sentence should feature *hegemony;* the second, *itinerary;* the third, *foregrounding;* the fourth, *privilege* used as a verb . . . There should be plenty of *de-* or *dis-* prefixes, beginning with *deconstruction* and *dismantling,* and as many *-ize* suffixes, such as *problematize, valorize, contextualize, totalize.* A good way to begin your *discourse* (you must always call it that) is with a nod toward Derrida, an allusion to de Man, and a determination to call into question some *binary opposition* . . . *male* and *female, nature* and *culture, center* and *periphery* . . .[24]

A cogent reservation should be registered: some essays and books are important regardless of inept language. I once complained to an editor about a book published by his university press, which I found unreadable. He put me in my place with a single remark. "Yet, the title does quite well with us." Sales might not constitute an argument, but does indicate an audience; and even the most cynical observer would not imagine that professors buy these books exclusively for conformist reasons. Why do they? Beyond the most general answer—they find them provocative or interesting—little can be specified. The point should be conceded, however. Readability cannot—should not—be the only lens we use to inspect scholarship. Nor should it be abandoned.

As with so much radical scholarship, leftists break with the very theories they appeal to. The easy or ostentatious references to seditious thought from Marx to Nietzsche and Freud ignore the fact that these masters often—not always—were wonderful writers, and ruthless critics of pedantry and obscurantism. The original rebels did not obsessively salute their own complexity and difficulty, and scorn journalists and the educated public. If anything they did the reverse; they scorned the pedants, and turned to the public. The new academics invoke their names and ideas, and surrender their prose and precision.

The French took the first steps in rendering critical theories coded communications for the initiated. To explain why the land of Descartes became a prose junkyard requires a sociology of French intellectuals more than an understanding of the progress of thought. In any event, their American disciples enthusiastically followed. On the graph of readable prose the line that connects Marx to Althusser and his American followers; Freud to Lacan and his American followers; and Nietzsche to Derrida and his American followers goes straight down.

While many of his passages shine, few argue that Marx was a great stylist. He spent much effort, and hundreds of pages, however, attacking bombast. His *German Ideology* is little more than a six-hundred-page attack on philosophical pomposity. He counseled "how to proceed if you want to appear German, profound and speculative." "First of all, an abstraction is made from a fact; then it is declared that the fact is based on the abstraction." He gave an example:

> *Fact:* The Cat eats the mouse.
> *Reflection:* Cat-nature, mouse-nature, consumption of mouse by cat = consumption of nature by nature = self-consumption of nature.
> *Philosophic presentation of the fact:* Devouring of the mouse by the cat is based upon the self-consumption of nature.[25]

Moreover, Marx knew something else forgotten by those who appeal to his writings: it is possible to write in different fashions for different audiences. He wrote not simply dense volumes like *Capital* but daily journalism and polemical books and pamphlets for a wider public. Works like *The Communist Manifesto, The Eighteenth Brumaire,* and *The Civil War in France* stand at the furthest remove from scholasticism. And even *Capital* is hardly a linguistic death valley; it contains many splendid passages. Marx himself admitted that "no one can feel the literary shortcomings of *Capital* more strongly than myself"; and he went on to quote with pride reviews that praised its "clearness" and "unusual liveliness." "In this respect the author in no way resembles . . . the majority of German scholars, who . . . write their books in a language so dry and obscure the heads of ordinary mortals are cracked by it."[26]

Is it necessary to argue that the writings of Nietzsche and Freud shine with clarity and wit? Much of their importance derives from their open and engaging prose; they were less specialists, than antispecialists. Obviously some of their writings are difficult; some are dense, especially Nietzsche's, but in the main, they address themselves to educated readers, not specialists. Even when Nietzsche raises the issue of obscure texts, he raises it sharply. "It is by no means an objection to a book," he wrote, "when someone finds it unintelligible: perhaps this might just have been the intention of the

author—perhaps he did not *want* to be understood by 'anyone.' "
Authors, he continues, sometimes seek only "the ears of those who
are acoustically related to them." As for "my own case,—I do not
desire that either my ignorance, or the vivacity of my temperament,
should prevent me being understood by *you,* my friends."[27]

Throughout his writings, Nietzsche scorned the feebleness and
timidity of professors. "Consider the historical student," he wrote
in *The Use and Abuse of History.* "He has the 'methods' for original work, the 'correct ideas' and the airs of the master . . . A little
isolated period of the past is marked out . . . He cleverly applies
his method and produces something," but what is it worth? The
"wisdom is rotten." The young savant has become just a cog in the
"factory of science."

> I am sorry to use the common jargon about slaveowners and taskmas-
> ters . . . but the words 'factory,' 'labor market,' 'auction sale,' 'practi-
> cal use,' and all the auxiliaries of egoism come involuntarily to the lips
> in describing the younger generation of savants.

They are already "exhausted hens." "They can merely cackle
more than before, because they lay eggs oftener; but the eggs are
always smaller though their books are bigger."[28]

Freud, of course, was a superb stylist, a lucid and engaging
writer, as Bruno Bettelheim showed in *Freud and Man's Soul.* Biog-
raphers note that the only award he won during his life was literary, the Goethe Prize in 1930. From his case histories to his theoretical speculations, his prose shimmered. He once regretted that his
case histories "should read like short stories and that, as one might
say, they lack the serious stamp of science." One of his case histories begins this way:

> In the summer vacation of the year 189- I made an excursion in the
> Hohe Tauern [in the Alps] so that for a while I might forget medicine
> and more particularly the neuroses. I had almost succeeded in this when
> one day I turned aside from the main road to climb a mountain which
> lay somewhat apart and which was renowned for its views and for its
> well-run refuge hut. I reached the top after a strenuous climb and,
> feeling refreshed and rested, was sitting deep in contemplation of the
> charm of the distant prospect. I was so lost in thought that at first I did
> not connect it with myself when these words reached my ears. "Are you
> a doctor, sir?" But the question was addressed to me, and by the rather
> sulky-looking girl of perhaps eighteen who had served my meal and had

been spoken to by the landlady as "Katharina." Coming to myself I replied: "Yes, I'm a doctor: but how did you know that?"[29]

This is Freud: not a short story or the opening of a novel or caper. Nor is it an American Freudian or psychoanalytic literary critic. While his theoretical speculations lacked this eloquence, Freud regularly pitched his writings to the nonspecialist, and in fact unsuccessfully fought the specialists, the medical doctors. "It is not without satisfaction," he stated in his first lecture in the United States, "that I have learnt that the majority of my audience are not members of the medical profession. You have no need to be afraid that any special medical knowledge will be required for following what I have to say."[30]

In several of his writings he leavened his reflections by including an "opponent" who raises objections to his train of thought. "An enquiry," he explained, "which proceeds like a monologue" may evade criticism by becoming overdecisive. "I shall therefore imagine that I have an opponent who follows my argument with mistrust, and here and there I shall allow him to interject some remarks." Nor was this simply a ploy. Freud gave the "opponent" many pages to vigorously denounce his argument. " 'That sounds splendid! A race of men who have renounced illusions,' " sputters the opponent. " 'We seem now to have exchanged roles: you emerge as an enthusiast . . . I stand for the claims of reason . . . What you have been expounding seems to me to be built upon errors . . .' "[31]

Even Adorno can be defended against his devotees. The easy references to his convoluted and abstract sentences malign his oeuvre. From the iridescent aphorisms of *Minima Moralia* to the polemical *Jargon of Authenticity* Adorno's work explodes academic prose. If anything, his writing is deliberately anti-academic, a term he once embraced. A student protested that Adorno's criticism of Heidegger was too polemical, lacking collegiality; Adorno replied that if philosophy is to be more than a trite enterprise, it must "burst the concept of the academic."[32] Virtually all of his sentences display a compressed energy and corrosive intellect worlds apart from standard American academic prose. Pedantic references, indifferent sentences, and empty abstractions do not litter his writings. His incomparable essay "Cultural Criticism and Society" opened this way:

To anyone in the habit of thinking with his ears, the words "cultural criticism" [*Kulturkritik*] must have an offensive ring, not merely because, like "automobile," they are pieced together from Latin and Greek. The words recall a flagrant contradiction. The cultural critic is not happy with civilization, to which alone he owes his discontent.[33]

On the other hand, Fredric Jameson, who highly esteems Adorno, writes in a peculiar American baroque: a gray mash of half-written sentences punctuated by tooting horns and waving pennants. A chapter in his book on Adorno begins with this sentence:

In fact, far from being an "open" or aleatory composition, [Adorno's] *Negative Dialectics* imitates—as over a great distance, with radically different building materials, and in that "prodigious erosion of contours" of which Gide, following Nietzsche, likes to speak—the plan of Kant's *Critique of Pure Reason*. (I am tempted to say that it *wraps* it as a postmodern reconstruction—glass shell, arches—wraps an older monument; except that Adorno is not postmodern and the more fitting analogy would be what Thomas Mann does to Goethe's *Faust*.)[34]

The point needs no reinforcement; to move from Freud, Nietzsche, and Marx to their French interpreters and American followers is to enter a different universe. The pedantry, self-satisfaction, and academicism which the original critical theorists despised metastasizes in the disciples, where it threatens to become not simply a lesion but the whole of their work. In the name of subversion the new academics throttle language, confounding rigor mortis with rigor. In the 1950s Edmund Wilson wondered how someone could be "set up as an authority on teaching the young when he was not himself sufficiently well-educated to have mastered the rudiments of writing." These thoughts breathe of simpler times, especially Wilson's suggestion that English professors might improve the writing of their colleagues.

As for my experience with articles by experts in anthropology and sociology, it has led me to conclude that the requirement, in my ideal university, of having the papers in every department passed by a professor of English might result in revolutionizing these subjects—if indeed the second of them survived at all.[35]

The issue is more than style. The new academics see themselves not simply at but as the cutting edge. They celebrate themselves, their prose, ideas, and professionalism. If this is radicalism, it is a new type, for it looks very much like old-fashioned progressivism or twentieth-century liberalism. This is not necessarily bad. As the hopes for socialism and revolution recede, if not dissipate, leftist intellectuals redefine their role; they view themselves as what they are, college teachers and scholars with academic debates, curricula, and hiring their realities.

So far so good: this might be dubbed a victory for realism or truth. Leftist intellectuals no longer pretend they are peasants or workers or guerrillas. Yet they slide from an old to a new illusion; they are not outsiders heaving dynamite, but insiders cracking codes. They become cheerleaders with a difference. When they laud campus progress, professionalism, and scholarship, they are advancing a radical agenda. They justify an insular academicism in the name of revolution.

Andrew Ross, a Princeton English professor, presents the new program. He writes that "the mantle of opposition" no longer belongs to an autonomous avant-garde, or urban intellectuals or bohemians. To whom does it belong? Professors. A "reactionary consensus" loyal to "narratives of decline" bemoans the fragmentation and academization that Ross applauds; now professors subvert disciplines.

> Professional intellectuals who are not self-loathing have come to insist that it is necessary to examine their institutional affiliations in order to understand and transform the codes of power which are historically specific to their disciplinary discourses. In this respect, the recent generation of poststructuralist thinkers each applied themselves, in ways unavailable to the classical Marxist tradition, to the kinds of critique necessary for examining and redefining the intellectual's relation to the institution.[36]

Ross hits all the buttons: the new academics are the new radicals; departmental corridors are the new trenches; the tools of specialist scholarship are the new means of warfare; and the combatants, "the recent generation of poststructuralist thinkers," surpass their dotty predecessors. Old fogies committed to "narratives of decline" fail to see the brighter future. In one way or another, the new academics repeat, and revel, in these themes.

In a recent collection on academics, Bruce Robbins, an English professor, exults over the successes of professors. An unfolding debate, Robbins informs us, takes up "the institutional forms the energies of the 60s have taken." Of course, Robbins rejects the "narrative of decline." He is upbeat, like other critical theorists, since the sixties led to one evident achievement: left-wing English professors. He trumpets that the title of a recent book by the English professor Paul Bové, *Intellectuals in Power*, "can no longer seem a contradiction in terms."[37]

The phrase "intellectuals in power" or "intellectuals in politics" may be no contradiction. Thirty years ago James Joll wrote a book titled *Three Intellectuals in Politics*. The subjects of Joll and Bové's books suggest the progress of self-delusion. Joll surveyed the careers of people like Léon Blum, the French socialist Prime Minister, who led a Popular Front government during the Spanish Civil War; and Walther Rathenau, a German industrialist and sometime government official in World War I. These were people who not simply wrote and thought about matters of the mind but played roles in the state; they were intellectuals in power. A couple of decades later, who are the intellectuals in power to American English professors? English professors.[38]

More recently, Theodore Draper has reflected on "intellectuals in politics." Who are his subjects? Not English professors but people like Woodrow Wilson, Daniel Moynihan, and Henry Kissinger, individuals with "actual service in government." Apart from entering governments or political movements, Draper doubted intellectuals have power. "Intellectuals may have influence but they almost never have power."[39]

The new academics endlessly repeat that we are in the midst of an exciting explosion of "theory," as if all theories were the same and all were good. The fetish of theory, like that of complexity, anoints the professionals, keeping out the unaccredited. It also testifies to the thriving idealism of postmaterialists. Subversive theories explode in the campus quads, thrilling the academics. "Gray, my dear friend, is every theory / And green alone life's golden tree," instructs Mephistopheles the student in Goethe's *Faust*.[40]

"Philosophy is blooming," roars a philosopher. It has "never before been in as great shape as it is today. All topics are available; all its applications are legitimate; all methods are feasible; all interdisciplinary connections are accessible." If this is not enough, we are told that more philosophers live today than "there have been from the dark beginnings of history up to 1900." Another cheerleader enthuses, "We are seeing the emergence of a vital academic left counterculture. One consequence is a veritable explosion of new theoretical paradigms for political and cultural critique."[41]

Progress bewitches the new academics; although they appeal to theories that repudiated it, they write under the star of relentless improvement. Nietzsche and Freud held dim views of progress; and the Marxism of Lukács and Gramsci that filtered into European thought repudiated the idea of mechanical advancement. The American followers, again, blithely reverse this, revealing their unbreakable links to positive thinking; they twitch at any hint of "narratives of decline." To imply that something might be lost in history; that things may worsen: these violate the first principle of progress.

Jonathan Culler, a Cornell University English professor, also protests "the crisis narratives" that blame professionalization and academization. Culler stoutly maintains "we must assert the value not just of specialization but of professionalization also, explaining how professionalization makes thought possible." Culler turns misty-eyed on the virtues of specialization; it gives rise to "serious" "works of criticism or scholarship," not to be confused with "newspaper articles," "works of popularization," or "especially commentary." It leads to the judicious and democratic judgments by peers.

> While reducing capriciousness and favoritism in important decisions, this progress in professionalism shifts power from the vertical hierarchy of the institutions that employ a critic to a horizontal system of evaluation. Critical writing, which is the medium of exchange of this system, thus becomes central to the professional situation and identity of teachers of literature.[42]

In themselves these statements are hardly noteworthy. Yet not a public relations official, but a leading literary critic offers these banal celebrations of academic professionalism. Moreover, this is a critical theorist in the school of Marx, Freud, Nietzsche, Derrida, Baudrillard, and Foucault, whose teachings challenge capitalism, hierarchy, domination, and hegemony. Appropriated by American academics, what does a mountain of subversive thought add up to? Gushings over bureaucratization and professionalization. Advertisements for themselves, their positions, and their universities.

Once critical theorists denounced the market as corrupting

thought. No longer. With some exceptions postmodern subversives now sing its praises.[43] "Critical writing" is "the medium of exchange" for the new scholars, states Culler, which means that attacking hierarchy and patriarchy spells cash and promotion. Culler loves the free market because it leads to competition and innovation. He applies the wisdom of Capitalism 101 to competing departments and scholars. "Competition for money and positions" encourages "innovative enterprises"; and competition between schools "creates a situation in which departments are expected to vie with departments at other universities for eminence, both by attempting to hire their most distinguished critics and by encouraging their members to seek greater professional standing." Again, these statements are unexceptional—if made about the frozen pizza industry or a football franchise.

Culler's survey of "Criticism and the American University" reads like a guide for the investor in the futures market of criticism. What schools or individuals look promising? Harvard has been in the "doldrums." Berkeley, though its emphasis has shifted, has remained a "major" force. "Duke, which in 1985–7 repeated on a grander scale Buffalo's experiment of the 1960s, hiring a number of distinguished senior literary theorists, will provide an interesting test of the possibility of creating a new theoretically-orientated program that will have a decisive impact on literary studies." Investors take note. Instruct your broker to buy Duke critical theory futures.

The lingo of theoretical breakthroughs and explosions partakes of the language of the market because it is a market. Talk of new paradigms slips into the idiom of new items and new marketing strategies. Advanced theory sounds very much like advanced capitalism. Theoretical innovations "can occur only if we reflect critically and boldly about just what the new developments mean and about how they may be capitalized on to devise new meanings for 'collective research in the humanities.' "

In other words, states J. Hillis Miller, a leading critical theorist, we need more money, travel, and computers in order to advance thought. "Technological developments such as tape recorders, xeroxing, word processing computers, and relatively inexpensive telephoning and travel by jetplane obviously are necessary to make this possible."[44] This is the wisdom of critical thinking in a postindustrial age: critical thought "obviously" requires air travel, xeroxing, and computers. These insights are uncomfortably close to the remarks of Professor Zapp, David Lodge's satire of a hustling academic in *Small World*. "There are three things which have revolutionized academic life in the last twenty years," notes Zapp. "Jet travel, direct-dialling telephones and the Xerox machine." "The radical academic," comments Harold Fromm, "exhibits the verbal trappings and forms of Marxist renunciation while acting as paradigmatic acquisitive capitalist."[45]

At the end of the radical theorizing project is a surprise: a celebration of academic hierarchy, professions, and success. Never has so much criticism yielded so much affirmation. From Foucault the professors learned that power and institutions saturate everything. Power is universal; complicity with power is universal, and this means university practices and malpractices are no better or worse than anything else. After decades of imported skepticism, critical theorists simply defend the facts of elitism and professionalism; the arguments turn tautological and circular. We do what we do; and we are who we are. The effort to deconstruct ideas and values leads to blessing the sociology of power.

With Stanley Fish, a leading Duke University English professor, this conclusion is spelled out. In the name of radical understanding the facts are heralded as the final understanding. Fish argued against the policy in academic journals of "blind submission." In evaluating articles for publication, professional journals send submissions to experts or "referees" for judgment; in order to eliminate or minimize bias, the author's name is removed. Inasmuch as the author is unknown, in principle equality is established. An article submitted by a new assistant professor at Nowheresville Community College will be judged in exactly the same manner as that by a Harvard chaired professor.

Fish objects. "Blind submission" assumes an essay can be judged on its "intrinsic merits"; it posits a neutral process of selection. This is a fiction; everything is biased and "political." For this reason who wrote an essay and what position this person holds in the profession are relevant. "Merit is inseparable from the structure of the profession and therefore the fact that someone occupies a certain position in that structure cannot be irrelevant to the assessment of what he or she produces." In other words, the sociology and the politics of the profession constitute the judgment of merit. The writings of chaired professors at major universities are obviously more valuable than writings by Professor Nobody at Nowhere

State. Why? Because they are chaired professors. Fish does not mince words. "I am against blind submission because the fact that my name is attached to an article greatly increases its chance of being accepted."[46]

The rank careerism would be difficult to surpass, which is hardly altered by Fish's commitment to left and liberal causes. Status and prestige within a profession determine the value of one's contribution, which is evaluated by one's status and prestige. Fish does not deplore, but praises this woeful situation. Like Culler, he easily uses the language of the market; and as with Culler, what first might appear as a denunciation is actually a celebration of intellectual marketing. To a small-fry critic complaining that Fish is swallowing the little guys, Fish retorts: Of course. Referring to Foucault and other French luminaries, Fish gives an elementary lesson in intellectual capitalism. Like anyone else, Fish sells his stuff.

> The truth is that professional capital, like any other, can only grow by being expended; professional critics must put their funds into circulation if they are to see them increase. In the case of this profession, circulation means (among other things) reading for journals and presses, writing recommendations, refereeing for presses and foundations, merchandising one's graduate students, recruiting for one's department, organizing conferences, appearing at conferences.[47]

Some are not as upbeat about this state of affairs. Terry Caesar is a professor at what he calls a "second-rate" university (Clarion University in Pennsylvania), where they teach a lot and publish little. He reflects on the elitism endemic to literary studies. The same scholars who attack hierarchy embrace it; the same professors who "deconstruct" and "decenter" structures of domination praise academic structures of domination. The leading journals print articles and letters from leading professors at leading schools. When Caesar engages an eminent theorist in conversation at a conference, he or she quickly loses interest upon learning where Caesar teaches.

Caesar served on a humanities committee with some luminaries from Yale and UCLA. They were to judge and fund candidates' proposals; institutional affiliations were supposed to be irrelevant. As Caesar learned quickly, this was not exactly the case. The institutional affiliation of the candidate mattered most. At one point Caesar argued for the proposal of a candidate from Bates College, a small liberal arts school. After all, the candidate had published several books. The UCLA professor would have none of it. First of all, Bates had no graduate school; second of all, Bates and its candidate were second-rate. "UCLA looked right at me . . . 'Put it this way. All right, he's got books. But if he were any good would he still be at Bates?' "

> I couldn't answer. I was speechless, silenced: everything rises that deserves to rise, because if it hasn't risen it hasn't deserved to . . . What's first-rate is finally and fatefully separable from what's second-rate, or else it wouldn't be first-rate.[48]

Gerald Graff's *Beyond the Culture Wars* is one of the first book-length replies to the conservative critics of higher education. Graff is well equipped for the role. He is an English professor who teaches at a major university; he has written several books about the state of literary criticism, and in recent years he has lectured widely about the canon and curriculum. He advocates "teaching the conflicts." The very disputes about the curriculum should inform the curriculum. Students must be brought into the debate as to what books and authors should be taught. An honest discussion about the controversy will draw students to the materials; they will begin to understand the issues that permeate reading and writing.

Beyond the Culture Wars evidences Graff's openness, good sense, and desire to engage an audience. From its first sentence, Graff shows a willingness to break with academic mandarinism. "The insularity of my department, my courses and my circle of professional contacts," he notes, has kept outsiders at bay. "The very organization of academic life works against [clarity]." His book is an effort to step out, correct the misconceptions, and offer some ideas. In many ways Graff is successful. His book is plainly written and argued. He makes a good case for enlarging the curriculum to include disputes about it.

Clarity is not the problem; and I will leave aside Graff's curriculum recommendations to consider his larger orientation. As a major public statement by a left literary critic, *Beyond the Culture Wars* is not marred but permeated by an ethos that it shares with much critical thought, academic boosterism. Graff shows himself as less a critic than a cheerleader of professional life. This is not a foible or weakness, but structures his argument and approach. Graff recommends the approach, words, and style of elite English professors as the cure for university ills.

Even as he gulps the fresh air, Graff repeats a familiar gripe: journalists and their readers cannot understand what academics are up to. "Few readers of the popular press are in a position to recognize misrepresentations of academic practices." Graff illustrates one misconception, what he calls "the myth of the vanishing classics," that circulates in newspapers. Graff states that this myth is "provably false," if only journalists took the trouble to check the evidence. As a case in point he cites a declaration that Alice Walker's novel *The Color Purple* is taught in more English courses than Shakespeare's plays.

Graff aptly shows that this sentence is quoted and requoted in the press, as if it were proof of something. No one checks the facts, as Graff will do, conclusively showing it is false. How does Graff do this? He canvasses the courses taught over several years in the English Department at Northwestern University, and finds that many more students read Shakespeare than Alice Walker.

Yet Graff is no more convincing than the journalists he decries. For starters, Graff uses "course description pamphlets," not actual syllabuses, to find out what titles are being read. These pamphlets are hardly reliable as a tally of titles. Produced by a department for prospective students, they may list books, but not all the books or the books for that particular semester. Moreover, when Graff states that he found "eight courses that required at least six plays by Shakespeare," we see the hand on the scale. Big English Departments have upper-level courses on Shakespeare, which English majors might take, but the issue really is what is taught in the introductory English classes, the only literature most students will get. Here Graff has nothing to say.

The real problem is what Graff omits: how relevant is the curriculum of Northwestern, an elite private school, for the curriculum of the rest of the United States? "The curriculum of students at elite colleges," to again cite Clifford Adelman, "is so different from that followed by the other 97% that it is irrelevant to discussions."[49] Even if this is overstated, some recognition of his privileged sample is necessary, but for Graff the whole world looks very much like the leafy suburb where Northwestern is located (and where Graff taught). "There is no reason to think Northwestern is exceptional," he states, when there is every reason. What's his proof? Duke University, where students are also reading Shakespeare.[50]

Whether Alice Walker is taught more than Shakespeare is probably beside the point. But Graff comes out firing; this allegation is "provably false." The journalists and conservative critics are sloppy and fail to check things out. Insider academics like Graff know what's up. He'll show lazy academy bashers what a real argument looks like. Here are the facts, but Graff has few facts; he is hardly persuasive.

The real concern of Graff lies elsewhere, advancing a curriculum that confronts conflicts. His argument rests on the model of elite English professors with their penchant for theoretical disputes. Some object to the ode to theory; Graff surmises that the "hostility" to theory is powerful because it is based on "resentment" and "anxieties" of modern life. "To those who have never reconciled themselves to the academization of literature," Graff writes, the obsession with theory seems like a betrayal of the common reader and literature. Graff has more than reconciled himself to "the academization of literature." He wants to spread it; he believes in it; he loves it.

Graff's enthusiasm is infectious: he loves everything about academia: jargon, colleagues, and conferences. These are his reference points. They are also his weakness, for his argument proceeds sociologically; it is circular and self-validating. We should teach students to talk, think, and write as we do. Why? Because this is what we do. We are professionals, major professors at major universities, and growing up means learning what adults like us do.

The truism parades its banality. Success is proof. Why should the academic status quo be elevated to a religion? Graff barely asks. As with Stanley Fish, the "discipline" determines what is to be thought or said. Students should be taught to join or at least follow what the "discipline" is doing. What is the discipline doing? It is doing what it is doing. A more conformist project could hardly be imagined.

Students must become aware of the "discourse community" and its "agenda of problems, issues and questions." Otherwise they will not know what to say or write. Even in choosing a paper topic, a student must have "a sense of what *other people* are saying, of what the state of the discussion is." One can almost hear Professor Graff reproaching a student, "No, no, don't do a paper on 'the idea of the soul in Emerson.' We don't do that any longer. The profession has moved on. We do gender now, and race and hierarchy."

Students also need "special help to produce a kind of literary-critical talk" or professional jargon. Why? Because the profession uses jargon as a useful "shorthand." "If I say 'We need to problematize that distinction,' it saves" a much wordier formulation. Moreover, academic jargon subverts bourgeois hegemony. "Often underlying such jargon, however, is a kind of alienation device like those employed by the playwright Bertold Brecht—a deliberate attempt to alienate readers from their normal expectations."

This is good. Brecht sought to block the identification of an audience with characters by making stage actions and utterances appear "strange" or "alien." This "new artistic principle" would lead audiences to historical awareness; they would understand the transience of bourgeois society and "the necessity and the possibility of remodelling society."[51] In academic writing, left professors use the same principle. The unsuspecting reader picks up an essay of criticism anticipating the graceful prose of Matthew Arnold or Alfred Kazin; instead he or she is assaulted by the blaring horns and backfiring of an academic roadster. Chastened, the reader draws back, understands bourgeois illusions and the need for socialist transformation.

If you believe this, you'll believe anything. Academic prose does not draw on the alienation effect but the love of alienation. Graff becomes lyrical about jargon, but his argument is always instrumental. We talk and write with jargon, and if you want to join the big time, you have to learn the codes and passwords. Graff is not shy; for all the chatter about "discourse" and "problematize" the bottom line is power and money and jobs. Like Culler, Fish, and other critical theorists, Graff embraces the intellectual market.

> The ability to . . . command the discourse about what texts and other social phenomena mean, to control what has come to be called "spin" —these are important forms of symbolic capital in a society where information is increasingly a key source of power. It seems time to come to terms with this fact . . . If we recognize that the control of spin can be an important issue in presidential elections, we should also be able to recognize that it is an issue in reading and teaching literature . . .

Nor does he stop with jargon, spin, and accumulating capital. Graff blesses the new scholarship. The usual complaint that scholarship is overspecialized and unreadable misses the point. Graff loves the stuff. Nowadays standard scholarship broaches big issues on gender or hierarchy, unlike the traditional scholarship. "To be sure, humanities research still *looks* as specialized as ever because its paradigm-shattering arguments are still couched in highly-specialized vocabularies." But a doctoral dissertation like "The Construction of Gender in the Later Romantic Lyric" is actually "broad, generalized, and ambitiously political."[52]

Finally, Graff loves academic conferences; and he hopes they can be replicated in undergraduate life.

> I would like to round off this discussion . . . by outlining an idea that is not yet in widespread use . . . This would be an adaption of the academic conference or symposium to the needs of the undergraduate curriculum. One often senses in the heightened atmosphere of today's professional conferences that the eagerness with which these events are attended stems from the fact that they are providing the kind of intellectual community that is sadly missing from the home campus . . .

Graff prescribes hustling conferences of upscale professors fleeing their campuses as the cure, not the disease. He confuses networking with teaching, back-scratching with scholarship, jargon with thinking. The scramble for self-advancement, not the crackle of thought, heats up the atmosphere at professional conferences.[53]

For most of the twentieth century, left-wing professors in the United States were a rare, if not endangered species. Small and homogeneous faculties were inhospitable to radicals. Typically American leftist intellectuals were writers and editors, not professors. Moreover, during national crises universities regularly purged the few radical professors. From the firing of Scott Nearing at the University of Pennsylvania in 1915 through McCarthyism in the 1950s, higher education sent its radical teachers packing.

With the expansion of the universities and a shift in political temperament in the 1960s, this changed. Only in a few fields, however, did a left achieve anything like a presence. What kind of presence? With what kind of impact? Conservatives have long attributed the unraveling of America to radical professors, and sometimes journalists and film people. The left professors agree with this exalted appreciation of their role. They see themselves as the cutting edge of the movement for social justice and reform. They do not take kindly to skepticism about their impact or genius. In *The Last Intellectuals* I raised some questions about the academization of intellectuals and their public profile. From *The New Republic* to *The Village Voice* and *New Left Review* leftist professors howled. "Look at me! Look at us!" they cried. "We're smart, hip, important, and influential!" I was accused of a class A felony in the criminal code of progressivism: nostalgia. For the new academics things only get better.

Some things do get better; and left academics do some of the pushing. The most successful new areas like Feminist and African-American Studies are a product of extra-campus movements, and in turn influence those movements, but that influence is difficult to define. The impact of academic radicals is most evident on campuses themselves. Black, feminist, gay, and Latino groups constitute political and intellectual campus realities that cannot be ignored.

Their strength is simultaneously their weakness; their causes become exclusively campus causes—curriculum, hiring, speech codes. If this makes sense, it also evidences a narrowing. David Bromwich recounts an incident at the Yale Law School. A white student was raped in New Haven by two black men; afterward black law students found racist messages in their mailboxes. From this emerged race-sensitivity workshops at Yale run by outside race consultants, which were backed by the administration and students, and a boycott of classes, as if the Law School itself were the assailant or guilty party. Bromwich comments:

> In the early sixties, law students like these, both black and white, would have seized any occasion to throw their weight on the liberal side of struggles in real communities, where people spend more than three years, where they are compelled to live and to die. But for such students now, the struggle they know what to do with takes place in a community exactly the size of a law school.[54]

Incessant leftist bleating and self-aggrandizement should not provoke a blanket dismissal. Over the last thirty years the accumulated activity of younger academics has renovated several disciplines; this is no mean accomplishment. Gary B. Nash, a UCLA history professor, remarks on the "wholesale changes" in history. A few decades ago, American history rarely went beyond political events and the happenings of a white male society. Now "African-American history, women's history, and labor history are taught in most colleges and universities." Other schools teach Asian-American, Native American, and Latino history. Nash notes that the *Harvard Guide to Afro-American History,* when completed, will list thousands of books, articles, and dissertations, "an enormous flowering of scholarship."[55]

Revitalized and enlarged scholarly fields enrich us all, but especially teachers and students. Of course, students do not remain students forever; and students have parents and friends. For these reasons new teachings make their way through society. The line dividing education and society blurs. Especially in secondary schooling, the new scholarship causes waves as it leads to revised textbooks.[56]

The charge that left professors are narrowly engaged with their disciplines and campuses can be convincingly answered by pointing to the millions of students who take courses, passing on to other stations in life. Many left professors justify their politics by their students and teaching. The impact of teaching, however, remains incalculable. Moreover, the most prominent left professors work at the best schools, where teaching is minimal.

The bulk of teaching proceeds at the much maligned "second-rate" universities and the community colleges. If teaching is the object, why not teach at these schools? Many liberals and leftists do; we infrequently hear from them, since they have little time to publish and explain themselves. The others, who teach at elite schools, do not address teaching at a popular institution as a political choice. On occasion, a leftist pities himself, suffering the "contradiction" of teaching a few elite students about mass suffering. "Poor me," laments Louis Kampf, an MIT English professor, "I have a nifty little job at a big famous place, but I feel depressed . . . For years I've written articles telling people that universities are . . . the ideological servants of the ruling elites." No need to worry. As Professor Struggle explains, after wine and a pasta dinner he felt better.[57]

A larger public knows, or doesn't know, of radical professors because of their writings, which include more than scholarly articles and monographs; they encompass textbooks, opinion pieces, and sometimes films and popular books. It would be wrong to dismiss this collective oeuvre; through Feminist Studies, social history, Latino and African-American Departments, and revised canons it percolates throughout higher education and society. On the other hand, one need not be a doomsayer to wonder about the quality of the scholarly writing—its pretentiousness, cynicism, jargon, elitism, and cheerleading—and the dearth of public writing.

Early in the century William James pondered the role of colleges and the college-educated; he could not be very precise. Colleges should have something to do with producing better individuals, cultivating a certain tone, and aiding democracy. He feared colleges were failing on these scores; and he wondered if the popular and literary magazines of the day, the so-called ten-cent magazines, were taking up the slack. "It would be a pity," he wrote in 1908,

> if any future historian were to have to write words like these: "By the middle of the twentieth century the higher institutions of learning had lost all influence over public opinion in the United States. But the mission of raising the tone of democracy, which they had proved so lamentably unfitted to exert, was assumed with rare enthusiasm . . . by a new educational power . . . private literary adventures, commonly designated in the market by the affectionate name of ten-cent magazines."[58]

7

CONCLUSION: LOW-TECH

EUROPEANS MISTAKENLY BELIEVE, wrote Benjamin Rush in 1786, that the American Revolution is over. "This is so far from being the case that we have only finished the first act of the great drama." What else is on the agenda? Something much more difficult than defeating armies: transforming "our principles, opinions and manners." This transformation requires the "knowledge and virtue" that only education provides. "Let our common people be compelled by law to give their children (what is commonly called) a good English education . . . Let us have colleges in each of the states, and one federal university under the patronage of Congress."[1]

The new American government not only entertained creating a federal or national university, as Rush proposed, but in the 1780s began setting aside land that would be sold to support higher education. This effort crested with the 1862 Land-Grant or Morrill Act; for each congressional representative the federal government earmarked 30,000 acres that would be sold for the benefit of a state university. As Morrill put it, "The bill proposed to establish at least one college in every state . . . accessible to all."[2]

From the Universities of Arizona, California, and Connecticut to those of Massachusetts, Vermont, West Virginia, Wisconsin, and Wyoming, sixty-nine of America's leading universities were founded or developed on this basis. Moreover, Congress passed and President Lincoln signed this act "during one of the darkest hours of the Civil War." To one historian it represented "an embodiment of the whole democratic dream." Another called it "a remarkable example of forward-looking legislation in the midst of calamity."[3]

Nowadays calamities thwart forward-looking legislation. For decades the commitment and confidence that infused American educators have been ebbing. Cries of collapse mislead, however; there is no collapse. Higher education in particular and education in general proceed along a track they have been on. That is the problem. Everywhere the tickets are getting pricier; the lines, at some stations, longer; the gates higher; and the frustrations deeper.

The density of problems explodes conventional schemas of blame. Who is responsible for high school students who work at outside jobs? Or proliferating preprofessional illiberal courses in colleges? Or the jump in tuition? Or intensifying campus enmities? No single group can be charged. Yet complexity is not another word for fate; it does not mean that nothing or no one is responsible. Society deploys resources that convey messages. Columbia University closed its geography and linguistics programs at the same time that it built a multimillion-dollar new Center for Engineering and Physical Science Research. Isn't this a comment about the humanities?

Across the nation the byword is "cutbacks": fewer teachers, courses, and funds. I visited East Los Angeles Community College, a vibrant and busy place with a Latino and Asian-American student body. Unlike some community colleges, the school is not tucked away in a reclaimed airport, but sits amid the community; local and sometimes national politicians stop by to give speeches and to be seen on campus. However, increasingly thousands of students cannot enroll in the courses they want and need, and they cannot afford to go elsewhere. "What do you think happens to the students we turn away?" asked an administrator. She answered her own question. "They end up in the streets, and then in jail. It would be cheaper to expand the college than the jails."

The obvious turns elusive. Over the centuries the greatest advances in public health have been relatively simple, democratic, and "low-tech": clean water, vaccinations, decent food, sanitary disposal of waste. It is tempting to view education in a similar light. A thousand studies and ten thousand reports and what is necessary is nothing fancy: decent classrooms, good libraries, devoted teachers, small classes, committed students, low tuition. If these were in place, hostilities over schooling, curriculum, affirmative action, racism, and free speech would shrink; pools of acrimony would drain away.

These are not in place. If anything, the simplicities seem further and further out of reach. The physical plant decays; teachers are distracted; classes too large; resources too little; costs too high; students angry. As America moves toward a new century, how is it we can no longer provide these essentials? In a five-year period Americans bought 51 million microwave ovens, 85 million color televisions, 48 million VCRs, and 23 million cordless telephones, all for an adult population of 180 million. We have 4 billion square feet of land devoted to shopping malls, about 16 square feet for every individual.[4] Yet we are no longer able even to maintain safe and sound classrooms. In the 1990s the simple realities of past education appear more and more utopian. This might stand as a comment for a society that many dub postmodern, its inability to provide the basics of a premodern society.

Conservatives want us to return to old educational verities, and leftists to advance to new ones. Both may be right. Yet both ignore the ingression of the market that makes a mockery of a return or advance; both avoid the commercialism that constricts a liberal education; both sidestep the invidious elitism that poisons civil life. Too often the controversy on education settles on secondary, not primary issues. Heated arguments unfold about which books should be taught or what language offends what group; but few books are taught—and fewer read—and the general din overpowers all language.

Secondary issues are not fraudulent, but they displace more fundamental realities. Arguments over the curriculum or canon easily substitute for more pressing problems of classes too large or resources too scanty; they bypass the obvious, the widespread demise of a curriculum. Disputes over free speech and correct language shift attention from an unraveling social fabric to talking about talk and monitoring psyches. Oddly, both conservatives and leftists prefer this terrain, which may testify to an inescapable psychologizing of American society. As society turns opaque and ill, we obsessively check our psychological health. As education sickens, we keep tabs on self-esteem.

Multiculturalism, tolerance, and relativism can hardly be considered diversionary topics. Nor are they the same. The great figures in European tolerance despised autocratic power and injustice. They were hardly relativists in the popular sense; they used the facts of social diversity to fight against despotism. Their vigorous defense of tolerance is much more than an edifying tale from the past; the lesson of the three rings must be continuously taught to a world more practiced in fratricide than fraternity.

However, multiculturalism is a box that contains too many items. The superiority of history textbooks and literary anthologies that represent more voices and peoples can hardly be doubted; this is indubitably true for primary and secondary schooling. Yet in higher education multiculturalism takes on another meaning. Where there is no common curriculum, additional studies spell more choices but also separate studies. Women study women; African-Americans study African-Americans; Latinos study Latinos. This not only lends itself to a new provincialism; it feeds a separatism that is turning prickly and hostile. At the end of multiculturalism a primitivism returns, thinking by blood, race, and sex.

Perhaps the campus battles over multiculturalism also mislead, for the many "cultures" in the United States are not so different, and the differences are probably diminishing. Though academic multiculturalists do not acknowledge it, the point is not especially abstruse. Few can or even want to escape the American cultural steamroller. For instance, an extensive survey of Hispanic social, political, and economic beliefs discovered that "a driving commitment to be part of American society shapes attitudes among Hispanic groups more than a sense of ethnic identity."[5]

This is hardly an argument against Latino or Chicano Studies. Nor is it proof that we live in a homogeneous universe. In campus settings, however, cultural differences get magnified and fetishized. Cultural labels easily substitute for rethinking an identity threatened by modernization; individuals instantly gain a label and a cause. Moreover, as with correct speech, academic legitimation of cultural identity consoles for the injustices that some groups have suffered.

In the end, however, educational conflicts would ebb if the instructional infrastructure were solid and secure, which is far from the case. Today society cannot even provide the cultural space and quiet essential for learning. Anyone who teaches knows that outside a classroom one jackhammer, or just one lawn mower, drowns talk and reflection. A liberal education, wrote Leo Strauss, "consists in learning to listen to still and small voices."[6] Like the other simplicities, however, the leisure and cultural room necessary to listen is increasingly rare, if not obsolete; the space crumples under the barrage of money, pressing needs, and even violence and arms. We are all too busy, preoccupied, worried, and afraid.

Once upon a time, to even mention learning and guns in a single sentence would jar. No longer. In 1992, teachers and authorities confiscated almost 400 guns in Los Angeles schools alone, including 33 in elementary school.[7] In the first months of 1993, two students were killed by other students in class. Nor is the violence confined to urban high schools. Gun-packing students have killed students and professors in Massachusetts and Iowa colleges.[8] A safe school, once an assumption beyond discussion, has become a program for the future.

A worsening situation spurs an elite—chosen and self-chosen—to redouble efforts to gain access to the few educational oases. This accelerates the free fall of the rest of the system. As the most ambitious, moneyed, and talented depart, they abandon public education and the bulk of higher education to their own, diminishing resources. The democratic promise of education, always a partial tease, turns cruel and mocking. All the ills of society—the violence, economic injustices, and inequalities—cannot be foisted on education. If it is to mean anything, however, a liberal education cannot forget these ills as it remembers itself.

NOTES

Preface

1. "Means and Objects of Common-School Education," in *Life and Works of Horace Mann,* vol. 2: *Educational Writings of Horace Mann* (Boston: Lee & Shepard, 1891), pp. 83–84.

2. Henry Louis Gates, Jr., *Loose Canons* (New York: Oxford University Press, 1993), p. 19.

3. The first organized freshman orientation seems to have been at the University of Maine in 1923; see Henry J. Doermann, *The Orientation of College Freshman* (Baltimore: Williams & Wilkins, 1926), pp. 101–2; "New Greetings for Freshman as Life and Campus Change," New York *Times,* August 28, 1991, p. A1.

4. "Politically Correct" [editorial], *The Wall Street Journal,* November 26, 1990, p. A10.

5. Hilton Kramer, "Notes and Comments," *New Criterion,* November 1991, p. 2.

6. Thomas B. Edsall and Mary D. Edsall, *Chain Reaction: The Impact of Race, Rights and Taxes on American Politics* (New York: Norton, 1991), p. 286.

7. Jonathan Kozol, *Savage Inequalities* (New York: HarperCollins, 1992), p. 202.

8. Mark Edmundson, "The Academy Writes Back," in *Wild Orchids and Trotsky: Messages from American Universities,* ed. M. Edmundson (New York: Penguin, 1993), p. 6.

9. Judith Frank, "In the Waiting Room," in *Wild Orchids and Trotsky,* p. 148.

10. Noah Webster, "On the Education of Youth in America" [1790], in *Essays on Education in the Early Republic,* ed. Frederick Rudolph (Cambridge: Harvard University Press, 1965), p. 45.

11. Russell Jacoby, "General Education Is Antistudent, Antiknowledge," *Chicago Maroon,* January 14, 1964, p. 6.

Several paragraphs in the following chapters have been taken from my previous writings on education, mainly from "The Lost Intellectual: Relativism and the American Mind," *New Perspectives Quarterly,* Winter 1988, and "The Greening of the University," *Dissent,* Spring 1991.

CHAPTER 1   Office Management 101

1. Andrew Carnegie, *The Empire of Business* (New York: Harper & Brothers, 1906), p. 80.
2. Cited in and see David O. Levine, *The American College and the Culture of Aspiration, 1915–1940* (Ithaca: Cornell University Press, 1986), pp. 137–40.
3. U.S. Department of Education, National Center for Educational Statistics, *The Condition of Education, 1991,* vol. 2: *Postsecondary Education* (Washington, D.C., 1991), pp. 12, 62.
4. Henry Adams, *The Education of Henry Adams* (New York: Modern Library, 1931), pp. 305–6.
5. "Report of the Committee of Nine," cited in Richard Hofstadter, *Anti-Intellectualism in American Life* (New York: Vintage, 1963), p. 334.
6. U.S. Department of the Interior, Bureau of Education, *Cardinal Principles of Secondary Education* (Washington, D.C.: Government Printing Office, 1918), pp. 30, 13.
7. David Snedden, "Progress Towards Sociologically Based Civic Education," *Journal of Educational Sociology,* 3 (1930): 482–83; Walter H. Drost, *David Snedden and Education for Social Efficiency* (Madison: University of Wisconsin Press, 1967), pp. 114–15; Herbert M. Kliebard, *Forging the American Curriculum* (New York: Routledge, 1992), pp. 44–46. For an overview of "life adjustment" at the end of the 1940s, see Federal Security Agency, Office of Education, *Vitalizing Secondary Education* (Washington, D.C.: Government Printing Office, 1951), and *Education for Life Adjustment,* ed. H. R. Douglass (New York: Ronald Press, 1950).
8. Hofstadter, *Anti-Intellectualism,* p. 341; Lawrence A. Cremin, *American Education: The Metropolitan Experience, 1876–1980* (New York: Harper & Row, 1988), p. 546.
9. Loren Baritz, *The Good Life: The Meaning of Success for the American Middle Class* (New York: Harper & Row, 1990), p. 220; "Crisis in Education," *Life,* March 24, 1958, pp. 25–33.
10. U.S. Congress, Senate, *Science and Education for National Defense,* Hearings before the Committee on Labor and Public Welfare, 85th Congress, Second Session, January 1958, p. 2; Landon Y. Jones, *Great Expectations: America and the Baby Boom Generation* (New York: Ballantine, 1981), pp. 61–62; and see, generally, Barbara B. Clowse, *Brainpower for the Cold War: The Sputnik Crisis and National Defense Act of 1958* (Westport, Conn.: Greenwood Press, 1981).
11. Abraham Flexner, *Universities: American English German* [1930], intro. Clark Kerr (New York: Oxford University Press, 1968), pp. 55, 44.
12. Irving Babbitt, *Spanish Character and Other Essays* (Boston: Houghton Mifflin, 1940), pp. 217–28; I. Babbitt, "English and the Discipline of Ideas"

[1920], In *Representative Writings*, ed. George A. Panichas (Lincoln: University of Nebraska Press, 1981), p. 63. For a general overview that includes chapters on Flexner and Babbitt, see Michael R. Harris, *Five Counterrevolutionists in Higher Education* (Corvallis: Oregon State University Press, 1970).

13. Irving Babbitt, "President Eliot and American Education" [1929], in *Spanish Character and Other Essays*, pp. 217–18, 222, 216. See Bernd Lüking, *Der amerikanische "New Humanism"* (Frankfurt am Main: Peter Lang, 1975), and J. David Hoeveler, Jr., *The New Humanism: A Critique of Modern America* (Charlottesville: University Press of Virginia, 1977), esp. pp. 81–124.

14. Allan Bloom, *The Closing of the American Mind* (New York: Simon & Schuster, 1987), pp. 338, 341.

15. *The Common-Sense Guide to American Colleges 1991–1992*, ed. Charles Horner, P. Pyott, and S. B. Loux (Lanham, Md.: Madison Books, 1991), p. 241.

16. Dinesh D'Souza, *Illiberal Education: The Politics of Race and Sex on Campus* (New York: The Free Press, 1991).

17. Flexner, *Universities*, p. 179.

18. Michael B. Paulsen, "Curriculum Change at Liberal Arts Colleges," *Liberal Education*, 76/2 (1990): 2.

19. Eric L. Dey, Alexander W. Astin, and William S. Korn, *The American Freshman: Twenty-five-Year Trends* (Los Angeles: Higher Education Research Institute, UCLA, 1991), p. 27. In the last several years, business majors have registered small declines.

20. "Earned Degrees Conferred by U.S. Institutions, 1990–91," *Chronicle of Higher Education*, June 2, 1993, p. A25. These mark small changes from previous years; see *Digest of Educational Statistics, 1991*, National Center for Educational Statistics, U.S. Department of Education, Washington, D.C., 1991, table 235.

21. Clifford Adelman, *Tourists in Our Own Land: Cultural Literacies and the College Curriculum* (Washington, D.C.: U.S. Department of Education, 1992), pp. 23–24, 29–30.

22. "Humanities Not a Major to Bank On," Los Angeles *Times*, March 17, 1988, p. 1.

23. Michael A. Russo, "Perspectives: Communications, an Undergraduate Major for the Liberal Arts, *Liberal Education*, 75/4 (September–October 1989): 40.

24. Matthew Arnold, *Culture and Anarchy*, ed. J. Dover Wilson (Cambridge, Eng.: Cambridge University Press, 1963), pp. 62, 51.

25. Raymond Williams, *Culture and Society 1780–1950* (Garden City, N.Y.: Anchor Books, 1960), pp. 120–21.

26. J. S. Mill, "Civilization" [1836], in *Collected Works of John Stuart Mill*, vol. 18, ed. J. M. Robson (Toronto: University of Toronto Press, 1977), pp. 138–43.

27. W. E. B. Du Bois, *The Souls of Black Folk*, in *Three Negro Classics*, intro. J. H. Franklin (New York: Avon, 1965), pp. 241, 268, 269–70. See Arnold

Rampersad, *The Art and Imagination of W. E. B. Du Bois* (New York: Schocken, 1990), pp. 68–90.

28. W. E. B. Du Bois, "Does Education Pay?" [1891], in *Writings by W. E. B. Du Bois in Periodicals Edited by Others*, ed. H. Aptheker, vol. 1: *1891–1909* (Milwood, N.Y.: Kraus-Thomson, 1982), pp. 6–7.

29. Adelman, *Tourists in Our Own Land*, pp. 24, vi.

30. U.S. Department of the Interior, *Cardinal Principles of Secondary Education*, p. 15.

31. Sebastian de Grazia, *Of Time, Work and Leisure* (New York: Twentieth Century Fund, 1962), p. 7.

32. Josef Pieper, *Leisure: The Basis of Culture*, trans. A. Dru (New York: New American Library, 1963), p. 20.

33. Bruce A. Kimball, *Orators and Philosophers: A History of the Idea of Liberal Education* (New York: Teachers College Press, 1986), p. 13.

34. Cicero, "Discussions at Tusculum (V)," in Cicero, *On the Good Life,* ed. M. Grant (London: Penguin, 1987), p. 56.

35. Here I am following Kimball, *Orators and Philosophers*, pp. 229–32.

36. John Henry Cardinal Newman, *The Idea of a University*, ed. M. J. Svaglic (Notre Dame: University of Notre Dame, 1982), pp. 115–16.

37. Ibid., pp. 124–26.

38. "Inaugural Address Delivered to the University of St. Andrew" [1867], in J. S. Mill, *Essays on Equality, Law and Education*, ed. J. M. Robson (Toronto: University of Toronto Press, 1984), p. 218.

39. A. Dwight Culler, *The Imperial Intellect: A Study of Newman's Educational Ideal* (New Haven: Yale University Press, 1955), pp. 156–70, 225–26.

40. Scott Thomson, "How Much Do Americans Value Schooling?" *NASSP* [National Association of Secondary School Principals] *Bulletin,* October 1989, pp. 56–57.

41. Thomas Toch, *In the Name of Excellence: The Struggle to Reform the Nation's Schools, and Why It's Failing, and What Should Be Done* (New York: Oxford University Press, 1991), p. 241. See the illuminating study by Ellen Greenberger and Laurence Steinberg, *When Teenagers Work: The Psychological and Social Costs of Adolescent Employment* (New York: Basic Books, 1986).

42. Juliet B. Schor, *The Overworked American* (New York: Basic Books, 1993), pp. 25–27.

43. "Too Old, Too Fast?" *Newsweek,* November 16, 1992, pp. 80–88.

44. De Grazia, *Of Time, Work and Leisure,* p. 327. See Witold Rybczynski's engaging reflections on leisure and society, *Waiting for the Weekend* (New York: Penguin, 1992), esp. pp. 210–26.

45. *Student Fees, Access, and Quality: Prospects and Issues for the 1992–93 Budget Process,* California Postsecondary Education Commission, p. 19; Arthur Hauptman, "Thoughts on State Financing of Higher Education," *Policy Perspectives* (Pew Higher Education Research Program), 4/2 (March 1992): 8B.

16. Division of Student Academic Services, *Annual Student Profile. 1990-91*, p. 6.

47. Institute for the Study of Social Change, *The Diversity Project: Final Report* (Berkeley: University Printing, 1991), p. 3.

48. A. Bartlett Giamatti, *A Free and Ordered Space: The Real World of the University* (New York: Norton, 1988), pp. 18–20.

49. Andrew Ross cited in Anne Matthews, "Deciphering Victorian Underwear and Other Seminars," *New York Times Magazine*, February 10, 1991, p. 58.

50. Benjamin deMott, *The Imperial Middle* (New York: Morrow, 1990), p. 13.

51. Adelman, *Tourists in Our Own Land*, p. 31. A "raree show" was a traveling exhibit carried from town to town in a box, a sort of peep show.

52. *Mission College Catalog 1992–1993*, p. 2. Jane Patton, "The Cultural Pluralism Program at Mission College," unpublished.

53. Steven Brint and Jerome Karabel, *The Diverted Dream: Community Colleges and the Promise of Educational Opportunity in America, 1900–1985* (New York: Oxford University Press, 1989), p. 6.

54. To confuse matters, they are also called universities, although none have their own doctorate programs. Collectively they are known as California State University in contrast to the University of California.

55. I offer more thoughts in Chapter 5.

CHAPTER 2   The Free Speech Movement, Part Two

1. Hal Draper, *Berkeley: The New Student Revolt* (New York: Grove Press, 1965), p. 43.

2. "The History of a Student Revolt," in *The Berkeley Student Revolt*, ed. Seymour Martin Lipset and Sheldon S. Wolin (Garden City, N.Y.: Anchor Books, 1965), p. 122.

3. Wolin, "Introduction," ibid., p. xii.

4. John Searle, "The Faculty Resolution," in *Revolution at Berkeley*, ed. Michael V. Miller and Susan Gilmore (New York: Dell, 1965), p. 94.

5. "The FSM Speaks," in *Berkeley Student Revolt*, pp. 201, 204–5; Sidney Hook, "Second Thoughts on Berkeley," in *Revolution at Berkeley*, p. 126.

6. Draper, *Berkeley*, p. 13; Mario Savio, "An End of History," in *Revolution at Berkeley*, p. 239.

7. Paul Jacobs and Saul Landau, *The New Radicals* (New York: Vintage, 1966), p. 63.

8. Michael Novak, "The Larger Context: Thought Police," *Forbes*, October 1, 1990, p. 212.

9. Stanley Fish, "There's No Such Thing as Free Speech and It's a Good Thing, Too," in *Debating P.C.: The Controversy over Political Correctness on College Campuses*, ed. Paul Berman (New York: Dell/Laurel, 1992), pp. 231; Catherine A. MacKinnon, *Feminism Unmodified* (Cambridge: Harvard University Press, 1987), pp. 138–39; Felice Yeskel, "Campuses Out of the Closet," *Against the Current*, March–April 1992, p. 39.

10. Justice Scalia, *"R.A.V. v. City of St. Paul,"* *Daily Appellate Report,* June 23, 1992, p. 8398; Professor Lawrence quoted in "Campus 'Hate Speech' Codes in Doubt," *Chronicle of Higher Education,* July 1, 1992, p. A22.

11. All quotes from R. Emmett Tyrrell, Jr., "PC People," *The American Spectator,* May 1991, pp. 8–9.

12. Ellen W. Schrecker, *No Ivory Tower: McCarthyism and the Universities* (New York: Oxford University Press, 1986), p. 174.

13. Robert Justin Goldstein, *Political Repression in Modern America* (Cambridge, Mass.: Schenkman, 1978), p. 376; David Caute, *The Great Fear: The Anti-Communist Purge under Truman and Eisenhower* (New York: Simon & Schuster, 1978), p. 406.

14. Diane Ravitch, *The Troubled Crusade: American Education, 1945–1980* (New York: Basic Books, 1983), p. 101.

15. Allan Bloom, *The Closing of the American Mind* (New York: Simon & Schuster, 1987), p. 324. See also John P. Roche, "Was Everyone Terrified? The Mythology of 'McCarthyism,' " *Academic Questions,* 2/2 (Spring 1989): 64–79. Roche does not go so far as Bloom, but contests the impact of McCarthyism.

16. Paul F. Lazarsfeld and Wagner Thielens, Jr., *The Academic Mind: Social Scientists in a Time of Crisis* (Glencoe, Ill.: Free Press, 1958), pp. 37.

17. Ibid., pp. 69–71; see, generally, Lionel S. Lewis, *Cold War on Campus: A Study of the Politics of Organizational Control* (New Brunswick, N.J.: Transaction Books, 1988), pp. 22–23. Robert M. MacIver, *Academic Freedom in Our Time* (New York: Columbia University Press, 1955), p. 21.

18. See Schrecker, *No Ivory Tower,* pp. 292–93; "Sir Moses I. Finley" [obituary], New York *Times,* July 11, 1986, p. D18.

19. The conservative journal *Heterodoxy* offers a case: an assistant professor of sociology discharged from Dallas Baptist University because of "transgressing feminist orthodoxy." See David John Ayers, "My Days and Nights in the Academic Wilderness," *Heterodoxy,* 1/8 (January 1993): 1.

20. Jane Sanders, *Cold War on the Campus: Academic Freedom at the University of Washington, 1946–64* (Seattle: University of Washington Press, 1979), pp. 96–97.

21. See Julius Lester, "Academic Freedom and the Black Intellectual," and W. E. B. Du Bois Department of Afro-American Studies, "Don't Believe the Hype: Chronicle of a Mugging by the Media," both in *Black Scholar,* 19/6 (November–December, 1988): 17–43.

22. "Taking Offense," *Newsweek,* December 24, 1990, p. 48.

23. Paul Selvin, "The Raging Bull of Berkeley," *Science,* 251 (January 25, 1991): 371. Some of these actions happened after the *Newsweek* report.

24. Evan Gahr, "Political Correctness," *National Catholic Reporter,* April 5, 1991, p. 4.

25. Charles J. Sykes and Brad Miner, "Sense and Sensitivity," *National Review,* March 18, 1991, p. 31.

26. " 'Politically Incorrect' Complain of Ostracism," *Observer* (Case Western Reserve University), April 26, 1991, p. 1.

27. My account is drawn from "The Education of Dr. Alan Gribben," Dallas

Morning News, June 17, 1991, p. 1C; "Professor Leaves In the Wake of Course Debate," Austin *American-Statesman,* May 30, 1991, p. A1; Gregory Curtis, "Behind the Lines," *Texas Monthly,* May 1990, pp. 5–6.

28. Peter Collier, "Incorrect English: The Case of Alan Gribben," *Heterodoxy,* 1/2 (May 1992): 9.

29. Ibid., p. 9.

30. R. Emmett Tyrrell, Jr., "A Bizarre Province: Preliminary Findings for *The American Spectator*'s Amnesty in Academia Campaign," *The American Spectator,* November 1991, pp. 16–18.

31. Edward Hoagland, "Fear and Learning in Vermont," New York *Times,* June 15, 1991, p. L23; "Bennington Essayist Ran Afoul of the Campus 'Thought Police,' " Boston *Globe,* July 11, 1991, p. 57; "Faculty Personnel Review Committee: Findings and Recommendations: Edward Hoagland Academic Freedom Grievance" (unpublished, undated); Robert Stone (PEN) to Elizabeth Coleman (President, Bennington), June 26, 1991 (copy).

32. James Sellers [letter], *The Wall Street Journal,* December 17, 1990, p. A9.

33. Robert Miner, "War in Heaven or War Against the West: The Controversy in the Rice Department of Religious Studies," *Rice Sentinel,* April 1991, pp. 8–11; and letters by Sellers to RJ, November 20, 1991; May 30, 1992.

34. Tyrrell, "A Bizarre Province," pp. 16–18.

35. All information from Ken Fireman, " 'Political Correctness' in Dispute," *Newsday,* May 12, 1991, p. 34, and David Beers, "PC? B.S.," *Mother Jones,* September–October 1991, pp. 35, 64.

36. Jon Wiener, "What Happened at Harvard," *The Nation,* September 30, 1991, pp. 384–88.

37. For another case of a student blocked from attending a class, see Gerard Arthus, "First Muzzled, Then Jailed: The Trials of a Student Who Dared to Challenge His Professor," in *Academic License: The War on Academic Freedom,* ed. Les Csorba III (Evanston: UCA Books, 1988), pp. 189–95. This case has ended in a lawsuit; the school refuses to comment.

38. All my information is drawn from the account by Terry Tang, " 'Women 200,' " *Seattle Weekly,* April 6, 1988, pp. 29–33.

39. All information from Jon Wiener, " 'Rape by Innuendo' at Swarthmore," *The Nation,* January 20, 1992, pp. 44–47.

40. Nat Hentoff, "The ACLU and Mr. Hyde," Washington *Post,* March 23, 1991.

41. David Markowitz, Press Alert, American Council on Education, March 28, 1991.

42. Lionel S. Lewis and Philip G. Altbach, "Political Correctness, Campus Malaise," *Times Higher Education Supplement,* February 28, 1992.

43. Bloom, *The Closing of the American Mind,* pp. 313–14.

44. Dietrich Orlow, *The History of the Nazi Party: 1933–1945* (Pittsburgh: University of Pittsburgh Press, 1973), p. 164.

45. On the takeover of a building by black students at Cornell, see *Divided We Stand: Reflections on the Crisis at Cornell,* ed. Cushing Strout and David I. Grossvogel (Garden City, N.Y.: Doubleday, 1970).

46. Dinesh D'Souza, *Illiberal Education: The Politics of Race and Sex on Campus* (New York Free Press, 1991), p. 217.

47. At least according to his notes, Tocqueville picked up the idea of the "tyranny of the majority" from the American Jared Sparks. Yet Sparks seems to have thought of this "tyranny" solely in governmental terms: the majority might oppress the minority by passing laws. See Alexis de Tocqueville, *Oeuvres Complètes,* ed. J.-P. Mayer, vol. 5 (Paris: Gallimard, 1957), p. 96. Moreover, Sparks later criticized Tocqueville on exactly this point. ". . . Tocqueville often confounds the majority with public opinion . . ." Sparks to William Smyth, October 13, 1841, cited in Herbert B. Adams, *Jared Sparks and Alexis de Tocqueville* (Baltimore: Johns Hopkins University Press, 1898), pp. 43–44.

48. Mill, *On Liberty,* pp. 63, 73, 135. See John C. Rees, *John Stuart Mill's "On Liberty"* (Oxford: Oxford University Press, 1985), pp. 75–87.

49. Benjamin R. Barber, *An Aristocracy of Everyone* (New York: Ballantine, 1992), p. 83.

50. Daniel Pipes, *The Rushdie Affair: The Novel, the Ayatollah, and the West* (New York: Birch Lane/Carol Publishing, 1990), pp. 109–10. Rushdie is cited by Pipes.

51. Timothy Garton Ash, *The Uses of Adversity: Essays on the Fate of Central Europe* (New York: Vintage, 1990), p. 117.

52. See Craig R. Smith, *Freedom of Expression and Partisan Politics* (Columbia: University of South Carolina Press, 1989), pp. 87–117, for an argument that federal monitoring of the content of electronic media is an obsolete and confused project.

53. "The Tennessee Anti-Evolution Act," cited in *D-Days at Dayton: Reflections on the Scopes Trial,* ed. Jerry R. Tompkins (Baton Rouge: Louisiana State University Press, 1965), p. 3.

54. Nat Hentoff, *The First Freedom: The Tumultuous History of Free Speech in America* (New York: Delacorte, 1980), pp. 3–54.

55. Scott Henson, "The Education of Dinesh D'Souza," *Texas Observer,* September 20, 1991, pp. 6–9; Louis Menand, review of *Illiberal Education, New Yorker,* May 20, 1991, pp. 101–7; Dinesh D'Souza, *Falwell: Before the Millennium* (Chicago: Regnery Gateway, 1984), pp. 112–13; Jerry Falwell cited in Carol Flake, *Redemptorama: Culture, Politics and the New Evangelicalism* (New York: Penguin, 1985), pp. 45–46.

56. Cited in and see Frances FitzGerald, *Cities on a Hill* (New York: Simon & Schuster, 1986), p. 160.

57. My sources for this are "Liberty University Questions Freedom of Religion," *Equinox,* September 6, 1991, p. 17; "Liberty Expels Students for Religious Beliefs," *U: The National College Newspaper,* February 1992, p. 6; and "Jerry Falwell Statement Regarding United Pentecostal Church, Lynchburg, Virginia," press release, Jerry Falwell Ministries, September 16, 1991. The figure on federal and state financial aid to Liberty comes from "Falwell's College Alters Mission to Keep It Alive," New York *Times,* August 19, 1992, p. A14.

58. Falwell cited in "U.S. Supreme Court," *Newsletter on Intellectual Freedom,*

May 1988, pp. 95–96; Jerry Falwell, *Listen, America!* (Garden City, N.Y.: Doubleday, 1980), pp. 205–6.

59. William F. Buckley, Jr., *God and Man at Yale: The Superstitions of "Academic Freedom"* (Chicago: Regnery, 1951), pp. 182–83, 190.

60. Roger Kimball, *Tenured Radicals* (New York: Harper & Row, 1990), pp. xiv, xviii.

61. Cited in and see Milton Mayer, "The Red Room," *Massachusetts Review,* 16 (1975): 520–50.

62. "Clash at U. of C," Chicago *Daily Tribune,* May 14, 1935, p. 1; " 'Red' Teachings Told by Niece of Walgreen's," Chicago *Daily Tribune,* May 25, 1935, p. 1.

63. One odd note: Walgreen later had a change of heart and became a university benefactor. See Mary Ann Dzuback, *Robert M. Hutchins* (Chicago: University of Chicago Press, 1991), pp. 163–66.

64. See *The American Small Businessman* by John H. Bunzel (New York: Knopf, 1962), pp. 236–37.

65. "A Declaration," *Educational Reviewer,* 1/1 (July 15, 1949): 1; and the *Reviewer*'s editor, Lucille C. Crain, "What Is Taught Your Children," *Educational Reviewer,* 2/2 (October 15, 1950): 1.

66. Ben W. Palmer, review of *Roots of Political Behavior,* ed. R. C. Synder and H. W. Wilson, *Educational Reviewer,* 2/2 (October 15, 1950): 4.

67. Felix Wittmer, *Conquest of the American Mind: Comments on Collectivism in Education* (Boston: Meador, 1956), pp. 37–38.

68. Colin Clark cited in E. Merrill Root, *Collectivism on the Campus: The Battle for the Mind in American Colleges* (New York: Devin-Adair, 1955), p. 6.

69. Root, *Collectivism on the Campus,* pp. 369–70.

70. Norma and Mel Gabler, of Educational Research Analysts, cited in People for the American Way, "The Texas Connection: Countering the Textbook Censorship Crusade," in *The First Freedom Today,* ed. Robert B. Downs and Ralph E. McCoy (Chicago: American Library Association, 1984), p. 95. See the introduction (pp. 1–15) to People for the American Way, *Attacks on the Freedom to Learn: 1990–1991 Report* (Washington, D.C.: People for the American Way, 1991). This organization publishes an annual list of "attacks on the freedom to learn." "Recent efforts to remove or restrict access to school library or instructional materials have been most associated with politically conservative or fundamentalist religious views." Henry Reichman, *Censorship and Selection: Issues and Answers for Schools* (Chicago: American Library Association, 1988), p. 27.

71. American Library Association, "Some People Consider These Books Dangerous," pp. 5, 36.

72. Richard M. Weaver, *Ideas Have Consequences* (Chicago: University of Chicago Press, 1948).

73. National Rifle Association, advertisement, "While Time Warner Counts Its Money, America May Count Its Murdered Cops" (various newspapers); NRA, news release, "NRA Blasts Ice-T, Time Warner Music," June 11,

1992; Chuck Philips, "The Uncivil War," Los Angeles *Times,* July 19, 1992, Calendar, p. 77.

74. Cited in and see *Rebel Voices: An I.W.W. Anthology,* ed. J. L. Kornbluh (Ann Arbor: University of Michigan Press, 1964), pp. 94–95.

75. Nat Hentoff, " 'Speech Codes' on the Campus," *Dissent,* Fall 1991, p. 546.

76. "A Preliminary Report on Freedom of Expression and Campus Harassment Codes," *Academe,* May–June 1991, and "On Freedom of Expression and Campus Speech Codes," *Academe,* July–August 1992.

CHAPTER 3   Say the Right Thing

1. Horace E. Scudder, *Noah Webster* (Boston: Houghton Mifflin, 1882), p. 213.

2. J. Witherspoon, "The Druid" [1781], reprinted in *The Beginnings of American English,* ed. M. M. Mathews (Chicago: University of Chicago Press, 1931), pp. 17–18.

3. Webster to Canfield, January 6, 1783, in *Letters of Noah Webster,* ed. Harry R. Warfel (New York: Library Publishers, 1953), p. 4.

4. The speller assumed the name *The American Spelling Book* only in a later edition. See, generally, E. Jennifer Monaghan, *A Common Heritage: Noah Webster's Blue-Back Speller* (Hamden, Conn.: Archon Books, 1983). *The American Spelling Book* cited in Richard J. Moss, *Noah Webster* (Boston: Twayne, 1984), p. 29.

5. Noah Webster, *Dissertations on the English Language* [1789] (Menston, Eng.: Scolar Press, 1967), p. 20.

6. Ibid., pp. 106–7.

7. Ibid., pp. 25–27.

8. Ibid., p. 397.

9. See Brian Weinstein, "Noah Webster and the Diffusion of Linguistic Innovations for Political Purposes," *International Journal for the Sociology of Language,* 38 (1982): 85–108. Moss, *Noah Webster,* p. 7.

10. Dennis E. Baron, *Grammar and Good Taste: Reforming the American Language* (New Haven: Yale University Press, 1982), p. 239. See also John Ayto, "English: Failures of Language Reforms," in *Language Reform,* vol. 1, pp. 85–100 (see note 75 below).

11. H. L. Mencken, *The American Language,* 4th ed. (New York: Knopf, 1962), pp. 388–89.

12. See James Milory and Lesley Milroy, *Authority in Language: Investigating Prescription and Standardisation* (London: Routledge, 1985); John Wesley Young, *Totalitarian Language: Orwell's Newspeak and Its Nazi and Communist Antecedents* (Charlottesville: University Press of Virginia, 1991), p. 228.

13. All cited in Allen Walker Read, "Words Indicating Social Status in America in the Eighteenth Century," *American Speech,* 9 (1934): 207; Albert Matthews, "Hired Man and Help," *Transactions: Colonial Society of Massachusetts,* 5 (1897–98): 250–51; Mencken, *Supplement I,* pp. 580–81; Lucy

Maynard Salmon, *Domestic Service* [1097] (New York: Arno Press, 1977),
pp. 59, 55. See also Kenneth Cmiel, *Democratic Eloquence* (Berkeley: University of California Press, 1990), p. 41; *Dictionary of American English on
Historical Principles,* ed. William A. Craigie, vol. 2 (Chicago: University of
Chicago Press, 1940), pp. 1250–51.

14. Lowell to Briggs, February 18, 1848, in *Letters of James Russell Lowell,* ed.
C. E. Norton (New York: Harper & Row, 1894), p. 105. See Martin
Duberman, *James Russell Lowell* (Boston: Houghton Mifflin, 1966),
pp. 72–80.

15. Patricia J. Williams, *The Alchemy of Race and Rights* (Cambridge: Harvard
University Press, 1991), p. 20.

16. James Fenimore Cooper, *The American Democrat,* ed. G. Dekker and L.
Johnston (New York: Penguin, 1989), pp. 173–77.

17. Keith Allan and Kate Burridge, *Euphemism and Dysphemism* (New York:
Oxford University Press, 1991), p. 13. For a generally positive view of
euphemisms, see *Fair of Speech: The Uses of Euphemism,* ed. D. J. Enright
(New York: Oxford University Press, 1985).

18. "Politics and the English Language," in George Orwell, *A Collection of
Essays* (New York: Harcourt Brace Jovanovich, 1953), pp. 166–67; "As I
Please" [March 17, 1944], in Orwell, *The Collected Essays, Journalism and
Letters,* vol. 3 (Harmondsworth: Penguin, 1970), ed. S. Orwell and I.
Angus, p. 133. For a critical assessment of Orwell's analysis of language, see
W. F. Bolton, *The Language of 1984: Orwell's English and Ours* (Oxford:
Basil Blackwell, 1984), esp. pp. 188–224.

19. "On Being an American," in H. L. Mencken, *Prejudices: A Selection,* ed.
J. T. Farrell (New York: Vintage, n.d.), pp. 117–18.

20. Nathaniel Hawthorne, *Our Old Home* (Boston: Houghton Mifflin, 1907),
p. 140.

21. Mencken, *The American Language,* 4th ed., pp. 284–94; *Supplement I,*
pp. 580, 565–95.

22. W. L. George, *Hail, Columbia!* (London: Chapman & Hall, 1923), p. 95.
George also tackled the "servant problem." They are in "a queer state of
mind . . . They . . . seem to suffer under a sense of intolerable grievance
because they are servants. They seem to think that to serve is to lose
caste . . ." (p. 169).

23. Citations from Albert H. Marckwardt, *American English* (New York: Oxford University Press, 1958), pp. 114–16, and Thomas Pyles, *Words and
Ways of American English* (New York: Random House, 1952), pp. 134–37.

24. Some of these are taken from the compendium of craziness, Henry Beard
and Christopher Cerf, *The Officially Politically Correct Dictionary and
Handbook* (New York: Villard, 1992), pp. 24, 58.

25. Rosalie Maggio, *The Bias-Free Word Finder: A Dictionary of Nondiscrimi-
natory Language* (Boston: Beacon, 1992), p. 154.

26. Kim Mizrahi and Patricia Rozee, *Guide to Inclusive Language: Suggestions
for Improved Communications* (California State University Long Beach:
President's Advisory Commission on the Status of Women, 1991), p. 7.

27. Maggio, *The Bias-Free Word Finder,* pp. 31, 241–42.

208   *Notes*

28. Ambrose Bierce, *The Devil's Dictionary* [1911] (New York: Dover, 1958), pp. 56, 88.
29. P. Neilson [1830] cited in Matthews, "Hired Man and Help," p. 251.
30. Salmon, *Domestic Service*, p. 157.
31. *The Simplified Letter* (Philadelphia: National Office Management Association, n.d., perhaps 1956), unpaged.
32. Allan and Burridge, *Euphemism and Dysphemism*, p. 197.
33. Cited in Dwight Bolinger, *Language: The Loaded Weapon* (London: Longman, 1980), p. 130.
34. Maggio, *The Bias-Free Word Finder*, pp. 202, 258; Casey Miller and Kate Swift, *The Handbook of Nonsexist Writing*, 2nd ed. (New York: Harper & Row, 1988), p. 160.
35. "Bias Concerns in Test Development," in *Assessing Basic Academic Skills in Higher Education: The Texas Approach,* ed. Richard T. Alpert, W. P. Gorth, and R. G. Allan (Hillsdale, N.J.: Lawrence Erlbaum, 1989), p. 181. As a booklet, this chapter has been widely distributed, and itself draws upon university and publishers' guides to "bias-free" test material and publishing.
36. Howard J. Ehrlich, *Campus Ethnoviolence: A Research Review,* Institute Report no. 5 (Baltimore: National Institute Against Prejudice and Violence, 1992), p. 7.
37. John H. Bunzel, *Race Relations on Campus: Stanford Students Speak* (Stanford: Stanford Alumni Association, 1992), pp. 25–34, and Sally Cole, "Beyond Recruitment and Retention: The Stanford Experience," in *The Racial Crisis in American Higher Education,* ed. P. A. Altbach and K. Lomotey (Albany: State University of New York Press, 1991), pp. 218–29.
38. Violent racial collisions on campus usually include drinking, fraternities, and nonstudents. See Jon C. Dalton, "Racial and Ethnic Backlash in College Peer Culture," in *Racism on Campus,* ed. Jon C. Dalton [San Francisco: Jossey-Bass, 1991], p. 6.
39. Charles R. Lawrence III, "If He Hollers Let Him Go: Regulating Racist Speech on Campus," *Duke Law Journal,* 1990 (1990): 473.
40. Unless otherwise noted, references in this and the following paragraph are drawn from Lawrence, "If He Hollers Let Him Go"; Mari J. Matsuda, "Public Response to Racist Speech: Considering the Victim's Story," *Michigan Law Review,* 87 (August 1989): 2320–81; Mari J. Matsuda, "Language as Violence v. Freedom of Expression," *Buffalo Law Review,* 37 (1988–89): 359–64; Richard Delgado, "Words That Wound: A Tort Action for Racial Insults, Epithets, and Name-Calling," *Harvard Civil Rights–Civil Liberties Law Review,* 17 (1982): 133–81; Richard Delgado, "Campus Antiracism Rules: Constitutional Narratives in Collision," *Northwestern University Law Review,* 85 (1991): 343–87.
41. ACLU's Robert Sedler cited in Holly Metz, "Bad Apples, Evil Deeds," *Student Lawyer,* February 1990, p. 37; and see Nadine Strossen, "Regulating Racist Speech on Campus: A Modest Proposal?" *Duke Law Journal,* 1990 (1990): 557–58.

42. Randall L. Kennedy, "Racial Critiques of Legal Academia," *Harvard Law Review,* 102 (June 1989): 1780.

43. G. Jiyun Lee, "Racism Comes in All Colors: The Anti-Korean Boycott in Flatbush," *Reconstruction,* 1/3 (1991): 72.

44. Nat Hentoff, *Free Speech for Me—But Not for Thee* (New York: HarperCollins, 1992), p. 170.

45. Catherine A. MacKinnon, *Feminism Unmodified: Discourses on Life and Law* (Cambridge: Harvard University Press, 1987), pp. 201, 208–9, 155–56.

46. See "Lust Horizons" and "Nature's Revenge," in Ellen Willis, *No More Nice Girls: Countercultural Essays* (Middletown, Conn.: Wesleyan University Press, 1992), pp. 3–18.

47. Judge F. Easterbrook cited in and see Chapter 29 in Edward de Grazia, *Girls Lean Back Everywhere: The Law of Obscenity and the Assault on Genius* (New York: Vintage, 1993), pp. 577–621.

48. "Furor on Exhibit at Law School Splits Feminists," New York *Times,* November 13, 1992, p. B12.

49. Daniel Y. Nah, "Assaulted by PC," *Daily Bruin,* January 6, 1992, p. 10.

50. Bunzel, *Race Relations on Campus,* p. 68.

51. Harold R. Isaacs, *Idols of the Tribe* (Cambridge: Harvard University Press, 1989), p. 87.

52. Results of survey, author Sandra Cisneros, and co-author of the survey, Rodolfo de la Garza, all cited in "What's the Problem with 'Hispanic'? Just Ask a 'Latino,'" New York *Times,* November 15, 1992, p. E6.

53. John Leo, "Racism on American College Campuses," *U.S. News & World Report,* January 8, 1990, p. 53. According to Leo, the report offers three dozen offensive remarks; in his count, only five are racially stereotyped or prejudiced.

54. Ehrlich, *Campus Ethnoviolence,* pp. 8–10; Howard J. Ehrlich, Fred L. Pincus, and Cornel Morton, *Ethnoviolence on Campus: The UMBC Study,* Institute Report no. 2, October 1987 (Baltimore: National Institute Against Prejudice and Violence), p. 5.

55. Bunzel, *Race Relations on Campus,* pp. 39–42.

56. Ehrlich, Pincus, and Morton, *Ethnoviolence on Campus,* p. 11.

57. The figure of 150,000 for 1960 is from *Minorities on Campus,* ed. M. F. Green (Washington, D.C.: American Council on Education, 1989), p. 1. No source is given. Reliable numbers of blacks in higher education before the 1970s are difficult to nail down. Some ideas can be gleaned from the historical statistics on "school enrollment, by Age, Race and Sex," but this does not distinguish between secondary and postsecondary schooling; see U.S. Bureau of the Census, *Historical Statistics of the United States,* Part II: Colonial Times to 1970, Bicentennial Edition, pp. 370–71. On increases of blacks in predominantly white schools, see Alan Colón, "Race Relations on Campus," in *The Racial Crisis in American Higher Education,* ed. Altbach and Lomotey, pp. 69–88; David Karen, "The Politics of Class, Race and Gender: Access to Higher Education in the United States, 1960–1986," *American Journal of Education,* 99 (February 1991): 208–37.

58. G. D. Jaynes and R. M. Williams, Jr., *A Common Destiny: Blacks and American Society* (Washington, D.C.: National Academy Press, 1989), pp. 338–40.

59. Lowell cited in Stephen Steinberg, *The Academic Melting Pot* (New York: McGraw-Hill, 1974), pp. 22–23.

60. Mary F. Berry and John W. Blassingame, *Long Memory: The Black Experience in America* (New York: Oxford University Press, 1982), pp. 286–87.

61. Figures from U.S. Bureau of the Census, *Historical Statistics of the United States,* Part II, pp. 716–19.

62. Seymour Martin Lipset and David Riesman, *Education and Politics at Harvard* (New York: McGraw-Hill, 1975), p. 146.

63. "Massachusetts Campus Is Torn by Racial Strife," New York *Times,* October 18, 1991, p. 8.

64. Walter C. Farrell, Jr., and Cloyzelle K. Jones, "Recent Racial Incidents in Higher Education," *Urban Review,* 20 (1988): 215.

65. V. A. C. Gatrell, "The Decline of Theft and Violence in Victorian and Edwardian England," in *Crime and the Law: The Social History of Crime in Western Europe Since 1500,* ed. V. A. C. Gatrell et al. (London: Europa Publications, 1980), p. 243.

66. *R.A.V., Petitioner* v. *City of St. Paul,* 90-7675 (U.S. Supreme Court, June 22, 1992).

67. Matsuda, "Public Responses to Racist Speech," pp. 2336–38.

68. Donald Meyer, *The Positive Thinkers* (Garden City, N.Y.: Anchor/Doubleday, 1966), p. 148.

69. "Interview with John Vasconcellos," *Esteem,* 4/3 (June 1990): 14.

70. See, generally, Andrew M. Mecca et al., *The Social Importance of Self-Esteem* (Berkeley: University of California Press, 1989); this book surveys the findings in many fields. In his introduction Neil J. Smelser states, "One of the disappointing aspects of every chapter in this volume . . . is how low the associations between self-esteem and its consequences are in research to date" (p. 15).

71. Surveying the education literature on self-esteem and achievement in *The Social Importance of Self-Esteem,* Martin V. Covington notes the "low magnitude of association" (p. 79).

72. Harold W. Stevenson and James W. Stigler, *The Learning Gap: Why Our Schools Are Failing and What We Can Learn from Japanese and Chinese Education* (New York: Summit, 1992), p. 128; Harold W. Stevenson, "Learning from Asian Schools," *Scientific American,* December 1992, pp. 71–72.

73. Educational Testing Service, *A World of Difference: An International Assessment of Mathematics and Science* (Princeton: ETS, 1989), pp. 10, 14, 24; *Learning Mathematics* (Princeton: ETS, 1992), table 1, pp. 66–68. The results of the latter study are not strictly comparable to the previous study inasmuch as in the results the question on being "good at mathematics" was grouped with several other attitude questions.

74. David Halberstam, *The Next Century* (New York: Avon, 1992), p. 160.

75. See, generally, Louis-Jean Calvet, *La Guerre des langues et les politiques*

linguistiques (Paris: Payot, 1987), and the five-volume collection *Language Reform/La Réforme des langues/Sprachreform,* ed. I. Fodor and C. Hagège (Hamburg: Buske Verlag, 1983–   ). For a classification of "language planning," see Robert L. Cooper, *Language Planning and Social Change* (New York: Cambridge University Press, 1989), esp. pp. 122–56. Brian Weinstein in *The Civic Tongue: Political Consequences of Language Choices* (New York: Longman, 1983) emphasizes the political and deliberate aspect of language formation and shifts.

76. Johnson cited in Paul Fussell, *Samuel Johnson and the Life of Writing* (New York: Norton, 1986), p. 215. Webster, in a undated manuscript, quoted in K. Alan Snyder, *Defining Noah Webster* (Lanham, Md.: University Press of America, 1990), p. 37.

CHAPTER 4   Fabulous, Foreign, and Dead

1. *The Autobiography of Lincoln Steffens* (New York: Harcourt, Brace, 1931), p. 111.

2. See Verne A. Stadtman, *The University of California 1868–1968* (New York: McGraw-Hill, 1970).

3. Gerald Graff, *Professing Literature: An Institutional History* (Chicago: University of Chicago Press, 1989) and see, generally, Burton J. Bledstein, *The Culture of Professionalism: The Middle Class and the Development of Higher Education in America* (New York: Norton, 1976), esp. pp. 287–300.

4. For a discussion of the piece and context, see Irvin Ehrenpreis, *Swift: The Man, His Work, and the Age,* vol. 1 (Cambridge: Harvard University Press, 1962), pp. 226–37. However, Ehrenpreis sees Swift's contribution to the dispute as more aesthetic than substantial.

5. Jakob Burckhardt, *The Civilization of the Renaissance in Italy* (New York: Modern Library, 1954), p. 128. Of course, Burckhardt's formulations are dated. Yet even as Hans Baron criticizes Burckhardt he offers formulations not very distant from the Swiss historian; see Hans Baron, *In Search of Florentine Civic Humanism,* vol. 2 (Princeton: Princeton University Press, 1988), pp. 32–33, 155–81.

6. Miriam Kosh Starkman, *Swift's Satire on Learning in "A Tale of a Tub"* (Princeton: Princeton University Press, 1950), p. 3.

7. Aeneae Silvii, *De Liberorum Educatione,* trans. and intro. Joel S. Nelson (Washington, D.C.: Catholic University of America Press, 1940), pp. 187–89. Eight years later, Aeneas himself wrote a history of Bohemia.

8. Eugen Weber, *Peasants into Frenchmen* (Stanford: Stanford University Press, 1976), p. 333.

9. Otto von Bismarck, cited in and see Konrad H. Jarausch, *Students, Society and Politics in Imperial Germany* (Princeton: Princeton University Press, 1982), p. 218.

10. See Theodore C. Smith, *The Life and Letters of James Abram Garfield,* vol 2: *1877–1882* (New Haven: Yale University Press, 1925), pp. 777–820.

Historians of education attribute to him an aphorism about the president of Williams College, where Garfield went to school. "The ideal college is Mark Hopkins on one end of a log and a student on the other." For Hopkins, see Frederick Rudolph, *Mark Hopkins and the Log: Williams College, 1836–1872* (New Haven: Yale University Press, 1956); for these aphorisms of Garfield, see pp. 225–27.

11. Garfield, "College Education: Address Before the Literary Societies of the Eclectic Institute, Hiram, O., June 14, 1867," in B. A. Hinsdale, *President Garfield and Education* (Boston: James R. Osgood & Co., 1882), pp. 289–91, 300–1.

12. "Observations upon the Study of the Latin and Greek Languages," in Benjamin Rush, *Essays, Literary, Moral and Philosophical* (Philadelphia: Thomas and William Bradford, 1806), p. 25.

13. See "To Friends of the Federal Government: A Plan for a Federal University" (October 29, 1788), in *Letters of Benjamin Rush*, ed. L. H. Butterfield, vol. 1: *1761–1792* (Princeton: Princeton University Press, 1951), pp. 492–93.

14. Jefferson to George Ticknor, July 16, 1823, in *The Writings of Thomas Jefferson*, ed. H. A. Washington, vol. 7 (New York: John C. Riker, 1857), pp. 300–1.

15. Cited in and see David B. Tyack, *George Ticknor and the Boston Brahmins* (Cambridge: Harvard University Press, 1967), pp. 111–13.

16. Francis Wayland cited in Walter C. Bronson, *The History of Brown University 1764–1914* (Providence: Brown University, 1914), p. 266.

17. Philip Dorf, *The Builder: A Biography of Ezra Cornell* (New York: Macmillan, 1952), p. 288. The statement was put on the university seal. In fact, Andrew D. White, Cornell's first president, backed off from a complete elective system; see Glenn C. Altschuler, *Andrew D. White—Educator, Historian, Diplomat* (Ithaca: Cornell University Press, 1979), pp. 69–74; Andrew D. White, *Autobiography,* vol. 1 (New York: Century Co., 1905), pp. 360–76.

18. "What Is Liberal Education?" (1884), in *Charles W. Eliot: The Man and His Beliefs,* ed. William Allan Neilson, vol. 1 (New York: Harper & Brothers, 1926), pp. 43–44.

19. Ibid., pp. 45–47, 65.

20. "Emerson" (1903), in *Charles W. Eliot: The Man and his Beliefs,* vol. 2, p. 517.

21. "The Freedom to Choose" (1906), in ibid., pp. 544–45.

22. Henry James, *Charles W. Eliot,* vol. 1 (Boston: Houghton Mifflin, 1930), p. 209.

23. Samuel Eliot Morison, *Three Centuries of Harvard 1636–1936* (Cambridge: Harvard University Press, 1936), pp. 344–45.

24. Hugh Hawkins, *Between Harvard and America: The Educational Leadership of Charles W. Eliot* (New York: Oxford University Press, 1972), p. 96.

25. Harold Stearns, *The Confessions of a Harvard Man* [retitled reprint of *The Street I Know,* 1935] (Sutton West: Paget Press, 1984), pp. 63, 69.

26. Claude M. Fuess, *The College Board: Its First Fifty Years* (New York: Columbia University Press, 1950), p. 3.

27. Helen L. Horowitz, *Campus Life* (Chicago: University of Chicago Press, 1987), pp. 101–2.

28. Paul Fanlund, "A School That Does Without," New York *Times,* "Education Life," January 10, 1993, p. 19.

29. Michael Tulley and Roger Farr, "Textbook Evaluation and Selection," in *Textbooks and Schooling in the United States,* ed. David L. Elliott and Arthur Woodward (Chicago: University of Chicago Press, 1990), pp. 164–65.

30. See Caroline Cody, "The Politics of Textbook Publishing, Adoption and Use," in *Textbooks and Schooling,* pp. 127–45.

31. For an older discussion, but still pertinent, see Frances FitzGerald, *America Revised: History Schoolbooks in the Twentieth Century* (New York: Vintage, 1980).

32. On the California controversy on K–6 textbooks, see Robert Reinhold, "Class Struggle," *New York Times Magazine,* September 29, 1991, pp. 26 ff.

33. Lawrence A. Cremin, *Popular Education and Its Discontents* (New York: Harper & Row, 1990), p. 19. Cremin qualifies this statement: "except for a few highly select institutions."

34. Laurie L. Lewis and Elizabeth Farris, *Undergraduate General Education and Humanities Requirements* (Higher Education Survey Reports, no. 7, January 1989), pp. 3–5.

35. Herbert Lindenberger, "On the Sacrality of Readings Lists: The Western Culture Debate at Stanford University," in his *The History in Literature* (New York: Columbia University Press, 1990), pp. 156–57; *Stanford University Bulletin: Courses and Degrees 1991–1992,* pp. 348–50; Daniel Gordon, "Inside the Stanford Mind," *Perspectives* (AHA newsletter), 30/4 (April 1992): p. 1–8; "Program in Culture, Ideas and Values: Required Readings 1990–1991," Stanford University; "Better Late Than Never: Text of CUS Compromise as Adopted," *Campus Report,* April 6, 1988, p. 8; *Approaching Stanford* (information bulletin for incoming freshmen), pp. 60–66.

36. "Virtually all institutions . . . require students to take freshman composition . . ." Bettina J. Huber and David Laurence, "Report on the 1984–85 Survey of the English Sample: General Education Requirements in English and the English Major," *ADE Bulletin,* 93 (Fall 1989): 31.

37. Mike Rose, *Lives on the Boundary: The Struggles and Achievements of America's Underprepared* (New York: Free Press, 1989), pp. 198–99.

38. Janice Gohm Webster, "Composition Courses: No Experience Necessary?" *ADE Bulletin,* 93 (Fall 1989): 41.

39. George F. Will, "Radical English" (1990), reprinted in *Debating P.C.,* ed. Paul Berman (New York: Laurel/Dell, 1992), p. 261.

40. Linda Brodkey, "Contingent Pedagogy and Exigent Publicity," unpublished paper, delivered MLA, December 1991, San Francisco.

41. Linda Brodkey, telephone interview, February 28, 1992.

42. Linda Brodkey, "Tentative Syllabus for English 306 and Table of Contents for the English 306 Course Pack," University of Texas, Austin, November 15, 1990.

43. Edward Berenson, "Beyond Multiculturalism" *Contentions,* 2/1 (Fall 1992): 52.

44. Frederick Rudolph, *Curriculum: A History of the American Undergraduate Course of Study Since 1636* (San Francisco: Jossey-Bass, 1977), p. 6. Since catalog descriptions are the easiest way to tabulate curriculum changes, many scholars first contend that they are unsatisfactory, and then with this caveat use them. For instance, J. B. Lon Hefferlin states, "Catalog copy is not always a reliable reflection of reality" (*Dynamics of Academic Reform* [San Francisco: Jossey-Bass, 1969], p. 205). However, he guesses that "catalog description of the courses" would eventually reflect "course reforms."

45. See "General Report of the Committee on Academic Freedom and Academic Tenure (1915)," as well as William W. Van Alstyne, "Academic Freedom and the First Amendment in the Supreme Court of the United States," and David M. Rabban, "A Functional Analysis of 'Individual' and 'Institutional' Academic Freedom under the First Amendment," all in *Law and Contemporary Problems,* 53/3 (Summer 1990): 393–406; 79–154; 227–303; and Walter P. Metzger, *Academic Freedom in the Age of the University* (New York: Columbia University Press, 1955), pp. 112–17.

46. Martin Kaplan, "The Wrong Solution to the Right Problem," in *In Opposition to Core Curriculum,* ed. James W. Hall (Westport, Conn.: Greenwood Press, 1982), p. 9.

47. Hazen Foundation 1968 report on higher education, cited in Ernest L. Boyer and Martin Kaplan, *Educating for Survival* (n.p: Change Magazine Press, 1977), p. 55.

48. Lionel Trilling, "The Uncertain Future of the Humanistic Educational Ideal," in *What Is an Educated Person,* ed. Martin Kaplan (New York: Praeger, 1980), p. 46.

49. Rudolph, *Curriculum,* p. 259.

50. George W. Bonham, "Toward One Human Experience," in *The Great Core Curriculum Debate* (New Rochelle, N.Y.: Change Magazine Press, 1979), p. 4.

51. Barry O'Connell, "Where Does Harvard Lead Us?" in *The Great Core Curriculum Debate* p. 29.

52. Ernst L. Boyer, *College: The Undergraduate Experience in America* (New York: Harper & Row, 1987), pp. 88–89.

53. From the *Western Review* of Cincinnati, 1820, cited in R. Freeman Butts, *The College Charts Its Course: Historical Conceptions and Current Proposals* (New York: McGraw-Hill, 1939), p. 11.

54. Irving Babbitt, *Literature and the American College: Essays in Defense of the Humanities* (Boston: Houghton Mifflin, 1908), p. 84.

55. Dinesh D'Souza, "The Legacy of Leo Strauss," *Policy Review,* Spring 1987, p. 36.

56. Allan Bloom, "Leo Strauss: September 20, 1899–October 18, 1973," *Political Theory,* 2/4 (November 1974): 372, 387.

57. Leo Strauss, *Liberalism Ancient and Modern*, foreword by Allan Bloom (Ithaca: Cornell University Press, 1968), p. 3.

58. Allan Bloom, *The Closing of the American Mind* (New York: Simon & Schuster, 1987), p. 344.

59. Edward H. Cotton, *The Life of Charles W. Eliot* (Boston: Small, Maynard, 1926), p. 277.

60. See Hugh Hawkins, *Between Harvard and America: The Educational Leadership of Charles W. Eliot* (New York: Oxford University Press, 1972), pp. 292–96.

61. *Fifteen Minutes a Day: The Reading Guide. The Harvard Classics*, ed. Charles W. Eliot (New York: P. F. Collier & Son, 1930), pp. 23, 63.

62. John Erskine, *The Memory of Certain Persons* (New York: Lippincott, 1947), pp. 341–43. See Daniel Bell, *The Reforming of General Education* (New York: Columbia University Press, 1966), pp. 13–14. For a discussion of Erskine and his ideas, see Joan Shelley Rubin, *The Making of Middlebrow Culture* (Chapel Hill: University of North Carolina Press, 1992), pp. 148–97.

63. Mortimer J. Adler, *Philosopher at Large: An Intellectual Autobiography* (New York: Macmillan, 1977), p. 25.

64. Ibid., p. 61.

65. Ibid., pp. 128–29; Harry S. Ashmore, *Unseasonable Truths: The Life of Robert Maynard Hutchins* (Boston: Little, Brown, 1989), pp. 86–87.

66. Adler, *Philosopher at Large*, p. 229.

67. James Sloan Allen, *The Romance of Commerce and Culture: Capitalism, Modernism and the Chicago-Aspen Crusade for Cultural Reform* (Chicago: University of Chicago Press, 1983), p. 106. See Allen's excellent chapter "Great Books and Cultural Reform," pp. 78–109.

68. Sidney Hyman, *The Lives of William Benton* (Chicago: University of Chicago Press, 1969), p. 247.

69. Herman Kogan, *The Great EB: The Story of the Encyclopaedia Britannica* (Chicago: University of Chicago Press, 1958), pp. 82, 105.

70. For this and other details of the economics of the Sears/EB connection, see Boris Emmet and John E. Jeuck, *Catalogues and Counters: A History of Sears, Roebuck and Company* (Chicago: University of Chicago Press, 1950), pp. 443–46.

71. James M. Wells, *The Circle of Knowledge* (Chicago: Newberry Library, 1968), p. 22.

72. Adler cited in Hyman, *Benton*, p. 287.

73. Adler, *Philosopher at Large*, p. 25.

74. *Fifteen Minutes a Day*, p. 17. Adler, *Philosopher at Large*, pp. 239–49.

75. Quoted in Hyman, *Benton*, p. 494.

76. "The Principles and Methods of Syntopical Construction," *The Great Ideas: A Syntopicon of Great Books of the Western World*, vol. 2 (Chicago: Encyclopaedia Britannica, 1952), pp. 1225–26.

77. Hyman, *Benton*, pp. 391–92.

78. Benton cited in Rubin, *Making of Middlebrow Culture*, p. 196.

79. Container Corporation of America, Catalog, *Great Ideas of Western Man*,

Traveling Exhibition (n.p., n.d.); and see, generally, Allen, *Romance of Commerce and Culture,* pp. 213–14.

80. Peggy Clifford, *To Aspen and Back: An American Journey* (New York: St. Martin's Press, 1980), p. 21.

81. Allen, *Romance of Commerce and Culture,* pp. 214–21.

82. "Appendix II: The Principles and Methods of Syntopical Construction," *The Great Ideas: A Syntopicon of Great Books of the Western World,* vol. 2, ed. Mortimer J. Adler (Chicago: Encyclopaedia Britannica, 1952), pp. 1221, 1299.

83. "The Idea of Equality," in *The Great Ideas Today 1968,* ed. R. M. Hutchins and M. Adler (Chicago: Encyclopaedia Britannica, 1968), p. 303.

84. All quotes from "The Book-of-the-Millennium Club" [1952], in Dwight Macdonald, *Against the American Grain* (New York: Vintage, 1965), pp. 243–61.

CHAPTER 5   Three Rings: Relativism, Relatives, and Wandering Yams

1. Black Hair as Culture and History was offered at Stanford; see the "The Cutting Edge of Multiculturalism" *The Wall Street Journal,* July 29, 1992.

2. Paul Johnson, *Modern Times* (New York: Harper & Row, 1983), p. 11.

3. *The Times* of London cited in Ronald W. Clark, *Einstein: The Life and Times* (New York: Avon, 1984), p. 297.

4. Eric Chaisson, *Relatively Speaking: Relativity, Black Holes and the Fate of the Universe* (New York: Norton, 1988), p. 59.

5. Cited in Clark, *Einstein,* p. 298.

6. S. Freud, *Civilization and Its Discontents,* in Pelican Freud Library, ed. J. Strachey, vol. 12 (Middlesex, Eng.: Penguin, 1985), p. 291.

7. Philip Rieff, *Freud: The Mind of the Moralist* (Garden City, N.Y.: Doubleday, 1961).

8. Modris Eksteins, *Rites of Spring: The Great War and the Birth of the Modern Age* (New York: Doubleday/Anchor, 1990), p. 258.

9. Janet Flanner cited in Phyllis Rose, *Jazz Cleopatra: Josephine Baker in Her Time* (New York: Doubleday, 1989), p. 31. Two earthshaking points: as Rose indicates (p. 274), thirty years after the event Flanner revised her original remarks; and the banana skirt did not appear in the 1925 "Revue Négre" but later in the Folies-Bergère.

10. Hitler, "The Cultural Renascence" [1937], in *Nazi Culture,* ed. G. L. Mosse (New York: Schocken, 1981), p. 12.

11. "Intolerance," in *Encyclopaedia of the Social Sciences,* vol. 8 (New York: Macmillan, 1932), p. 244.

12. Herodotus, *The Histories,* bk. iii/38–39, ed. A. R. Burns (New York: Penguin, 1972), pp. 219–20. See J. A. S. Evans, *Herodotus: Explorer of the Past* (Princeton: Princeton University Press, 1991), pp. 24–26, 140–42.

13. Plato, "Protagoras," *The Collected Dialogues of Plato,* ed. E. Hamilton and H. Cairns (New York: Pantheon, 1966), p. 309.

14. "The term 'sophist (*sophistēs*)' was not originally a term of abuse," writes a

historian of Greek philosophy. "When Herodotus calls Solon and Pythagoras sophists (I.29; IV.95) he is praising them as sages and men of wisdom (*sophia*) . . ." Jonathan Barnes, *The Presocratic Philosophers,* vol. 2: *Empedocles to Democritus* (London: Routledge & Kegan Paul, 1979), p. 146.

15. G. S. Kirk, J. E. Raven and M. Schofield, *The Presocratic Philosophers,* 2nd ed. (Cambridge, Eng.: Cambridge University Press, 1983), pp. 168–69; Kathleen Freeman, *The Pre-Socratic Philosophers* (Oxford: Basil Blackwell, 1966), pp. 93–97; Jonathan Barnes, *The Presocratic Philosophers* (London: Routledge & Kegan Paul, 1982), pp. 140–43.

16. Plato, "Theaetetus," *Collected Dialogues,* pp. 856–57. For a defense of Protagoras and relativism, see Joseph Margolis, *The Truth About Relativism* (Cambridge, Mass.: Basil Blackwell, 1991). Margolis considers Protagoras "the philosopher of the flux (of a profoundly changing world, not a chaos) and of the analysis of the nature and conditions of knowledge confined to that" (p. 82).

17. G. W. F. Hegel, *Hegel's Lectures on the History of Philosophy,* trans. E. S. Haldane and Frances H. Simson, vol. 1 (London: Routledge and Kegan Paul, 1974), pp. 367–68, 371.

18. W. K. C. Guthrie, *History of Greek Philosophy,* vol. 3 (Cambridge, Eng.: Cambridge University Press, 1969), p. 16.

19. Sextus Empiricus, *Outlines of Pyrrhonism,* trans. R. G. Bury (Buffalo: Prometheus Books, 1990), pp. 59–63 [I.145–66].

20. Paul Hazard's *The European Mind 1680–1715* [1935] (New York: World/ Meridian, 1963), pp. 10–11.

21. See Henry Vyverberg, *Human Nature, Cultural Diversity, and the French Enlightenment* (New York: Oxford University Press, 1989).

22. Montesquieu, *Persian Letters,* ed. C. J. Betts (New York: Penguin, 1977), pp. 284–85, 124–25, 165.

23. See, generally, David D. Bien, *The Calas Affair* (Princeton: Princeton University Press, 1960).

24. Marc Chassaigne, *Le Procès du Chevalier de la Barre* (Paris: Librairie Victor Lecoffre, 1920), pp. 154–55, and Voltaire's "Relation de la Mort du Chevalier de la Barre," in *Oeuvres de Voltaire,* ed. M. Beuchot, vol. 42 (Paris: Chez Lefèvre, 1831), pp. 361–82.

25. See Peter Gay, *Voltaire's Politics: The Poet as Realist* (New York: Vintage, 1965), pp. 273–308.

26. John Locke, *Epistola de Tolerantia/A Letter on Toleration,* ed. R. Klibansky (Oxford: Oxford University Press, 1968), p. 145. In his *Traité sur la tolérance,* ed. R. Pomeau (Paris: Flammarion, 1989), Voltaire draws on and recommends Locke (pp. 83, 168).

27. See Hans R. Guggisberg, "Wandel der Argumente für religiöse Toleranz und Glaubensfreiheit im 16. und 17. Jahrhundert," in *Zur Geschichte der Toleranze und Religionsfreiheit,* ed. H. Lutz (Darmstadt: Wissenschaftliche Buchgesellschaft, 1977), pp. 460–78.

28. See, generally, *Lessing und die Toleranz,* ed. Peter Freimark et al. (Detroit: Wayne State University Press, 1986).

29. Gotthold Lessing, *Laocoön, Nathan the Wise, Minna von Barnhelm,* ed. William A. Steel (London: Dent/Everyman's Library, 1970), p. 167.

30. See Traute Richter, "Die *Ring-Fabel* als Spiegel der gesellschaftlichen Entwicklung," in *Lessing Heute,* ed. E. Dvoretzky (Stuttgart: Akademischer Verlag Hans-Dieter Heinz, 1981), pp. 226–40, and Stuart Atkins, "Die Ringparabel in Lessings 'Nathan der Weise,' " in *Lessings "Nathan der Weise,"* ed. Klaus Bohnen (Darmstadt: Wissenschaftliche Buchgesellschaft, 1984), pp. 155–67; A. C. Lee, *The Decameron: Its Sources and Analogues* [1909] (New York: Haskell House, 1972), pp. 6–13.

31. The case for its Jewish origin and its lesson of tolerance is argued in Marcus Landau, *Die Quellen des Dekameron* (Stuttgart: J. Scheible's Verlagsbuchhandlung, 1884), pp. 183–87; and for much more extensive discussion, see Mario Penna, *La Parabola dei tre anelli e la tolleranza del Medio Evo* (Turin: Rosenberg and Sellier, 1953). See also Uve Fischer, "La Storia dei tre anelli," *Annali della Scuola Normale Superiore di Pisa:* Classe di Lettere e Filosofia, Series III, 3/3 (1973): 955–98, and Poul Borchsenius, *The Three Rings: The History of the Spanish Jews* (London: Allen & Unwin, 1963), pp. 9–17.

32. My account draws mainly on the reconstruction of events in Yosef H. Yerushalmi, *The Lisbon Massacre of 1506 and the Royal Image in the "Shebet Yehudah"* (Cincinnati: Hebrew Union College, 1976), pp. 8–16.

33. Gaston Paris, "La Parabole des trois anneaux," *Revue des Etudes Juives,* 11 (1885): 4. Although published in the early sixteenth century, Paris as well as other scholars believe that the *Shebet Yehudah* collects material from earlier centuries.

34. R. Salomo Aben Verga, *Schevet Jehuda,* trans. from Hebrew to German by M. Wiener (Hannover: Orient-Buchhandlung, 1924), pp. 107–8.

35. *Il Novellino: The Hundred Old Tales,* trans. E. Storer (London: George Routledge, n.d.), pp. 168–69. Giovanni Boccaccio, *Decameron,* trans. M. Musa and P. Bondanella (New York: Mentor/New American Library, 1982), pp. 36–38 [First day, third story].

36. Carlo Ginzburg, *The Cheese and the Worms: The Cosmos of a Sixteenth-Century Miller* (New York: Penguin, 1982), pp. 49–51, 127–28, 152.

37. "Torture" in Voltaire, *Philosophical Dictionary,* ed. Theodore Besterman (New York: Viking Penguin, 1972), p. 396.

38. Jean Said Makdisi, *Beirut Fragments* (New York: Persea Books, 1990), pp. 138, 149.

39. Harold R. Isaacs, *Idols of the Tribe: Group Identity and Political Change* (Cambridge: Harvard University Press, 1989), pp. 3–4.

40. Christopher Hitchens, "Appointment in Sarajevo," *The Nation,* September 14, 1992, pp. 237, 240.

41. Werner Sollors, *Beyond Ethnicity: Consent and Dissent in American Culture* (New York: Oxford University Press, 1986), pp. 89–91.

42. Walter Lippmann, *Public Opinion* [1922] (New York: Macmillan, 1960), pp. 86–87; David L. Lewis, *The Public Image of Henry Ford* (Detroit: Wayne State University Press, 1976), p. 120.

43. Ray Allen Billington, "Cultural Contributions versus Cultural Assimila-

tion," in *The Cultural Approach to History*, ed. Caroline F. Ware (New York: Columbia University Press, 1940), pp. 79. Billington witnessed the Ford event himself.

44. Frances Kellor, cited in and see Edward G. Hartmann, *The Movement to Americanize the Immigrant* [1948] (New York: AMS Press, 1967), pp. 112–33; John Higham, *Strangers in the Land* (New York: Atheneum, 1963), p. 243.

45. Ellwood P. Cubberley, *Changing Conceptions of Education* (Boston: Houghton Mifflin, 1909), p. 15.

46. Cited in and see, generally, John F. McClymer, "The Americanization Movement and the Education of the Foreign-Born Adult, 1914–25," in *American Education and European Immigrants: 1840–1940*, ed. B. J. Weiss (Urbana: University of Illinois Press, 1982), pp. 98, 112.

47. Henry Pratt Fairchild, *The Melting-Pot Mistake* (Boston: Little, Brown, 1926), p. 154. Emphasis in original; guidebook cited in Moses Rischin, *The Promised City: New York Jews 1870–1914* (Cambridge: Harvard University Press, 1962), p. 75.

48. "The Handicapped," in Randolph Bourne, *The Radical Will: Selected Writings*, ed. O. Hansen (New York: Urizen Books, 1977), pp. 73–74.

49. "Trans-National America" [1916], in Bourne, *The Radical Will*, pp. 248–64. See, generally, Bruce Clayton, *Forgotten Prophet: The Life of Randolph Bourne* (Baton Rouge: Louisiana State University Press, 1984), pp. 182–202.

50. "The Jew and Trans-National America" [1916], in Randolph Bourne, *War and the Intellectuals*, ed. C. Resek (New York: Harper & Row, 1964), pp. 124–33.

51. All quotes from letters and interviews in Sarah L. Schmidt, *Horace M. Kallen and the Americanization of Zionism*, PhD, University of Maryland, 1973, pp. 33–35. See also Milton R. Konvitz, "Horace Meyer Kallen (1882–1974)," in *The Legacy of Horace M. Kallen*, ed. M. R. Konvitz (Cranbury, N.J.: Associated University Press, 1987), pp. 16–17.

52. Horace M. Kallen, "Democracy *versus* the Melting-Pot," in his *Culture and Democracy in the United States* [1924] (New York: Arno Press, 1970), pp. 117, 119–23.

53. Kallen, *Culture and Democracy in the United States*, pp. 11, 41–43.

54. See Jay Wissot, "John Dewey, Horace Meyer Kallen and Cultural Pluralism," *Educational Theory*, 25 (1975): 186–96, and Larry C. Miller, "William James and Twentieth-Century Ethnic Thought," *American Quarterly*, 31 (1979): 533–55.

55. Horace Kallen in Sarah Schmidt, "A Conversation with Horace M. Kallen," *Reconstructionist*, 41 (November 1975): 29.

56. Schmidt, *Horace M. Kallen and the Americanization of Zionism*, p. 49. The quotations and account vary slightly from that in Schmidt, "A Conversation." Sollors cites from unpublished letters of Kallen tarnishing his image as a principled anti-racist coming to Locke's aid ("A Critique of Pure Pluralism," pp. 270–71). On Kallen's pluralism, see also Moses Rischin, "The

Jews and Pluralism," in *Jewish Life in America,* ed. G. Rosen (n.p: KTAV, 1978), pp. 61–91.

57. Jeffrey Conrad Stewart, *A Biography of Alain Locke: Philosopher of the Harlem Renaissance, 1886–1930,* PhD dissertation (unpublished), Yale University, 1979, p. 18. My information on the Locke family is drawn from Stewart's excellent account (pp. 12–24).

58. Benny Kraut, *From Reform Judaism to Ethical Culture: The Religious Evolution of Felix Adler* (Cincinnati: Hebrew Union College Press, 1979), pp. 11, 85.

59. Howard B. Radest, *Toward Common Ground: The Story of the Ethical Societies in the United States* (New York: Frederick Ungar, 1969), p. 37. For a discussion of Adler's ideas, Jane Addams, and the settlement house movement, see Rivka S. Lissak, *Pluralism and Progressives: Hull-House and the New Immigrants, 1890–1919* (Chicago: University of Chicago Press, 1989), pp. 166–71.

60. Alain Locke, "The New Negro," in his *The New Negro* (New York: Albert & Charles Boni, 1925), pp. 6–7, 14. The volume has recently been republished (*The New Negro* [New York: Atheneum, 1992]), with an introduction by Arnold Rampersad, who summarizes criticisms of Locke. Rampersad praises the illustrations in the book by Winold Reiss "for depicting the faces and figures of Harlem blacks as they had never been drawn before" (p. xviii). Unfortunately, he fails to mention that the new edition drops all the color plates by Reiss, including the opening one, "The Brown Madonna," and that of Locke himself.

61. Wallace Thurman, *Infants of the Spring* [1932] (Plainview, N.Y.: Books for Libraries Press, 1972), pp. 227–45.

62. Alain Locke "Values and Imperatives," in *American Philosophy Today and Tomorrow,* ed. H. M. Kallen and S. Hook (New York: Lee Furman, 1935), p. 312.

63. Cited in Stewart, *Locke,* p. 135.

64. "Pluralism and Ideological Peace," reprinted in *The Philosophy of Alain Locke,* ed. L. Harris (Philadelphia: Temple University Press, 1989), pp. 96, 98.

65. "Pluralism and Intellectual Democracy," in *Philosophy of Alain Locke,* p. 64. See Philip Gleason, *Speaking of Diversity* (Baltimore: Johns Hopkins University Press, 1992), pp. 60–62. Gleason is a valuable guide to the issues of pluralism and the melting pot.

66. John Higham, *Send These to Me: Immigrants in Urban America* (Baltimore: Johns Hopkins University Press, 1984), p. 198. Michael Paul Rogin, *The Intellectuals and McCarthy* (Cambridge: MIT Press, 1967), pp. 9–10.

67. Marianne Hirsch, *The Mother/Daughter Plot* (Bloomington: Indiana University Press, 1989), p. 17.

68. Isaac B. Berkson, *Theories of Americanization: A Critical Study* (New York: Teachers College, Columbia University, 1920), pp. 185–86.

69. Ibid., pp. 81, 83, 88.

70. Arthur Mann, *The One and the Many: Reflections on the American Identity*

(Chicago: University of Chicago Press, 1979), p. 143. This book is a provocative discussion of American immigration, identity, and pluralism.

71. Berkson, *Theories of Americanization*, pp. 89–90.
72. Edward W. Said, "The Politics of Knowledge," in *Debating P.C.*, ed. Paul Berman (New York: Laurel/Dell, 1992), pp. 173–74.
73. See Randall L. Kennedy's bracing "Racial Critiques of Legal Academia," *Harvard Law Review*, 102 (June 1989): 1745–1819.
74. Paul Lauter, "The Two Criticisms," in *Literature, Language, and Politics*, ed. Betty Jean Craige (Athens: University of Georgia Press, 1988), p. 9.
75. Orlando Patterson, *Ethnic Chauvinism: The Reactionary Impulse* (New York: Stein & Day, 1977), p. 174.
76. Benjamin R. Barber, *An Aristocracy of Everyone* (New York: Ballantine, 1992), p. 146.
77. Henry Louis Gates, Jr., *Loose Canons* (New York: Oxford University Press, 1993), p. 90.
78. See, generally, Werner Sollors, "A Critique of Pure Pluralism," in *Reconstructing American Literary History*, ed. Sacvan Bercovitch (Cambridge: Harvard University Press, 1986), esp. pp. 254–56.
79. Lawrence H. Fuchs, *The American Kaleidoscope* (Middleton, Conn.: Wesleyan University Press, 1990), p. 1; "Trends in Immigration," U.S. Department of Justice, *1990 Statistical Yearbook of the Immigration and Naturalization Service*, December 1991, pp. 13–36.
80. Ray Allen Billington, *The Protestant Crusade 1800–1860* (Chicago: Quadrangle, 1964), pp. 325–26.
81. H. G. Wells, *The Future in America* (New York: Harper & Brothers, 1906), pp. 43–47.
82. All figures from "Trends in Immigration," U.S. Department of Justice.
83. Mann, *The One and the Many*, pp. 76–78.
84. Park noted the vast variations in figures. One directory listed 57 Norwegian and 18 Japanese newspapers; others counted 115 Norwegian and 44 Japanese papers. See Robert E. Park, *The Immigrant Press and Its Control* (New York: Harper & Brothers, 1922), pp. 252–302.
85. Common Council for American Unity, *Foreign Language Publications in the United States* [mimeographed] (New York, 1958), unpaged; Edward Hunter, *In Many Voices—Our Fabulous Foreign-Language Press* (Norman Park, Ga.: Norman College, n.d. [1960?]), pp. 34, 44; Lubomyr R. Wynar and Anna T. Wynar, *Encyclopedic Directory of Ethnic Newspapers and Periodicals in the United States* (Littleton, Colo.: Libraries Unlimited, 1976), pp. 16–27. Wynar and Wynar discuss the reliability of earlier surveys of the foreign press. Some of their own calculations are not comparable to older figures, since they include "ethnic publications" in English. For an announcement of a "fourth stage" and an informed survey of the press of select ethnic groups, see *Ethnic Press in the United States*, ed. Sally M. Miller (New York: Greenwood Press, 1987). *The Oxbridge Directory of Ethnic Periodicals* (New York: Oxbridge, 1979) lists about 3,500 publications; but this also is not comparable to other figures because it includes both the United States and Canada, as well as black publications and other

ethnic publications in English. It should be noted that any discussion of the decline of foreign newspapers must consider the decline of all newspapers and their replacement by radio and television.

86. Mann, *The One and the Many,* p. 152.
87. James Crawford, *Hold Your Tongue: Bilingualism and the Politics of "English Only"* (Reading, Mass.: Addison-Wesley, 1992), pp. 21–22.
88. Fuchs, *The American Kaleidoscope,* pp. 327–30.
89. Mary C. Waters, *Ethnic Options: Choosing Identities in America* (Berkeley: University of California Press, 1990), pp. 91–92.
90. J. Hector St. John Crèvecoeur, *Letters from an American Farmer* [1782] (Garden City, N.Y.: Doubleday/Dolphin, n.d.), p. 49.
91. George Lipsitz, *Time Passages: Collective Memory and American Popular Culture* (Minneapolis: University of Minnesota Press, 1990), pp. 140–43.
92. Marcus Lee Hansen, "The Problem of the Third Generation Immigrant" [1937], in *American Immigrants and Their Generations,* ed. Peter Kivisto and Dag Blanck (Urbana: University of Illinois Press, 1990), pp. 194–95.
93. Ibid., p. 196; see Gleason, *Speaking of Diversity,* pp. 231–49.
94. Nathan Glazer and Daniel Patrick Moynihan, *Beyond the Melting Pot* (Cambridge: MIT Press, 1964), pp. v, 17.
95. Mann, *The One and the Many,* p. 39.
96. Ruth Benedict, *Patterns of Culture* (New York: Mentor, 1959), p. 134.
97. Nicholas Lemann, "Philadelphia: Black Nationalism on Campus," *The Atlantic,* 271/2 (January 1993): 47.
98. Gerald Early, "Their Malcolm, My Problem," *Harper's,* December 1992, p. 68.

CHAPTER 6   Journalists, Cynics, and Cheerleaders

1. Annette Leddy, "Academic Fashion in the Eighties," unpublished.
2. Paul Lauter, "Canon Theory and Emergent Practice," in *Left Politics and the Literary Profession,* ed. L. J. Davis and M. B. Mirabella (New York: Columbia University Press, 1990), p. 144. William Bennett was Secretary of Education under President Reagan.
3. Christopher Newfield, "What Was Political Correctness?" *Critical Inquiry,* 19 (1993): 315, 335.
4. David Bromwich, *Politics by Other Means: Higher Education and Group Thinking* (New Haven: Yale University Press, 1992), p. 119.
5. See John M. Olin Foundation, *1990 Annual Report,* New York; Jon Wiener "Dollars for Neocon Scholars," in his *Professors, Politics and Pop* (New York: Verso, 1991), pp. 99–103; and Sara Diamond, "Endowing the Right-Wing Academic Agenda," *Covert Action,* 38(Fall 1991): 46–49.
6. Paul Gottfried, *The Conservative Movement,* rev. ed. (New York: Twayne, 1993), p. 141. See his savvy discussion of shifts in conservative monies, "Funding an Empire," pp. 118–41.
7. Michael Berubé, "Public Image Limited," in *Debating P.C.,* ed. Paul Berman (New York: Laurel/Dell, 1992), pp. 127–28, 135.

8. Mark Edmundson, "The Academy Writes Back," in *Wild Orchids and Trotsky: Messages from American Universities,* ed. M. Edmundson (New York: Penguin, 1993), pp. 3, 6, 15. Joan Wallach Scott, "The Campaign Against Political Correctness," *Change,* November–December 1991, p. 33.

9. Barbara Herrnstein Smith "Introduction" to *The Politics of Liberal Education,* ed. D. J. Gless and B. H. Smith (Durham: Duke University Press, 1992), pp. 3–4.

10. All quotes cited in David Lehman, *Signs of the Times: Deconstruction and the Fall of Paul de Man* (New York: Poseidon, 1992), pp. 212–18.

11. G. W. F. Hegel, *The Phenomenology of Mind,* trans. J. B. Baillie (New York: Humanities Press, 1964), pp. 99–100.

12. Hegel to von Knebel, November 21, 1807, in *Hegel: The Letters,* ed. C. Butler (Bloomington: Indiana University Press, 1984), p. 145.

13. Judith Frank, "In the Waiting Room," in *Wild Orchids and Trotsky,* p. 130.

14. David Kaufmann, "The Profession of Theory," *PMLA,* 105 (1990): 525.

15. Fredric Jameson, *Marxism and Form* (Princeton: Princeton University Press, 1971), p. xiii.

16. Gayatri Spivak, "The New Historicism: Political Commitment and the Postmodern Critic," in *The New Historicism,* ed. H. Arum Veeser (New York: Routledge, 1988).

17. Parsons cited and "translated" in C. Wright Mills, *The Sociological Imagination* (New York: Oxford University Press, 1959), pp. 218, 30–31.

18. Stanley Aronowitz and Henry Giroux, *Postmodern Education* (Minneapolis: University of Minnesota Press, 1991), pp. 90–91.

19. Richard Wolff, reviewing my *The Last Intellectuals* in *Rethinking Marxism,* 20/1 (Spring 1989): 138–39.

20. James H. Kavanagh, *Emily Brontë* (Oxford: Basil Blackwell, 1985), pp. xii-xiv.

21. R. Radhakrishnan, "Toward an Effective Intellectual," in *Intellectuals: Aesthetics, Politics, Academics,* ed. Bruce Robbins (Minneapolis: University of Minnesota Press, 1990), pp. 66, 92.

22. Sande Cohen, *Historical Culture: On the Recoding of an Academic Discipline* (Berkeley: University of California Press, 1988), pp. 2, 46, 327. See my "A New Intellectual History?" *American Historical Review,* 97 (1992): 405–24.

23. William V. Spanos, *The End of Education* (Minneapolis: University of Minnesota Press, 1993), pp. xi, 218. As Spanos explains, the 1978 Harvard Report provoked his reflections, but the book has been much expanded and revised in the intervening years. He also notes that the manuscript was rejected by an Ivy League university press on "manifestly ideological grounds." Without the courageous University of Minnesota Press, he writes, his "oppositional project" would have not seen the light of day. Some courage.

24. Lehman, *Signs of the Times,* pp. 83–84.

25. Karl Marx and Frederick Engels, *The German Ideology* (Moscow: Progress Publishers, 1964), p. 530.

26. Karl Marx, "Postface to the Second Edition," *Capital*, intro. E. Mandel (New York: Vintage, 1976), p. 99.

27. Friedrich Nietzsche, *Joyful Wisdom*, intro. K. F. Reinhardt (New York: Frederick Ungar, 1964), p. 349.

28. F. Nietzsche, *The Use and Abuse of History*, intro. J. Kraft (New York: Bobbs-Merrill, 1957), pp. 45–46.

29. Josef Breuer and Sigmund Freud, *Studies on Hysteria*, trans. and ed. by J. and A. Strachey (New York: Penguin, 1980), pp. 231, 190.

30. S. Freud, *Two Short Accounts of Psycho-Analysis*, ed. and trans. J. Strachey (New York: Penguin, 1983), p. 32. On some of these issues, see my *The Repression of Psychoanalysis* (Chicago: University of Chicago Press, 1986).

31. S. Freud, *The Future of an Illusion*, trans. and ed. J. Strachey (New York: Norton, 1989), pp. 26, 65.

32. T. W. Adorno, *Philosophische Terminologie. Zur Einleitung*, vol. 1 (Frankfurt: Suhrkamp, 1973), pp. 161–66.

33. T. W. Adorno, *Prisms*, trans. S. and S. Weber (London: Neville Spearman, n.d.), p. 19.

34. Fredric Jameson, *Late Marxism: Adorno, or The Persistence of the Dialectic* (London: Verso, 1990), p. 73. See the essential review by Robert Hullot-Kentor in *Telos*, 89 (Fall 1991): 167–77.

35. Edmund Wilson, *A Piece of My Mind* (New York: Farrar, Straus and Cudahy, 1956), p. 164.

36. Andrew Ross, *No Respect: Intellectuals and Popular Culture* (New York: Routledge, 1989), pp. 210–11, 229.

37. Bruce Robbins, "Introduction," in *Intellectuals: Aesthetics, Politics, Academics*, pp. ix–xxvii. See my review in *Telos*, 85 (Fall 1990): 149–56.

38. James Joll, *Three Intellectuals in Politics* (New York: Harper & Row, 1960); Paul A. Bové, *Intellectuals in Power* (New York: Columbia University Press, 1986). There are other differences in these books. Joll wrote in English; Bové, an English professor, doesn't.

39. Theodore Draper, "Intellectuals in Politics," in his *Present History* (New York: Random House, 1983), pp. 400–26.

40. *Goethe's Faust*, trans. Walter Kaufmann (New York: Anchor Books, 1990), p. 207 [I, 2038–40]. "The most significant development in literary studies over the last twenty-five years," writes a critic of departmental cheerleading, "has been the boom in literary theory . . . That theory . . . separates the professor from the literary amateur and, in effect, bars the amateur from critical debate." Brian McCrea, *Addison and Steele are Dead: The English Department, Its Canon, and the Professionalization of Literary Criticism* (Newark: University of Delaware Press, 1990), p. 149.

41. Hector-Neri Castañeda, "Philosophy as a Science and as a Worldview," in *The Institution of Philosophy*, ed. Avner Cohen and Marcelo Dascal (La Salle, Ill.: Open Court, 1989), pp. 35, 39. Nancy Fraser, *Unruly Practices: Power, Discourse and Gender in Contemporary Social Theory* (Minneapolis: University of Minnesota Press, 1989), p. 2. What sort of "vital left academic counterculture" prospers in a society without a left or a counterculture?

42. Jonathan Culler, *Framing the Sign: Criticism and Its Institutions* (Norman: University of Oklahoma Press, 1988), pp. 30, 55.

43. Fredric Jameson is one exception; see his "Postmodernism and the Market," in his *Postmodernism* (Durham: Duke University Press, 1991).

44. J. Hillis Miller, "Face to Face," in *The States of "Theory": History, Art and Critical Discourse*, ed. D. Carroll (New York: Columbia University Press, 1990), p. 286.

45. David Lodge, *Small World* (New York: Warner Books, 1991), p. 50. Harold Fromm, *Academic Capitalism and Literary Value* (Athens: University of Georgia Press, 1991), p. 252. Lodge's book was first published in 1984.

46. Stanley Fish, "No Bias, No Merit: The Case Against Blind Submission," *PMLA*, 103 (1988): 739–48.

47. Stanley Fish, "Reply," *PMLA*, 104 (1989): 220.

48. Terry Caesar, "On Teaching at a Second-Rate University," *South Atlantic Quarterly*, 90/3 (Summer 1991): 458, 464–65. Reprinted in his *Conspiring with Forms* (Athens: University of Georgia Press, 1992).

49. Clifford Adelman, *Tourists in Our Own Land: Cultural Literacies and the College Curriculum* (Washington, D.C.: U.S. Department of Education, 1992), p. vi.

50. Graff also draws on two MLA surveys, but again these are mainly beside the point. One uses catalog descriptions of courses required for English majors at four-year colleges; the other surveys upper-level courses in literature. Neither of these bears on the basic English courses required for all AA or BA students.

51. Bertold Brecht, "Alienation Effects in Chinese Acting," in *Brecht on Theatre*, ed. John Willet (New York: Hill and Wang, 1964), pp. 96–98.

52. James Atlas is more convincing about the new scholarship; see his *The Book Wars* (Knoxville: Whittle Direct Books, 1990), pp. 51–52.

53. See Camille Paglia's devastating "Junk Bonds and Corporate Raiders," in her *Sex, Art and American Culture* (New York: Vintage, 1992).

54. Bromwich, *Politics by Other Means*, pp. 35–36.

55. Gary B. Nash, *Contentions*, 1/3 (Spring 1990): 2–3.

56. Nash has himself been involved in writing a new multicultural textbook series; see Robert Reinhold, "Class Struggle," *New York Times Magazine*, September 29, 1991, pp. 26 ff.

57. Louis Kampf, "Annals of Academic Life," in *Left Politics and the Literary Profession*, p. 309.

58. William James, "Social Value of the College-Bred," in James, *Writings 1902–1910* (New York: Library Classics of the United States, 1987), p. 1248.

CHAPTER 7   Conclusion: Low-Tech

1. Rush to Richard Price (May, 25, 1786), in *Letters of Benjamin Rush*, ed. L. H. Butterfield, vol. 1: *1761–1792* (Princeton: Princeton University Press, 1951), pp. 388–89.

2. "Documents Illustrative of American Educational History," in *Report of the Commissioner of Education,* 1892–93, vol. 2 (Washington, D.C.: Government Printing Office, 1895), pp. 1270–72, 1293–1312. Morrill cited in Edward Danforth Eddy, Jr., *Colleges for Our Land and Time: The Land-Grant Idea in American Education* (New York: Harper & Brothers, 1957), p. 34.

3. Allan Nevins, *The State Universities and Democracy* (Urbana: University of Illinois Press, 1962), p. 22. Eddy, *Colleges for Our Land and Time,* p. 35.

4. Figures from Juliet B. Schor, *The Overworked American* (New York: Basic Books, 1993), pp. 107–14.

5. "Poll Finds Hispanic Desire to Assimilate," New York *Times,* December 15, 1992, p. A1. The poll was the Latino National Political Survey and is called "the most extensive effort to measure Hispanic attitudes to date." Most of the survey was conducted in Spanish.

6. Leo Strauss, *Liberalism Ancient and Modern* (Ithaca: Cornell University Press, 1989), p. 25.

7. "Reseda Killing Escalates Attacks on L.A. District," Los Angeles *Times,* February, 24, 1993, p. B1.

8. See, generally, Anne Mathews, "The Campus Crime Wave," *New York Times Magazine,* March 7, 1993, pp. 38 ff.

INDEX

228 *Index*